Arduino MEGA 2560 Hardware Manual

A Reference and User Guide for the Arduino MEGA 2560 Hardware and Firmware

Warwick A. Smith

First Edition

Arduino MEGA 2560 Hardware Manual

A Reference and User Guide for the Arduino MEGA 2560 Hardware and Firmware
by Warwick A. Smith

Copyright © 2020, Warwick A. Smith. All rights reserved. No part of this work may be reproduced or transmitted in any form or by any means, electronic or mechanical, including photocopying, scanning, recording, or by any information storage or retrieval system, without the prior written permission of the copyright owner and publisher.

The information in this book is distributed on an "As Is" basis, without warranty. While every precaution has been taken in the preparation of this work, the author and publisher assume no responsibility for errors or omissions, or for loss or damages resulting from the use of the information contained herein.

Trademarks are property of their respective owners and are used in an editorial fashion with no intention of infringement of the trademark.

ISBN-13: 979-8-55041-240-4

Table of Contents

Introduction 15

Why Buy this Arduino MEGA 2560 Hardware Manual?...15

Difference to the Arduino Uno Hardware Manual..16

Target Audience...17

Prerequisites..18

Hardware Requirements..18

Software Requirements...18

What is Covered and What's Not Covered...19

How to Use this Book..19

Accompanying Resources...20

Disclaimer, Errors and Corrections...20

A Note from the Author...20

Chapter 1 • Arduino MEGA 2560 Overview 23

1.1 Arduino MEGA Description and Functionality...24

1.1.1 Arduino MEGA 2560 Board..24

1.1.2 Arduino MEGA 2560 vs. Arduino Uno...24

1.1.3 Uses of the Arduino MEGA 2560...26

1.1.4 Arduino MEGA 2560 Main Parts..27

    1.1.4.1 Main Microcontroller...27

    1.1.4.2 USB Connector..27

    1.1.4.3 External Power In..27

    1.1.4.4 Reset Button..28

    1.1.4.5 Header Sockets with Arduino Pins...29

    1.1.4.6 ON LED...29

    1.1.4.7 L LED...29

    1.1.4.8 TX LED (Transmit)...29

    1.1.4.9 RX LED (Receive)..29

    1.1.4.10 ATmega16U2 Microcontroller...29

    1.1.4.11 ICSP Header...30

    1.1.4.12 ICSP Header for ATmega16U2...31

  1.1.4.13 Mounting Holes..31
 1.1.5 Programming...31
 1.1.6 Extending the Hardware...33
  1.1.6.1 Add-on Boards: Shields..33
   Stacking Shields..34
   Shield Reverse Connection Protection..35
  1.1.6.2 Prototype Shields..35
  1.1.6.3 Strip-board..36
  1.1.6.4 Electronic Breadboard..36
  1.1.6.5 Custom PCB..37
 1.1.7 Open-Source and Licensing..38
 1.1.8 Third Party Compatible Boards...38
 1.1.9 Build Quality, Warranty and Safety...39
 1.1.10 Arduino and Genuino...40

1.2 Arduino MEGA 2560 Firmware..**40**
 1.2.1 USB Bridge Firmware..40
 1.2.2 Bootloader..41

1.3 Precautions During Handling and Usage..**42**
 1.3.1 Static Electricity..42
 1.3.2 Work Surface..44
 1.3.3 Power..44
 1.3.4 Voltage..44
 1.3.5 Handling..45
 1.3.6 Interfacing Precautions..45

1.4 Arduino MEGA 2560 History and Revisions..**46**

1.5 First Time Use and Basic Testing..**47**
 1.5.1 New Arduino MEGA 2560 Default Behavior..47
  1.5.1.1 Computer Drivers...47
  1.5.1.2 Arduino MEGA 2560 Hardware Behavior......................................48
   On LED...49
   RX LED and L LED on Some Systems..49
   Factory or User Loaded Sketch Running..49
 1.5.2 Loading a Sketch to an Arduino MEGA 2560......................................49
  1.5.2.1 Select Board, Processor and Port...50
  1.5.2.2 Loading a Test Sketch...51
   Open the Test Sketch..51

Upload the Sketch...51
Modify the Sketch..51
 1.5.2.3 Serial Port Demonstration...52
  Serial Port Sketch Example..52
  Serial Monitor Window...52
1.5.3 Basic Testing..54
 1.5.3.1 Visually Inspect the Board..54
 1.5.3.2 Power LED and Voltages..54
 1.5.3.3 Check Expected Default Behavior..55
 1.5.3.4 Is the Board Recognized by the Host Computer?...............................55
 1.5.3.5 Load a Test Sketch...55

1.6 Arduino MEGA 2560 References and Help..56
1.6.1 Installing Software...56
 1.6.1.1 Windows..56
 1.6.1.2 MAC OS X..56
 1.6.1.3 Linux..56
1.6.2 Getting Started, Examples and Reference...56
 1.6.2.1 Getting Started Guides...56
 1.6.2.2 Arduino Examples and Tutorials...57
 1.6.2.3 Building Breadboard Circuits..57
 1.6.2.4 Arduino Software Reference...57
1.6.3 Getting Help..57
1.6.4 Related Open-Source Projects..57
 1.6.4.1 Fritzing...57
 1.6.4.2 Wiring...58
 1.6.4.3 Processing...58
1.6.5 Arduino MEGA 2560 on the Web..59

1.7 Arduino MEGA 2560, DUE and MEGA ADK...59
1.7.1 Arduino DUE vs. Arduino MEGA 2560..59
1.7.2 Arduino MEGA ADK vs. Arduino MEGA 2560...60

Chapter 2 • Hardware Technical Information   61

2.1 Microcontroller..62

2.2 Atmel, Microchip and AVR..63

2.3 Memory..63
2.3.1 Flash Memory...64

- 2.3.1.1 Flash Memory Size...64
- 2.3.1.2 Flash Wear..64
- 2.3.1.3 Data Retention...64
- 2.3.2 SRAM..64
  - 2.3.2.1 Volatile Memory..64
  - 2.3.2.2 SRAM Size...65
- 2.3.3 EEPROM..65
  - 2.3.3.1 EEPROM Programming..65
  - 2.3.3.2 EEPROM Size...65
  - 2.3.3.3 EEPROM Wear...65
- 2.3.4 Adding External Memory..65
  - 2.3.4.1 SD Cards (SPI Interface)..66
  - 2.3.4.2 Flash and EEPROM Chips (SPI / TWI Interface)..............................68
  - 2.3.4.3 SPI Devices...68
  - 2.3.4.4 TWI and I²C Devices..69

2.4 Power and USB..69
- 2.4.1 USB Power..69
- 2.4.2 USB Connection and Cable..69
- 2.4.3 External Power..70
- 2.4.4 Battery Power..71
- 2.4.5 Operating Voltage...73

2.5 Operating Frequency...73

2.6 LED Indicators and Reset Button...74
- 2.6.1 ON LED..74
- 2.6.2 L LED..75
- 2.6.3 TX LED...75
- 2.6.4 RX LED...75
- 2.6.5 Reset Button...75

2.7 User Pin Headers..76
- 2.7.1 Power Pins..76
  - 2.7.1.1 GND Pins...76
  - 2.7.1.2 5V Pins...76
  - 2.7.1.3 3.3V Pin..77
  - 2.7.1.4 Vin Pin..77
- 2.7.2 IOREF Pin and Unconnected Pin...77
- 2.7.3 RESET Pin...78

2.7.4 Digital, PWM and Communication Pins..78
   2.7.4.1 Output Pins..78
   2.7.4.2 Pin Current Rating..80
   2.7.4.3 Input Pins..81
   2.7.4.4 PWM Pins...82
      PWM Example Sketch...83
      Calculating PWM Duty Cycle..84
      PWM Frequency..84
      PWM LED Control Example..84
   2.7.4.5 Communication Pins..84
      Serial Port / UART Pins to USB..85
      Serial Port / USART Pins..86
      TWI or I²C Pins...86
      SPI Pins...87
2.7.5 Analog In Pins...87
   2.7.5.1 Analog In Example Sketch...87
   2.7.5.2 Floating Analog Input Pin..88
   2.7.5.3 Calculating Analog In Voltage...88
   2.7.5.4 Analog In Pins Used as Digital I/O..88
2.7.6 AREF Pin and Internal ADC Reference Voltages..89

2.8 Programming Headers..90
2.8.1 MEGA 2560 with External Programmer on ICSP..90
2.8.2 Restore Bootloader with IDE and External Programmer............................91
2.8.3 ATmega16U2 ICSP Header...91
2.8.4 ICSP Programming Resources...92
2.8.5 Using an Arduino as an In-System Programmer..93

2.9 Shared Pins...93
2.9.1 Serial Port Pins..93
2.9.2 L LED Pin..93
2.9.3 TWI or I²C Pins..94
2.9.4 ICSP SPI Pins and Reset..94
2.9.5 JTAG Pins..95

Chapter 3 • Pin Reference and Interfacing   97

3.1 Pin Default and Alternate Functions..98
3.1.1 Shared TWI Pins..98

3.1.2 Shared SPI Pins..98
3.2 ATmega2560 to Arduino MEGA 2560 Pin Mapping.......................................99
    3.2.1 ATmega2560 Ports...101
    3.2.2 ATmega2560 Alternate Pin Functions..102
3.3 Pin Types and Interfacing...103
    3.3.1 Digital Input / Output Pins...103
        3.3.1.1 Pins as Outputs...103
            Why an LED Needs a Series Resistor..104
            How to Calculate a LED Current Limiting Series Resistor....................106
            Current Sourcing and Current Sinking..109
            Current Sourcing...109
            Current Sinking...110
            Current Limitation Per Pin..111
            I/O Port Current Source and Sink Limits..111
            Switching Heavier Loads with Transistors and Relays.........................115
        3.3.1.2 Pins as Inputs...118
            Pull-down Resistor...119
            Pull-up Resistor..121
            Internal Pull-up Resistors..122
    3.3.2 PWM Pins...123
    3.3.3 Analog Pins..124
    3.3.4 TWI Bus Pins..125
        3.3.4.1 TWI Interfacing Example..125
            TWI Pull-up Resistors...126
        3.3.4.2 Accessing TWI Devices in Software..127
    3.3.5 SPI Bus Pins...128
        3.3.5.1 SPI Bus Interfacing Example..130
        3.3.5.2 Accessing SPI Devices in Software..130
        3.3.5.3 Accessing SD Cards in Software...130
    3.3.6 Serial / UART Pins...131
        3.3.6.1 Hardware Serial Ports...131
            Using the USB Port / Serial Port 0..132
            Using Serial Port 1, Serial Port 2 and Serial Port 3.............................132
            Serial Port Reference...135
        3.3.6.2 Software Serial Port...135
    3.3.7 Power Pins...136

  3.3.7.1 GND Pins..136

  3.3.7.2 5V Pins...136

    USB 5V...137

    External Power to 5V Regulator..137

  3.3.7.3 3.3V Pin..137

  3.3.7.4 Vin Pin..137

 3.3.8 Reset Pin...138

 3.3.9 IOREF Pin..138

 3.3.10 AREF Pin...139

3.4 ICSP Header on Main Microcontroller...140

3.5 ICSP Header on USB Microcontroller..141

3.6 JP5 Header on USB Microcontroller..142

3.7 JTAG Pins...143

3.8 Finding the Datasheets...143

 3.8.1 ATmega2560 Datasheet..144

 3.8.2 ATmega16U2 Datasheet..144

 3.8.3 Datasheets for Other Components..144

Chapter 4 • Power Reference   145

4.1 Power Supply Specification...146

 4.1.1 Operating Voltage..146

 4.1.2 USB Power Input..147

 4.1.3 External Power Jack Input...147

 4.1.4 External Power Jack Pinout...147

 4.1.5 Vin Pin as Power Input...148

4.2 Power Circuit..148

 4.2.1 External Power In and 5V Regulator..148

 4.2.2 Power On Indicator LED..148

 4.2.3 USB Power In...148

 4.2.4 Automatic Switch...149

 4.2.5 3.3V Regulator...150

 4.2.6 Power Header Socket..150

 4.2.7 Differences Between the MEGA 2560 and Uno Power Circuits....................150

  4.2.7.1 External Power In and 5V Regulator..150

  4.2.7.2 Power On Indicator LED...150

    4.2.7.3 USB Power In..151

    4.2.7.4 Automatic Switch..151

    4.2.7.5 3.3V Regulator..151

4.3 Power Supply Protection..**151**

    4.3.1 Reverse Polarity Protection..152

    4.3.2 5V Regulator Protection Features..152

    4.3.3 3.3V Regulator Protection Features...152

    4.3.4 USB Overload Protection...152

Chapter 5 • MEGA 2560 Firmware and Bootloader   153

5.1 Updating the USB to Serial Bridge Firmware using DFU................**154**

5.2 Atmel Studio..**155**

5.3 USB Microcontroller Firmware..**157**

    5.3.1 Backing up the ATmega16U2 Firmware with Atmel Studio...........................157

    5.3.2 DFU Bootloader Firmware...159

    5.3.3 USB to Serial Bridge Firmware...159

    5.3.4 Programming the USB Microcontroller using ICSP..........................160

    5.3.5. ATmega16U2 Fuse Settings..161

5.4 Main Microcontroller Bootloader..**162**

    5.4.1 Backing up the ATmega2560 Firmware with Atmel Studio...........................162

    5.4.2 Bootloader Firmware – stk500v2..163

    5.4.3 Restoring the Bootloader..163

    5.4.4 ATmega2560 Fuse Settings..164

5.5 The RESET-EN Solder Jumper..**166**

5.6 Alternative Firmware Programming Methods..................................**168**

Chapter 6 • Circuit Diagram and Components   169

6.1 Circuit Diagram...**170**

    6.1.1 Block Diagram..170

    6.1.2 Main Microcontroller Circuit...171

    6.1.3 USB Microcontroller Circuit..171

    6.1.4 Power Supply Circuit...174

6.2 Component List...**174**

6.3 Component Positions on the Board..**177**

6.4 Getting an Electronic Copy of the Circuit Diagram.................................179

Chapter 7 • Fault Finding and Measurement — 181

7.1 Basic Fault Finding and Repair...182

7.2 Replacing the Main Arduino MEGA 2560 Microcontroller.........................182

    7.2.1 Replacement Part...183

    7.2.2 Removing the Old Microcontroller..183

    7.2.3 Soldering the New Microcontroller...184

    7.2.4 Loading the Bootloader..185

7.3 Voltage Measurements...185

    7.3.1 Powered from USB...186

        7.3.1.1 5V Test Points...186

        7.3.1.2 USB Power and 3.3V Circuit Test Points..................................186

        7.3.1.3 Measuring Voltage on the L and ON LEDs...............................188

    7.3.2 Powered from External Power Supply..188

7.4 Waveform Patterns and Measurement...189

    7.4.1 Testing for Presence of Microcontroller Clocks................................190

    7.4.2 Testing for PWM Waveforms..191

    7.4.3 Testing UART Outputs..194

    7.4.4 TWI Signals..196

    7.4.5 SPI Signals...198

Chapter 8 • Mechanical Dimensions and Templates — 201

8.1 Measurements, Tolerance and Scale...202

8.2 Length, Width and Mass...202

8.3 Mounting Hole Spacing and Size..204

8.4 Shape Dimensions..205

8.5 Header Positions...206

8.6 Shield Reverse Connection Protection...207

8.7 Using Strip-board as a Shield...208

8.8 Drill Template and KiCad Template..208

Chapter 9 • Arduino Shield Compatibility — 209

9.1 Shield Compatibility Considerations...210

9.2 Shield Compatibility Between Arduino Models..........................210
    9.2.1 Shield Size..........................210
    9.2.2 Shield Voltage..........................210
    9.2.3 SPI Pin Compatibility..........................211
    9.2.4 TWI Pin Compatibility..........................211
    9.2.5 Shield Stacking..........................211

9.3 Compatibility Between Four Arduino Models..........................211
    9.3.1 Arduino MEGA 2560..........................214
    9.3.2 Arduino Due..........................214
    9.3.3 Arduino Uno..........................215
    9.3.4 Arduino Zero..........................215

9.4 Arduino Shield Pin Compatibility..........................216
    9.4.1 TWI Pins..........................216
    9.4.2 SPI Pins..........................217
    9.4.3 Digital Pins..........................217
    9.4.4 Analog Pins..........................217
    9.4.5 Power Pins..........................217

9.5 Example of Shield Compatibility Problems..........................218
    9.5.1 Data Logger Shield Example..........................218
        9.5.1.1 Shield Power..........................219
        9.5.1.2 ICSP Connector..........................219
        9.5.1.3 TWI Pins..........................220
    9.5.2 Ethernet Shield Example..........................221
        9.5.2.1 Shield Power..........................221
        9.5.2.2 ICSP Connector and Stacking..........................221

Appendix A • Specifications Quick Reference   223

Index   227

Introduction

Welcome to the Arduino MEGA 2560 Hardware Manual, a reference and user guide for the Arduino MEGA 2560 hardware and firmware. This manual provides up to date hardware information for the Arduino MEGA 2560, the easy to use open-source electronics platform used by hobbyists, makers, experimenters, educators and professionals.

Why Buy this Arduino MEGA 2560 Hardware Manual?

After the success of the *Arduino Uno Hardware Manual, ISBN 1-54292-181-3*, by the same author, it was decided to make a hardware manual for the Arduino MEGA 2560. This is a natural progression, as the Arduino MEGA 2560 is the next most popular Arduino board after the Arduino Uno. Progressing from the Arduino Uno to the Arduino MEGA 2560 provides the user with more input/output pins, more communication ports and more memory which may be required by some Arduino projects.

As with the Arduino Uno Hardware Manual, there are four main reasons to buy this book besides just wanting a handy reference manual for the Arduino MEGA 2560 hardware and firmware for use on the workbench. A discussion of these reasons follows.

1) All the Hardware Information in One Place
Although information about the Arduino MEGA 2560 hardware is available online, it is spread out over many pages and websites. Having all of the Arduino MEGA hardware information in one place, in this concise guide, is convenient and a time saver. This is especially true for new Arduino users who may not even know what to look for when getting familiar with the Arduino MEGA 2560 hardware, for example, how to extend the hardware, how to add external data memory, how to connect hardware to Arduino pins in

current sinking and current sourcing configuration. It also includes practical information such as which firmware to load to the microcontroller on the MEGA 2560 board, should it be erased, and which other settings must be changed for it to work. In addition, this manual has detailed hardware technical information, a pin reference chapter, basic interfacing information, a power reference chapter, information on all firmware programs loaded on an Arduino MEGA 2560, the circuit diagram and component list, fault finding and testing steps, as well as hardware mechanical dimensions and measurements. It also includes a chapter on Arduino shield compatibility which was not included in the Arduino Uno Hardware Manual.

2) Integrity of Information

Information on the internet about Arduino or any other subject may or may not be technically correct. Discerning which information is correct and which is incorrect is a problem, especially for those users who are new to electronics. Even hardware specifications from Arduino themselves are often badly specified or even incorrectly specified. This manual provides hardware information on the Arduino MEGA 2560 that has been carefully checked and verified to be correct.

3) Presentation of Information

Each topic or subject in this book has been broken down into smaller parts and carefully explained and described. For this reason, each chapter contains many sections, each with its own sub-heading and section number for easy reference and cross-reference. Numerous illustrations and figures are included for easier understanding of explanations and for quick and easy reference.

4) Information Not Available Elsewhere

This book contains some information that is not available online, or is hard to find. It also offers unique views and illustrations of the hardware that reveal some interesting aspects of the Arduino MEGA 2560 hardware that is not obvious when looking at the circuit diagram or other sources of information.

Difference to the Arduino Uno Hardware Manual

For those readers who already own a copy of the *Arduino Uno Hardware Manual, ISBN 1-54292-181-3*, written by the same author, this section looks at the motivation for making a separate manual for the Arduino MEGA 2560, instead of combining the two in one book.

Introduction

There are some similarities between the Arduino Uno and Arduino MEGA 2560, but also many differences. It was felt that there are enough differences between the two boards to write a separate manual for each. A second reason for publishing two manuals is that it is much easier when working with an Arduino board, to pick up the correct manual for it, and not have to sift through the information for the Arduino board being used in a manual that covers more than one board or model. One can continue working with the board and specific manual knowing that everything in the manual applies to the board in use. The result of the decision to make a separate book for the Arduino MEGA 2560 is the manual that you now hold in your hands.

This manual follows the same basic layout and format as the Arduino Uno hardware manual, but has been written for the Arduino MEGA 2560. Although there are some sections in this book that are mostly the same as the Arduino Uno Hardware Manual, such as the section in chapter 1 on ESD, enough changes have been made to make owning this manual worthwhile for those readers who already own the Arduino Uno hardware manual. Some sections of the book that would be very similar to the Arduino Uno Hardware Manual have been extended, and new images and figures added. All this is in addition to including information on the obvious additional capabilities of the Arduino MEGA 2560. Finally, an extra chapter chapter has been added that deals with Arduino shield compatibility between different Arduino models, including the MEGA 2560, Uno, Due and Zero. This chapter was added to give the reader an understanding of why some shields only work with some Arduino models, and also to provide information for those readers wanting to design Arduino shields that are compatible across a number of different Arduino models.

To be perfectly clear, if you own an Arduino Uno, you will want to have the *Arduino Uno Hardware Manual* written by the same author. If you own an Arduino MEGA 2560, you will want this *Arduino MEGA 2560 Hardware Manual*. Because there are some similarities between the two boards, such as the power supply circuit, the Arduino MEGA 2560 Hardware Manual has been extended to make it more worthwhile for those readers who already own the Arduino Uno Hardware Manual.

Target Audience

This manual has been written for anyone interested in the Arduino MEGA 2560 who would like an easy to use hardware reference. Hobbyists, makers, experimenters, teachers, students, and professionals such as electronic engineers will all find this manual to be an invaluable reference.

Prerequisites

The Arduino MEGA 2560 is a more advanced board with enhanced features, and is usually purchased after the user has had some experience with an Arduino Uno, but this is not essential. It is assumed that the reader of this manual has at least used an Arduino on a basic level and has some basic knowledge of electronics. Basics of electronics are not explained, but it is assumed that the reader already has the knowledge to understand terms such as voltage and current, and knows what electronic components such as resistors and transistors are. Those readers who do not have this basic knowledge must at least be willing to learn, by using additional resources, be it via the internet or by using other books on the subject.

Hardware Requirements

At a minimum, an Arduino MEGA 2560 will obviously be required, as well as a computer with which to program the Arduino board. This book mainly references the Arduino MEGA 2560 revision 3 (REV3 or R3) board which is the latest Arduino MEGA 2560 at the time of writing. It also mentions earlier versions of the Arduino MEGA 2560 when necessary and makes some reference to clone or compatible boards. For advanced use and for programming firmware to the Arduino MEGA 2560, one of several USB programmers can be used – see the text for more details, but most users will not need to do this.

In the pin reference and interfacing chapter, an electronic breadboard and jumper wires are used to show how to interface LEDs, transistors, a relay, an external TWI memory chip and an SD card adapter. These are just interfacing examples and users will only need the components for a particular project or interfacing example that they are interested in. Hardware testing requires at least a multimeter. Some tests require an oscilloscope, but it is not essential for every user and is only used in a small section of the book.

Software Requirements

Without software, an Arduino MEGA 2560 does absolutely nothing. For this reason, although this is a hardware manual, the free Arduino IDE programming environment must be installed. This enables Arduino programs or sketches to be loaded to the Arduino MEGA 2560 to operate and test the hardware.

All software used in this book is either free and open-source, such as the Arduino IDE software, or free software that is not open-source. All software used can easily be downloaded from the internet at no cost. Other software, besides the Arduino IDE, is optional and will only need to be installed if required for certain tasks.

What is Covered and What's Not Covered

This book is primarily about hardware on an Arduino MEGA 2560 board, including technical information, a pin reference, power supply information, firmware details, circuits and parts list, fault finding and measurement, as well as mechanical information, but includes some software, in the form of user programs or sketches, in order to get the hardware to work. That being said, it does not cover software programming in great detail, but does provide references to the appropriate example sketches in the Arduino IDE and online documentation where necessary. Most of the functionality of an Arduino MEGA 2560 comes from the main microcontroller on the board. This microcontroller is covered by the text in the context of Arduino and how it is set up and used by the Arduino IDE and its libraries. Advanced use of some of the internal hardware in the main microcontroller that is not available in the Arduino IDE and libraries is not covered, except to provide a pin reference for these advanced features that shows which Arduino pins are mapped to advanced hardware. Users who want to use the advanced hardware that is not available in the Arduino IDE or libraries must reference the datasheet for the main microcontroller.

How to Use this Book

It is suggested that this book is first read through once to get a good idea of its contents and a better understanding of the Arduino MEGA 2560 hardware, it can then be used as a reference manual. Although this book has been written as a manual, it is not dry like some manuals or textbooks. Anyone interested in Arduino should find it an enjoyable read.

For electronic engineers or competent hobbyists who have used other microcontroller boards, but not an Arduino MEGA 2560, this book provides an easy introduction to the Arduino MEGA hardware that will get new users started quickly with the board. The first two chapters of the book are basically a hardware user manual, while the remaining chapters are more like a reference manual, although there is some overlap between the two. The exception is the last chapter that discusses Arduino shield compatibility between different Arduino models. This chapter is basically a stand-alone technical chapter.

When using the book for reference, use the index to find specific topics and use appendix A to quickly find technical specifications. Appendix A has a cross reference for each technical specification that references the same specification in the main text, which provides detailed information.

Each section in the book cross references related material in other sections and chapters. The table of contents is also useful for referencing information, as it is a list of every section in the book.

Accompanying Resources

Accompanying resources can be found on the supporting website wspublishing.net which includes links to all of the online resources so that they do not need to be typed in manually. Arduino software sketches used in the book are also available from the supporting website.

Disclaimer, Errors and Corrections

Although this manual is not an official Arduino manual, or endorsed by Arduino in any way, it has been written and thoroughly checked by a competent electronic engineer. The information in this manual has been carefully checked and proof read, but this is not a claim of infallibility, and this manual, like any work, is subject to typos and small errors that may have been missed during the proof reading process. In the event that you do find an error or typo, please use the accompanying website wspublishing.net to report it. This will be a big help to others as any corrections will be published on the supporting website.

A Note from the Author

Thank you for purchasing this Arduino MEGA 2560 hardware manual! I hope that you thoroughly enjoy reading this book and using it as a reference. For those readers who have an Amazon account, such as at amazon.com, please give an honest review of this book on the site. This provides feedback to the author that can be used to improve future versions of this manual. When writing a review, bear in mind that this book is an Arduino MEGA 2560 hardware manual and not a software or electronics book. Review the book contents in light of its title and stated purpose. Also bear in mind that some information in this book is repeated because of the layout of the book – with chapter 1 being an overview of the Arduino MEGA 2560, chapter 2 containing technical information and chapter 3 a pin reference, some information is repeated, but more details are added in each chapter. The alternative to this is to lump everything related together, in which case the book can not be laid out in an easier to read format that builds the information up from a top level view of the hardware followed by more details on each aspect of the hardware. Further to this, note that this book is not available in color because color printing of this book would increase its price by approximately four times.

Chapter 1 • Arduino MEGA 2560 Overview

Before taking a closer look at each aspect of the Arduino MEGA 2560 hardware in greater depth, it is necessary to get a top level overview and general understanding of the Arduino MEGA 2560. This chapter, together with chapter 2, can be thought of as a "hardware user manual" for the Arduino MEGA 2560 and covers all of the basics that are needed before a more comprehensive study of the Arduino MEGA 2560 hardware that is contained in the chapters that follow.

Included in this chapter is a general overview of the Arduino MEGA 2560, its main parts, and how to extend its hardware.

Basics of firmware, the software that comes factory loaded on a new Arduino MEGA 2560 board, is explained. The chapter wraps up with board handling precautions, a brief history of the Arduino MEGA 2560 and the hardware revisions that it has been through, some information on first time use, and basic testing.

In this Chapter

- A top level view of the Arduino MEGA 2560 hardware and functionality
- A brief look at the Arduino MEGA 2560 firmware and what it does
- Board handling and usage precautions
- Arduino MEGA 2560 history and revisions
- First time use and basic testing
- References to quickly find information on the Arduino MEGA 2560
- Major differences between Arduino MEGA 2560 and same sized Arduino boards

1.1 Arduino MEGA Description and Functionality

The Arduino MEGA 2560 is a single board computer that uses a microcontroller as its main processor to run software loaded via the Arduino IDE or other programming environment. It extends the capabilities and number of pins of the smaller Arduino Uno.

1.1.1 Arduino MEGA 2560 Board

Figure 1.1 shows the Arduino MEGA 2560 single board computer. The main microcontroller on the board is a surface mount device that is soldered to the top of the board. The main microcontroller is the 100-pin chip that can be seen above the text "POWER" and "ANALOG IN" in Figure 1.1.

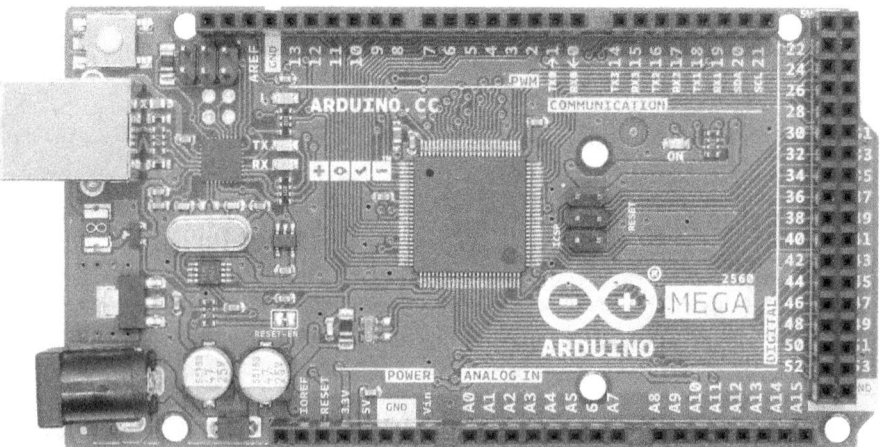

Figure 1.1: Top View of an Arduino MEGA 2560

1.1.2 Arduino MEGA 2560 vs. Arduino Uno

As the Arduino Uno is such a popular board, a comparison between an Arduino Uno and Arduino MEGA 2560 can be helpful. Arduino Uno boards come in two main types, the first has a through-hole mounted microcontroller. The second type is the Arduino Uno SMD board, where the main microcontroller is a surface mount device (SMD), meaning that it is soldered to the top layer of the board only. In comparison, an Arduino Uno with a through-hole mounted microcontroller has a socket soldered to the board that houses the main microcontroller. The socket is through-hole mounted, meaning that while the socket is placed on the top of the board, the legs or pins of the socket pass through holes in the board and are soldered to the board on the bottom layer. This allows the microcontroller to easily be unplugged from the socket on the board and replaced by a new microcontroller if necessary. This can't be done on the Arduino Uno SMD board. Figure 1.2 shows an Arduino Uno on the left and Arduino Uno SMD on the right.

Figure 1.2: Arduino Uno (left) and Arduino Uno SMD (right)

Arduino Uno boards with the main microcontroller housed in a socket are the most popular Arduino Uno boards, as users can replace the main microcontroller should it be damaged. Arduino MEGA 2560 boards are only available with a surface mount microcontroller. There is no through-hole version of the microcontroller used on Arduino MEGA 2560 boards, so the main microcontroller can not easily be replaced. This does not mean that it can't be replaced, it can be done with a rework soldering station and the necessary skills.

The main difference between Arduino Uno and Arduino MEGA 2560 boards is the size of the boards and number of pins, as can be seen in Figure 1.3 on the next page, which shows an Arduino Uno overlaid on an Arduino MEGA 2560. As can be seen in the figure, the Arduino MEGA 2560 is basically an extension of the Uno. Connectors or pins down the sides of the Arduino MEGA 2560 line up exactly with the same connectors on the Arduino Uno. Only the bottom right connector on the Uno is a 6-pin connector, whereas the Arduino MEGA extends this connector by using an 8-pin connector. At the right end of the Uno is a 6-pin connector (ICSP header), which also lines up with the same connector on the MEGA board. The Arduino MEGA 2560 has two additional 8-pin headers down its length, and a double row 36-pin connector at its end which is a 2 × 18 socket connector. By comparison, the Arduino Uno has a total of 32 socket connection points or "pins", while the Arduino MEGA 2560 has a total of 86. These totals exclude the 6-pin ICSP header.

The other major differences between the Uno and MEGA are the main microcontroller part numbers. Chapter 2 compares the microcontroller found on Arduino MEGA 2560 boards with the microcontroller found on Arduino Uno boards. For those readers wanting to know more about the hardware of the Arduino Uno, refer to the *Arduino Uno Hardware Manual, ISBN 1-54292-181-3*, by the same author.

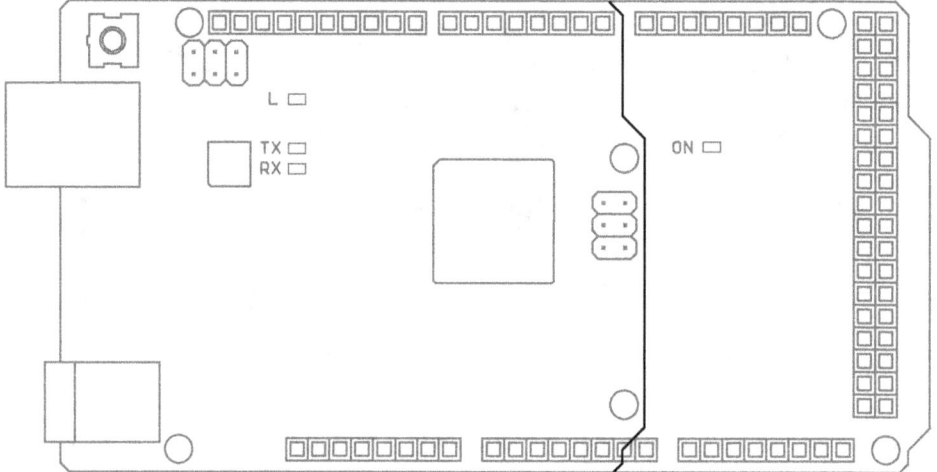

Figure 1.3: Arduino Uno Outline Overlaid on an Arduino MEGA 2560

1.1.3 Uses of the Arduino MEGA 2560

Arduino is based on the open-source Wiring project (wiring.org.co) which was originally intended for art and design students who wanted to use electronics in their projects. Originally the Wiring board and the first Arduino (before the Arduino MEGA 2560) were used in education for student projects. Arduino has become popular beyond its original design purpose and is now used by everyone from hobbyists, makers, hackers and educators, to engineers and other professionals.

Some examples of Arduino projects are 3D printer controllers, solar trackers for solar panel control, robots (many different kinds, including drawing robots and plotters), various light displays, clocks, electronic games, weather stations, vending machines and many more. A good place to look for Arduino projects, other than doing an internet search, is at the Arduino Project Hub (create.arduino.cc/projecthub) where projects that use the Arduino MEGA 2560 can be filtered using the products selection menu. Projects can also be filtered by category, difficulty and type. Other uses of an Arduino MEGA 2560 are for quick prototyping and testing of electronic components. For example, a temperature sensor can easily be wired to an Arduino MEGA 2560 and tested by writing a simple software sketch using the Arduino software programming environment (called the Arduino IDE). Temperature readings can then be displayed in the Serial Monitor window of the Arduino IDE to see whether the sensor is working.

1.1.4 Arduino MEGA 2560 Main Parts

Figure 1.4 on the next page shows the main parts of an Arduino MEGA 2560 that will be of interest to a normal user of the board. Each of these parts is described in more detail in the sections that follow.

1.1.4.1 Main Microcontroller

The main microcontroller (part number ATmega2560) runs sketches, or user programs, that are loaded to the Arduino from the Arduino IDE programming environment. Section 2.1 of the next chapter has more information on the main microcontroller of the Arduino MEGA 2560. The Arduino MEGA 2560 board gets its name from this microcontroller.

1.1.4.2 USB Connector

The USB connector is a standard type B connector and can be used to both power the Arduino MEGA 2560 and program it. USB programming is the default method of programming an Arduino MEGA 2560 when using the Arduino IDE software. Use an A to B USB cable for connecting the Arduino MEGA 2560 to a computer. This is the same type of USB cable used with an Arduino Uno.

A user program, called a sketch, can use the USB connection to send and receive serial data. This allows user programs to send data to, and receive data from a computer. The Arduino IDE has a utility called the Serial Monitor, which is one method that can be used to send and receive data over the USB link. Alternatively other serial terminal programs or custom software running on a computer can use the same link to communicate with the Arduino via USB.

1.1.4.3 External Power In

External DC (Direct Current) power with a voltage of between 7V to 12V can be applied to the external power connector of the Arduino MEGA 2560, allowing it to run stand-alone without the need of a computer connected to the USB port. When external power is supplied to the Arduino MEGA 2560 and the USB cable is plugged in for programming, the Arduino will automatically switch to using external power.

External power can be in the form of a DC power supply that converts mains power to low voltage DC, for example a "wall wart" power supply. Alternatively, a battery can be used, as long as the voltage is in the correct range of 7 to 12V. When connecting external power it is very important to get the polarity of the supply connected to the Arduino correctly. The center pin of the external power connector is positive on the Arduino MEGA 2560.

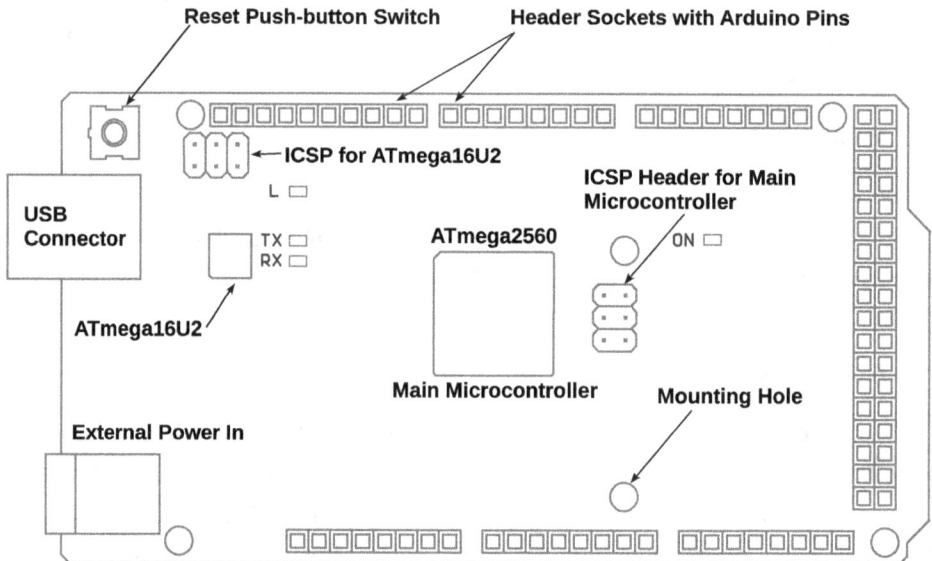

Figure 1.4: Main Parts of the Arduino MEGA 2560

1.1.4.4 Reset Button

A reset button next to the USB connector (next to the main microcontroller ICSP header on older boards, and on some compatible boards) allows manual resetting of the Arduino. Pressing the reset button will reset the main microcontroller, causing the software that is loaded on the main microcontroller to start running from the beginning.

After pressing the reset button, the bootloader software on the main microcontroller will start running. It will then start running whatever user sketch is currently in memory.

1.1.4.5 Header Sockets with Arduino Pins

Header sockets are found on either side, and on one end of the Arduino MEGA 2560. Each hole in the sockets is usually referred to as an Arduino pin. There are several types of pins, including power pins, analog input pins, digital pins and a few special pins. Section 2.7 of chapter 2 has more information on the pin types and functions.

1.1.4.6 ON LED

When power is supplied to the Arduino MEGA 2560, either from the USB connection, or from an external power supply, the ON LED will turn on, indicating that the Arduino MEGA 2560 is powered up.

1.1.4.7 L LED

The L LED is a user programmable LED connected to digital pin 13 on an Arduino MEGA 2560 (pin 13 also controls the L LED on Arduino Uno boards). In other words the L LED can be switched on and off by instructions or statements in any user sketch by controlling digital pin 13.

1.1.4.8 TX LED (Transmit)

When data is transmitted from the main microcontroller over the serial to USB link, the TX LED will flash or blink. This can be data transmitted by both the bootloader software and also a user sketch, if the user sketch transmits data on the serial port.

1.1.4.9 RX LED (Receive)

When data is received by the main microcontroller over the serial to USB link, the RX LED will flash or blink. Data received by the Arduino when the Arduino IDE is loading a sketch to the Arduino by communicating with the bootloader software, as well as any data sent to a user sketch both cause the RX LED to blink.

1.1.4.10 ATmega16U2 Microcontroller

An ATmega16U2 microcontroller in a tiny surface mount package can be found near the USB connector (see Figure 1.4). This microcontroller acts as a bridge between the USB connection and the main microcontroller for either programming the main microcontroller, or when a user sketch sends and receives serial data over the serial to USB link.

This microcontroller comes with factory loaded software, usually referred to as firmware, that gives it its functionality as a USB bridge. For most normal use, this microcontroller is never programmed by the end user.

1.1.4.11 ICSP Header

Most Arduino users won't need to use the ICSP header, except in the case where an extension board (or shield) is used with the Arduino that happens to connect to the ICSP header. Some advanced operations are available through the ICSP header and are described further in this section. New Arduino users may just want to browse through the rest of this section to see what the ICSP capabilities are, but it is not necessary to know about them for normal use. ICSP stands for In-Circuit Serial Programming.

The ICSP header is found near the middle of the board, at the right side of the ATmega2560 microcontroller with the USB connector at the left, and is wired to the main microcontroller. This header has two main uses. It is used by some extension boards (known as shields), such as Ethernet shields which have a connector under them that connects to this header in addition to the normal header pins around the sides of the board. The second use of the ICSP header is to connect an external USB programmer such as an Atmel-ICE, or any number of homemade or third party programming devices. An external programmer can be used to program the Arduino MEGA 2560 through the ICSP header as an alternative to using the default USB programming. This allows the full capacity of the program memory to be used – factory loaded bootloader software that is necessary for USB programming to work uses up some of the program memory (where sketches are loaded to). When using an external programmer, software sketches overwrite the bootloader and make use of the memory that it was occupying.

External programmers also allow the internal programmable fuse settings of the main microcontroller to be easily changed using software such as Atmel Studio. For normal use these fuses are left at their Arduino factory set values. A new bootloader can easily be programmed to the main microcontroller using an external programmer. This means that a board on which the bootloader was overwritten, after using an external programmer to load user sketches, can have its bootloader restored by an external programmer. The board will then be able to use USB programming again without the need of an external programmer.

Alternative programming tools such as Atmel Studio and others can be used to program the Arduino using plain C or C++. Some external programming tools that connect to the ICSP header have debugging capabilities, and when used in combination with Atmel Studio or other similar tools, allow single-step debugging and examination of the internal registers and variables of the main microcontroller. Those readers interested in learning the C language to program Arduino boards may be interested in the book *C Programming with Arduino ISBN 978-1-907920-46-2* by the same author and published by Elektor.

1.1.4.12 ICSP Header for ATmega16U2

A second ICSP header, found near the USB connector, connects to the ATmega16U2 microcontroller. Most Arduino users will never need to use this header. This header can be used to load software to the ATmega16U2 USB bridge microcontroller using the same tools described for the main microcontroller ICSP header. It can be used to update the ATmega16U2 firmware or for advanced users who are developing their own firmware for this microcontroller. An alternative to using this ICSP header to update the firmware on the ATmega16U2 is available, called DFU (Device Firmware Update) programming. DFU programming allows the ATmega16U2 to be programmed using the USB connection.

1.1.4.13 Mounting Holes

Six mounting holes can be found on the Arduino MEGA 2560. Four of these holes are near the corners of the board and two are found near the middle of the board. Four of these holes line up with the the mount holes of the Arduino Uno – two at the USB connector and two near the middle of the board, refer back to Figure 1.3. These holes can be used to mount the Arduino to a base plate or enclosure using screws, or bolts and PCB stand-offs.

1.1.5 Programming

Arduino programming software is available for Windows, Mac OS X and Linux, and is known as the Arduino IDE (Integrated Development Environment). Although this is a manual on the Arduino MEGA 2560 hardware, it is still necessary to have the Arduino IDE programming software installed and ready, as it is used to run various programs for testing the hardware and for demonstrating how the hardware works.

User written programs that are typed into the Arduino IDE are known as *sketches*. Sketches are the equivalent of the source code programs saved in files from other programming languages. Sketches are written in the editor window of the Arduino IDE where they can be verified to see if they contain valid code by clicking the Verify button. Valid sketches can be uploaded to an Arduino board using the Upload button in the Arduino IDE. Whenever the Verify or Upload button is clicked in the Arduino IDE, the build process of the sketch is started, which goes through preprocess, compile and link steps to convert the sketch into a file usable by the main microcontroller.

The Arduino IDE is free to download from www.arduino.cc/en/Main/Software where the correct download must be selected for the desired operating system. For Windows, there are three options for installing the Arduino IDE: by downloading and running the Windows installer, from the Microsoft Store, or via a ZIP file.

It is suggested to just download the ZIP file and extract the contents of the ZIP file (the folder found inside) to a convenient location, such as the desktop. Figure 1.5 shows the contents of the folder that was extracted from the ZIP file and then copied to the Windows desktop. Make sure to extract the folder from the ZIP file and not just open the ZIP file – first open the ZIP file and then drag and drop the folder from the ZIP file to the desktop.

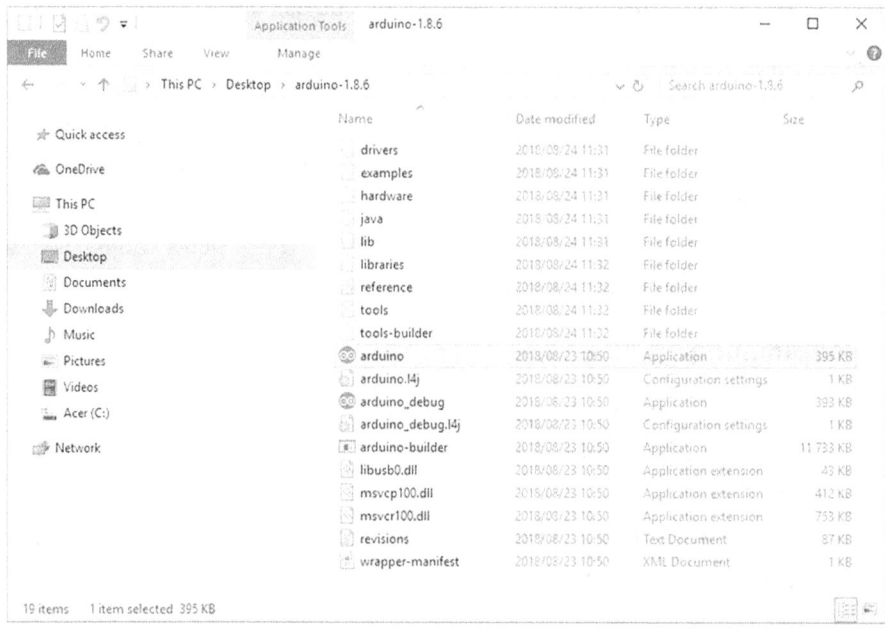

Figure 1.5: Arduino IDE Software Unzipped to a Folder on the Desktop

For those readers who may have already installed the Arduino IDE software using one of the other methods, this is not a problem. Having the Arduino software folder on the desktop does offer some advantages, but is mostly the preference of the author. One advantage is that it allows multiple versions of the IDE to be available on a single computer. It is possible that a newer version of an IDE can cause sketches of an older project to stop working. Building the same project using an older version of the IDE can resolve the problem. Although this type of software bug occurs rarely, it can and does still happen, hence the advantage of having different versions of the Arduino IDE on the same computer. For the purposes of this book, having the Arduino IDE software in an easy to find location on the desktop is convenient when we look at the firmware files that are located in this folder, rather than trying to find them in the file system. Users who have already installed the Arduino IDE using one of the other methods still have the option of downloading the ZIP file for the purpose of examining the software and easily finding the firmware files.

To start the Arduino IDE from the folder extracted from the ZIP file, simply open the folder and double-click the Arduino application file to run it. The Arduino application file can be seen highlighted in Figure 1.5. To remove the software from the computer, just delete the Arduino IDE folder. When a newer version of the software becomes available, the old version can either be left in place or deleted.

Alternative programming environments to the Arduino IDE are available, such as Atmel Studio, other free and commercial professional programming tools, and command line tools. This book uses the Arduino IDE software as the main method of programming the Arduino MEGA 2560. The Arduino IDE is the main or default way of programming Arduino boards, especially for new users.

1.1.6 Extending the Hardware

There are several ways to extend Arduino hardware including: buying add-on boards, using prototype boards, building circuits on strip-board, using an electronic breadboard and making a custom PCB (Printed Circuit Board). A description of each of these methods for extending Arduino MEGA 2560 hardware can be found in the sections that follow. Ultimately whichever method is used to extend the hardware, they all make use of the connector sockets found on each side of, and at the end of, the Arduino MEGA 2560. Hardware can be connected directly to any of the Arduino pins from the connector sockets, or use specific pins such as those that provide serial bus interfaces like SPI or TWI. SPI and TWI are explained further in section 2.3.4 – Adding External Memory, in the next chapter.

1.1.6.1 Add-on Boards: Shields

External add-on boards called *shields* that plug into the header sockets of the Arduino MEGA 2560 are used to extend the hardware of the board. Shields are available from Arduino as well as third party vendors, and include such functionality as Ethernet, WiFi, motor control, USB host support, relays, data logging, and more. Shields with two different form factor sizes can be plugged into Arduino MEGA 2560 boards. Those shields with the Arduino Uno form factor fit at the USB connector end of the MEGA 2560, using only the pins on this end of the board, and possibly the pins from the ICSP header in the middle of the board as well, as shown in Figure 1.6. Full-size shields that are the same size as the MEGA 2560 board are also available that connect to all of the pins on the MEGA 2560. Take note that not all small sized shields that work with Arduino Uno boards will work with Arduino MEGA 2560 boards, as is explained in the sections on the SPI bus in this manual, and in full detail in chapter 9.

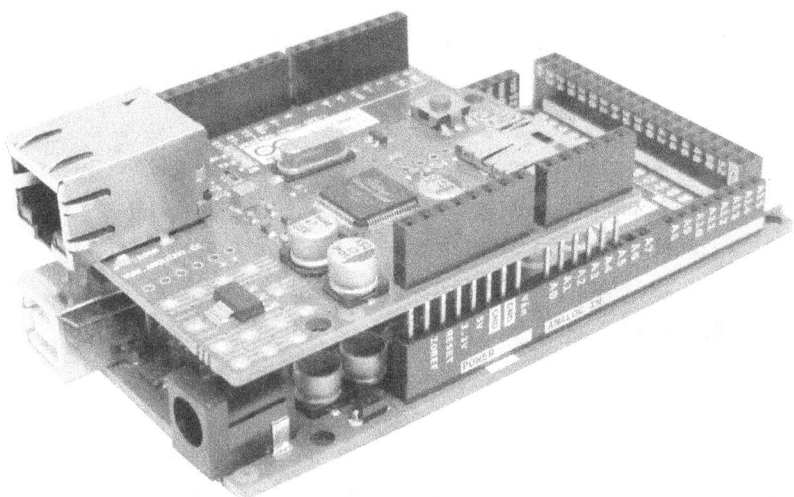

Figure 1.6: Arduino MEGA 2560 with Small Form Factor Ethernet Shield

Stacking Shields

Shields can be stacked one on top of the other to add multiple hardware functionality to an Arduino board. An example of a stack of shields is shown in Figure 1.7 on the next page. In this figure, a full-sized MEGA Proto shield is plugged into an Arduino MEGA 2560, and an Arduino Uno sized Ethernet shield is plugged into the MEGA Proto shield. The Ethernet shield is the small sized shield that fits both the Arduino MEGA 2560 and the Arduino Uno. This particular shield is compatible with both the Uno and MEGA 2560.

Stacking shields is only possible if the shields being used have long pinned connectors that provide pins at the bottom of the shield to plug into the board below, as well as sockets that allow a board to be plugged in above.

When connecting more than one shield to an Arduino, it is important to know which pins of the Arduino connectors are used by the shields. In some cases the pins can be shared, such as when the pins are used as a serial bus such as SPI or TWI. In other cases the shields may not be compatible if they both use one or more of the same pins.

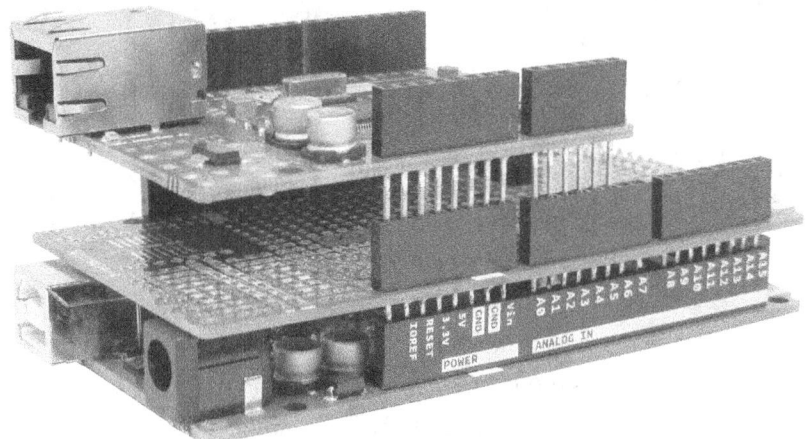

Figure 1.7: Arduino MEGA 2560 with Stacked Shields

Shield Reverse Connection Protection

To prevent shields from being inserted into an Arduino the wrong way around, one of the Arduino headers is spaced so that it is slightly offset from the headers on the other side of the board. This is essential for a classroom environment where hardware could easily be destroyed by students plugging in shields the wrong way around. For more information on the spacing of the headers on an Arduino MEGA 2560, see chapter 8, section 8.6.

1.1.6.2 Prototype Shields

Besides ready made and assembled shields, prototype shields are also available that allow custom circuits to be built on them by soldering the desired components to the board. These prototype shields are available from Arduino and from third party manufacturers. Figure 1.8 on the next page shows the Arduino MEGA PROTO shield REV3 that has the product code A000080 (store.arduino.cc/arduino-mega-proto-shield-rev3-pcb). As can be seen in the figure, prototype boards are blank circuit boards, to which connectors can be soldered so that the boards will plug into an Arduino MEGA 2560 like a shield does. Prototype shields have various holes and tracks to which components can be soldered to build a circuit.

Figure 1.8: Arduino MEGA PROTO Shield Revision 3

Prototype shields with the Arduino Uno form factor are also available, such as the PROTO Shield REV3, product code TSX00083 (store.arduino.cc/proto-shield-rev3-uno-size). Arduino Uno sized prototype shields can be fitted to an Arduino MEGA 2560 in the same way as other Arduino Uno sized shields do, at the USB connector end of the board.

1.1.6.3 Strip-board

Strip-board, such as Veroboard, that has been available to electronic hobbyists for many years can be used to make custom shields. The main problem with strip-board is that one of the Arduino MEGA 2560 headers is offset from the headers on the opposite side of the board, which means that the holes in the strip-board won't line up with the holes in the offset Arduino header, see chapter 8, sections 8.6 and 8.7 for more details. One option that allows strip-board to be used with an Arduino MEGA 2560 is to not use any pins from the offset header. Another option is more of a hack where long pins are soldered in the strip-board and bent to fit into the offset header.

1.1.6.4 Electronic Breadboard

Temporary circuits can be built on electronic breadboards which allows electronic components to be plugged into and removed from them. Breadboard circuits can be connected to Arduino MEGA 2560 pins via the header sockets using jumper wires, as can be seen in Figure 1.9, which shows two LEDs with series resistors connected to digital pins of an Arduino MEGA 2560. A software sketch can be written to control the two LEDs in the circuit, switching them on and off. Components and wires can be unplugged from a breadboard and reused, which is ideal for prototyping and educational use.

Chapter 1 • Arduino MEGA 2560 Overview

Figure 1.9: A Simple Breadboard Circuit Interfaced to an Arduino MEGA 2560

In addition to discrete electronic components, various modules are available that can also be plugged into a breadboard to build circuits. Packs of modules are available that include, for example, 30 modules of various types, such as LED modules, light sensors, tilt switches, temperature and humidity sensors, relays and others. Each module consists of a small circuit board with components soldered to it to make up the circuit. Modules have pins that are used to plug them into a breadboard.

1.1.6.5 Custom PCB

A shield in the form of a custom made PCB (Printed Circuit Board) can be designed and built. This method is more suited to those who have some experience with electronics, as it requires some circuit design skills and ability to use a suitable electronic CAD (Computer Aided Design) package. Also see Fritzing in section 1.6.4.1 in this chapter.

Figure 1.10: Homemade Custom PCB Shield

37

Options here are to either etch a board at home or in a work laboratory, or send the PCB design out to be professionally manufactured. KiCad (kicad-pcb.org) is an open-source EDA (Electronic Design Automation) software package that can be used to draw circuit diagrams and lay out PCBs. A KiCad template for an Arduino MEGA shield is provided with this book – see chapter 8, section 8.8 for details. Figure 1.10 shows an example of a custom homemade Arduino shield that was designed using KiCad. The shield in the figure is fitted to an Arduino MEGA 2560, but only uses the pins available on an Arduino Uno, so it fits to both the Uno and MEGA. This board extends beyond the normal Uno length.

1.1.7 Open-Source and Licensing

Arduino boards are open-source hardware which means that the design files for the hardware are available to examine and modify by anyone. The design files are licensed under a Creative Commons Attribution Share-Alike license which allows personal and commercial derivative works, but they must credit Arduino and release the derivative works under the same license. See creativecommons.org/licenses/ for more information on the various Creative Commons licenses.

The Arduino IDE software is also open-source which means that anyone can have access to the source code which can be examined and modified. Source code for the Java environment (used by the Arduino IDE software) is released under the GPL (General Public License). The C/C++ libraries are released under the LGPL (Lesser General Public License).

Arduino logos are **not** open-source, but are trademarks of Arduino AG. Use of the Arduino name is restricted and Arduino logos may not be copied. For more details, see the page www.arduino.cc/en/Trademark on the Arduino website.

1.1.8 Third Party Compatible Boards

Because Arduino is open-source, many third party Arduino boards are available including third party clone boards and boards that are compatible with the Arduino MEGA 2560. Figure 1.11 shows a board that is compatible with the Arduino MEGA 2560. This board is almost identical to earlier Arduino MEGA 2560 R3 or REV3 boards, except for some markings on the top silkscreen, which is the white writing on the board. Some compatible boards may offer additional features to the official Arduino boards. It can be seen that the board in Figure 1.11 is based on the older revision 3 layout because the reset button is next to the ICSP header, rather than next to the USB connector.

Figure 1.11: Arduino MEGA 2560 Compatible Board from a Third Party Manufacturer

Third party Arduino clones and Arduino compatible boards vary in quality from excellent to poor quality. Some of the cheaper boards, usually from China, are quite usable, but there is always the risk of getting a dud. For more information on the various spin-off boards including official boards, clones, derivatives, compatibles and even counterfeits, see the article blog.arduino.cc/2013/07/10/send-in-the-clones/ on the Arduino blog.

1.1.9 Build Quality, Warranty and Safety

Buying an official Arduino board manufactured by Arduino or one of its authorized manufacturers guarantees that the board will be a quality product, and that some of the money paid for the board will go back into supporting the Arduino community, such as for further hardware development, documentation and hosting of the support forums. A full list of official Arduino boards can be found at www.arduino.cc/en/Main/Products on the Arduino website.

For more information on Arduino board compliance and for the warranty statement, see www.arduino.cc/en/Main/warranty where probably the most important clause is with regards to safety-critical applications. This clause (clause 1.5) follows, verbatim as it was found on the Arduino website at the above link at the time of writing.

" 1.5 Arduino LLC products are not authorized for use in safety-critical applications where a failure of the Arduino LLC product would reasonably be expected to cause severe personal injury or death. Safety-critical applications include, without limitation, life support

devices and systems, equipment or systems for the operation of nuclear facilities and weapons systems. Arduino LLC products are neither designed nor intended for use in military or aerospace applications or environments, nor for automotive applications or the automotive environment. The Customer acknowledges and agrees that any such use of Arduino LLC products is solely at the Customer's risk, and that the Customer is solely responsible for compliance with all legal and regulatory requirements in connection with such use. "*

1.1.10 Arduino and Genuino

A dispute over the trademark "Arduino" caused Arduino to split into two companies. A new Arduino company was started with a new website at arduino.org and the original Arduino company with the original arduino.cc website. The folks at arduino.cc owned the Arduino trademark in the USA, but not outside of the USA. They then came up with the name *Genuino* to use for boards that sold outside the USA, in order to sidestep the trademark issue, and the name *Arduino* for boards sold in the USA.

Genuino was just a re-branding in order for the original team to be able to sell Arduino boards outside the USA. The whole legal battle has since been resolved and there is now only one Arduino website – arduino.cc and they own all of the trademark rights to the Arduino brand name.

Arduino have since dropped the use of the name *Genuino*. In the Arduino IDE, when selecting a target board, the name *Arduino/Genuino* used to appear next to some of the boards. The name *Arduino* is now used exclusively and Genuino does not appear in the IDE.

1.2 Arduino MEGA 2560 Firmware

As explained earlier in this chapter, the Arduino MEGA 2560 has two microcontrollers – one that acts as a USB to serial bridge and the other is the main microcontroller that runs user loaded programs or sketches. Each of these microcontrollers comes with factory loaded software, usually referred to as firmware in embedded systems such as Arduino.

1.2.1 USB Bridge Firmware

Firmware in the ATmega16U2 chip sets this microcontroller up as a virtual serial port, which is usually referred to as a virtual COM port on a Windows computer. It acts as a bridge between the USB port of the Arduino MEGA 2560 and the serial port or UART of the main microcontroller. When the serial port driver loads on the host computer after plugging the Arduino MEGA 2560 into a USB port, the Arduino looks like a serial port to any software that is running on the computer. The ATmega16U2 microcontroller and its firmware replaces the FT232RL USB to UART bridge chip from FTDI (www.ftdichip.com) found on the original *Arduino MEGA* before the *Arduino MEGA 2560*. Some clone or compatible boards still use the FTDI, or similar chip. Note that revision 1 and revision 2 Arduino MEGA 2560 boards used the ATmega8U2 chip, but all new Arduino MEGA 2560 revision 3 boards use the ATmega16U2.

With the ATmega16U2 and its firmware acting as a USB to serial port bridge, the Arduino IDE can communicate with the bootloader firmware on the main microcontroller of the Arduino MEGA 2560. This allows new sketches to be loaded to the Arduino MEGA 2560. The USB to serial bridge also allows user sketches to communicate over the USB port with software running on the computer, for example with the Serial Monitor window of the Arduino IDE.

1.2.2 Bootloader

Bootloader software, or firmware, is factory loaded to the main microcontroller (part number ATmega2560) of a new Arduino MEGA 2560. Fuses in the ATmega2560 are also factory programmed so that it boots up in the required state. When the Arduino is switched on or powered up, the first code that runs is the bootloader code. Typically, a bootloader waits a short time for a message over the serial port to see whether the user is loading a new sketch from the Arduino IDE. If a message is not received, program execution then starts at the part of memory where user sketches are loaded. In other words, it starts running whatever user sketch is found in memory. If a message is received that tells the Arduino that a sketch is ready to be uploaded from the Arduino IDE, the bootloader will receive the new sketch, byte by byte, and load it to the user sketch area of memory.

After a new sketch has been loaded to the Arduino from the Arduino IDE, the bootloader will start running the new sketch. From a user point of view, the Arduino simply runs a user sketch from memory when powered up or reset, and a new sketch can be loaded to the Arduino at any time by using the Arduino IDE and USB connection. Because the USB bridge chip on the Arduino MEGA 2560 has control of the reset line of the main microcontroller, the Arduino IDE can reset the microcontroller to force the bootloader to start running when a new sketch is to be loaded.

1.3 Precautions During Handling and Usage

Some precautions when handling and using an Arduino are listed below. The list does not include general workshop safety advice, but rather some things to think about before using or handling an Arduino board. For general or workshop related safety training, refer to other safety related texts which may have country or region specific advice and regulations.

1.3.1 Static Electricity

Electronic components and circuit boards, such as the Arduino MEGA 2560, can be damaged or partially damaged by static electricity, known as ESD (Electrostatic discharge). Static electricity can be stored in the human body or clothing and can discharge into a circuit board when touched, or when a person is very near to a circuit board, but not yet touching it. Static charge build-up is usually more likely to occur in dry regions and/or during dry periods of the year. Clothing made from wool, nylon or polyester can generate static electricity.

Most modern circuit boards that are susceptible to being damaged by static electricity are packaged in silver anti-static, or static shielding bags to protect them from static electricity when being shipped or stored. They usually have an ESD warning sticker attached to them. Arduino boards don't ship in anti-static bags, but are supplied in a box.
It is true that components are less susceptible to static electricity damage after they are soldered in place on a circuit board, and Arduino boards seem to be robust in this regard. The problem is that one can never easily tell what damage static electricity will do because it is so variable in occurrence and charge strength. Some areas or regions have very low occurrences of static electricity and it may not be a problem most of the year. Users may get away with not even being aware of ESD problems in these areas. The important point is to be aware that static electricity can damage a board such as an Arduino and certain electronic components, and to take as many precaution as are feasible, depending on the individual situation and budget.

Note that not all electronic component are static sensitive. Passive parts such as capacitors, resistors and inductors are not static sensitive. Usually semiconductor devices such as microcontrollers, and other integrated circuits will be static sensitive, while parts like transistors may or may not be, depending on the device type. Refer to the datasheet from the manufacturer of the specific device for information on whether an electronic component is static sensitive or not. Many static sensitive devices have a certain amount of protection built into them to try to harden them against ESD. Again, see the datasheet for the specific device and details on built-in ESD protection.

Ideally circuit boards should be handled by persons using a grounded anti-static mat on the work surface and using a grounded anti-static wrist strap. A grounded wrist strap ensures that any static electricity in the human body is discharged to ground. A grounded mat on the work surface creates a static free environment for working with electronics. In professional environments, in addition to anti-static work surfaces and wrist straps, floors are covered with anti-static mats and personnel wear anti-static clothing and use ESD safe tools. At the very least, static electricity should be discharged from the body by touching a grounded metal surface before handling static sensitive equipment or devices.

For the hobbyist and makers on a budget, get a small bench-top anti-static mat and wrist strap for working with Arduino and electronics. Mats have studs that are used to ground them through the earth connection of a wall plug. Anti-static wrist straps connect either to ground through a wall plug or to a stud on an already grounded mat. Wrist straps have an internal 1MΩ resistor to protect the user should the ground point accidentally become live.

The list that follows is a summary of precaution to take when handling any static sensitive equipment.

- Avoid wearing clothing that generates static electricity
- Store static sensitive boards is silver ESD shielding bags
- Leave static sensitive components in their protective packaging until needed
- Use a grounded anti-static mat on the workbench and a grounded wrist strap
- If anti-static equipment is not available, discharge static electricity from the body on a grounded metal surface
- Avoid touching the metal parts on a circuit board – hold the board on its sides
- Be aware of environmental conditions that increase the possibility of static electricity, including low humidity air from air conditioners

1.3.2 Work Surface

Avoid metal workbenches, even if painted, as any scratches could expose the conductive metal and short circuit the Arduino board underneath. One solution to this problem is to cover the top of the workbench with an anti-static, or ESD safe mat. Keep the work surface free of wires and small component that could easily end up under the Arduino causing a short circuit of the exposed solder joints on the bottom of the board.

1.3.3 Power

When connecting a prototype circuit, extension shield or doing any other wiring on the Arduino, make sure that the power to the Arduino is disconnected. Only power up the Arduino after finishing any wiring. Also be sure to check the wiring, especially polarity, before applying power to the system. When changing hardware connected to an Arduino, it is best to first load the default Blink sketch, or even better to load a blank sketch to overwrite the currently loaded sketch. This is because Arduino pins can individually be configured as inputs or outputs. Driving an output pin in a sketch for one hardware configuration, and then changing the hardware before loading a new sketch could result in the Arduino pin driving into an output from the new hardware, which may result in a short circuit. Loading a blank sketch is a precaution that should be taken unless you are absolutely sure that the new hardware configuration won't be damaged by the currently loaded sketch.

1.3.4 Voltage

Arduino MEGA 2560 boards are rated at 5V (five volts). This voltage is the voltage that the circuitry of the Arduino operates at and the voltage levels that its output pins will drive and its input pins can handle being applied to them. Make sure that a higher voltage is not applied to any Arduino pin and that any circuit connected to the Arduino can handle 5V – watch out for devices that can only handle lower voltages such as 3.3V.

3.3V devices can be connected to an Arduino MEGA 2560, but must use the appropriate voltage level shifters on its pins, and must use a 3.3V supply voltage, such as from the Arduino 3.3V pin. Various voltage level shifters are available, or can be built from transistors and resistors.

Although the Arduino operates at 5V, the external power supply can have a voltage of between 7V to 12V. An on-board regulator steps this voltage down to 5V.

1.3.5 Handling

Most handling precautions have to do with ESD safety as already discussed in section 1.3.1 – Static Electricity. When handling an Arduino or other circuit board it is better to pick the board up by its edges. This not only avoids touching metal parts which could be a path for ESD, but also prevents getting oils, sweat or dirt from the fingertips on the metal parts. Metal parts will eventually become dull and corroded if handled frequently. It is better to handle Arduino boards and electronic component as little as possible and avoid touching metal parts of the Arduino or electronic components. Leads of component can start to become less conductive or more resistive once they start corroding or start to get a build-up of grime. Although it is impossible to build circuits, especially breadboard circuits, without touching metal component leads at some time, the main point here is to be aware that touching them can eventually cause corrosion and dirt build-up, and to try and avoid touching them as much as possible.

1.3.6 Interfacing Precautions

Interfacing in electronics refers to the interconnecting of circuits or systems. Connecting an external circuit or component to an Arduino is an example of interfacing. When interfacing with an Arduino MEGA 2560 or any other electronic system, certain precautions must be taken. Most of the precautions have to do with an understanding of basic electronics, such as not trying to draw too much current from an Arduino pin, not interfacing circuits to the Arduino that operate at too high voltages without proper isolation, and properly overrating components used in interface circuits. Many beginner Arduino users have not had the advantage of first getting an education in electronics, so may be at risk of damaging their Arduino or interface circuit.

One of the most important rules that beginners need to know is that when connecting an LED to an Arduino, a resistor of the appropriate resistance must always be used in series with the LED so that the LED does not draw too much current from the Arduino pin, which can damage both the LED and the Arduino. If damage is done in this way to an Arduino MEGA 2560, the main ATmega2560 microcontroller would need to be replaced. As already pointed out, this is difficult to do without professional rework equipment.

Unfortunately an earlier Arduino board, the Arduino NG, had a series resistor connected between a pin on the main microcontroller and Arduino digital pin 13. On this particular board, an external LED could directly be connected between pin 13 and the GND pin next to it, by inserting it directly into these two connections on the header socket of the board.

The LED could then be switched on and off from a user sketch and not be damaged because of the on-board series resistor. This led to people assuming that an LED could be directly connected between pin 13 and GND of any other Arduino board. This wrong information is found on the internet and even printed in recent books. Take note that <u>the Arduino MEGA 2560 does not have a series resistor connected to pin 13 on the board, and an LED can not safely be connected between pin 13 and GND without damaging it and/or the Arduino</u>.

Although this book does not teach basic electronics, it does teach interfacing principles and gives some basic interfacing examples in chapter 3. Learning electronics the hard way and burning out components and circuit boards is one way of learning. A better way is first to learn and understand how something works. New Arduino users are encouraged to learn as much about electronics and microcontrollers as possible. There are many electronics and Arduino related books and resources available to learn from.

1.4 Arduino MEGA 2560 History and Revisions

In March of 2009, the Arduino MEGA board was released – note that this was an Arduino MEGA and not Arduino MEGA 2560. The MEGA board used an ATmega1280 microcontroller and FTDI chip for USB.

Arduino MEGA 2560 boards were first released in September of 2010 as a successor to the 2009 Arduino MEGA. Arduino MEGA 2560 boards have the same form factor as the Arduino MEGA.

The Arduino MEGA 2560 has been through a few hardware revisions since its first release. An original Arduino MEGA 2560, which is now referred to as R1, REV1 or revision 1, was succeeded by a revision 2 board (R2 or REV2) and then a revision 3 board. Each hardware revision added some improvements to the design of the board. At the time of writing, revision 3 is the newest version of the Arduino MEGA 2560 and has been available since 2015. The revision number is sometimes written as R3 or REV3.

Currently the latest board is referred to as Rev3e in the schematic and build files and adds two components, an inductor L2 and capacitor C16, that older REV 3 boards don't have. These components form a filter on one of the main microcontroller power pins. REV3 boards have had some superficial changes since they were first released, but the revision number has not been incremented. Newer Arduino MEGA 2560 REV3 boards are a teal color, instead of the blue color of older REV3 boards. Newer REV3 boards have also had some changes to the silkscreen (the white letters and markings on the circuit board), both on the top and bottom of the board, so look different from older REV3 boards. The header sockets or connectors found at the edges of Arduino MEGA 2560 boards are now one-piece connectors with silkscreen labels on newer REV3 boards. Older revision 3 boards had three separate connectors or header sockets on each side of the board with no labels on the connectors. The most obvious difference between older REV3 boards and Rev3e boards is that the reset switch has been moved to the corner of the board next to the USB connector. On older REV3 boards, the reset switch is next to the ICSP header. Lastly, new Arduino MEGA 2560 REV3 boards now ship with a clear plastic base that houses the board and has additional mounting holes.

One of the more notable differences between the Arduino MEGA 2560 revision 3 board and the previous two revisions is that the microcontroller chip used as a USB to serial bridge was upgraded from an ATmega8U2 to an ATmega16U2. The difference between these two chips is that the ATmega8U2 has 8K of Flash program memory and the ATmega16U2 has 16K of Flash program memory. Another difference between the R3 board and previous Arduino MEGA 2560 revisions is that the number of pins on the header sockets at the edges of the board was increased, making the TWI pins available as SCL1 and SDA1 on the other end of the board, and adding an IOREF and unused pin.

1.5 First Time Use and Basic Testing

Be sure to have the Arduino IDE software installed or copied to the desktop or other convenient location as described in section 1.1.5 – Programming, before starting with this section.

1.5.1 New Arduino MEGA 2560 Default Behavior

Knowing the default behavior of an Arduino MEGA 2560 board can help to identify if a board is working properly, or if it is faulty. This also helps with the fault finding process when dealing with a board that is suspected of being faulty.

1.5.1.1 Computer Drivers

When plugging an Arduino MEGA 2560 into the USB port of a computer, drivers will be loaded by the operating system of the computer. A Windows 10 computer will display a notification message indicating that drivers are being loaded the first time that a new board is connected. Subsequent times, no messages will be displayed.

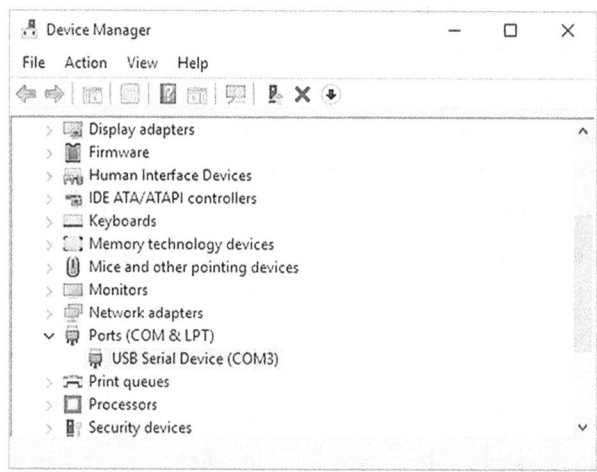

Figure 1.12: Arduino MEGA 2560 in the Windows 10 Device Manager

To check that drivers have loaded on a Windows 10 system, right click the Windows Start button, or menu icon, at the left of the bottom task bar, and then click Device Manager on the menu that pops up. This will open the Device Manager window. In the window, expand Ports (COM & LPT) by clicking the arrow at the left of it, and the Arduino should appear as a USB Serial Device with a COM port number as shown in Figure 1.12. COM port numbers found in the Device Manager may differ. They start at COM1, and can go up to COM15 and beyond. If there is more than one device under the Ports item in Device Manager, and you are not sure which device the Arduino MEGA 2560 is, leave Device Manager open and unplug the Arduino from the USB cable. The item that goes away is the Arduino. Plug the Arduino back in and it will appear back in the Device Manager window again.

1.5.1.2 Arduino MEGA 2560 Hardware Behavior

The following behavior is expected on a new official Arduino MEGA 2560 board. Bear in mind that software or firmware that controls the LEDs could be changed and updated in the future, so the LED behavior could change at some stage, however this is not highly likely. Also note that the bootloader software on an Arduino MEGA 2560 is different from the bootloader software on an Arduino Uno, so the startup behavior is slightly different between the two boards.

Boards that are not official Arduino MEGA 2560 boards such as clones or Arduino MEGA 2560 compatible boards are expected to behave in a similar way, but may have different software loaded on them, so may not behave exactly the same way.

On LED

After plugging an Arduino MEGA 2560 into an external power source, or into a computer using a USB cable, the first thing to look for is if the ON LED switches on. The ON LED indicates that the board is powered by 5 volts, either directly from the USB cable, or via the on-board regulator if external power is used.

RX LED and L LED on Some Systems

On some computers, such as Linux systems, the RX LED will blink rapidly for a burst, then switch off for a period, and repeat this burst 5 times, switching off after each burst. While the RX LED is behaving this way, the L LED stays on. Altogether, this startup delay takes around 8 seconds before the blink sketch, which is factory loaded on a new board, starts running (see next section). This delay and RX LED flashing does not occur when the board is plugged into a Windows computer, or powered directly from the external power connector instead of from USB.

Factory or User Loaded Sketch Running

On a new official Arduino MEGA 2560 board, the L LED will start to flash or blink slowly, on for 1 second and off for 1 second, as soon as the board is powered up. This is because the Blink sketch is factory loaded as a test and indicator to show that the Arduino is working. The Blink sketch is one of the example sketches that comes with the Arduino IDE software. Clone or compatible boards may or may not have the Blink sketch factory loaded. As mentioned in the previous section, when the board is powered from the USB connector on some computers, such as Linux systems, there is a significant delay before the default blink sketch starts running. The blink sketch starts running immediately on Windows computers and when the board is powered by an external power supply.

The first time that a user loads a new sketch, the default Blink sketch is overwritten. When the Arduino MEGA 2560 is powered up, the last uploaded user loaded sketch will run. The default Blink sketch can always be reloaded to the Arduino for testing purposes as is described in the next section.

1.5.2 Loading a Sketch to an Arduino MEGA 2560

Before loading a sketch to an Arduino MEGA 2560, start the Arduino IDE software. The correct Arduino board model and port must then be selected in the IDE. A sketch can then be written, or an example sketch opened, and loaded to the Arduino board. These steps are documented in the sections that follow.

1.5.2.1 Select Board, Processor and Port

With the Arduino IDE software started, plug the Arduino MEGA 2560 board into a USB port of the host computer. From the top menu, select Tools ▶ Board ▶ Arduino AVR Boards and then select Arduino Mega or Mega 2560 from the menu that pops out.

After Arduino Mega or Mega 2560 is selected, an item called Processor appears below the Board item on the menu. Make sure that ATmega2560 (Mega 2560) is selected for the Processor item. The two options that can be selected for the Processor setting are either ATmega2560 for *Arduino MEGA 2560* boards, or ATmega1280 for older *Arduino MEGA* boards. The full menu selection for the Processor setting is Tools ▶ Processor ▶ ATmega2560 (Mega 2560). This is different from the Arduino Uno where the processor does not need to be selected, and this option is not available on the menu.

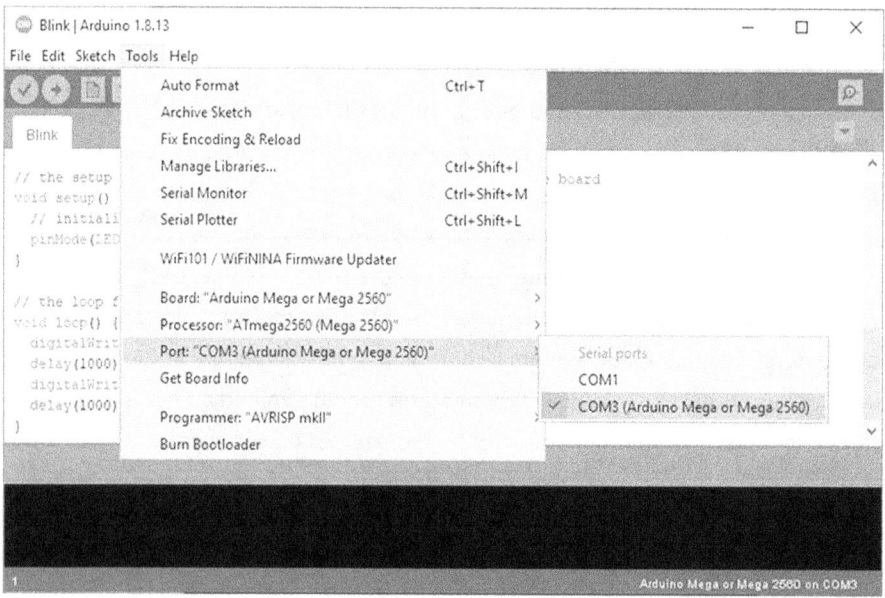

Figure 1.13: Setting up the Board, Processor and Port in the Arduino IDE

In order to be able to load a sketch to the board, the port that the board is configured as, must be selected. From the top menu, select Tools ▶ Port and then the port for the Arduino board on the menu that pops up. On a windows computer the port name will be in

Chapter 1 • Arduino MEGA 2560 Overview

the form COM3 (Arduino Mega or Mega 2560) where the number next to COM may be a different number, depending on which COM port number was assigned to the board.

Notice that after selecting the board, processor and port, the selected board, processor and port can be seen on the Tools menu, next to the Board:, Processor: and Port: items, when it is popped out, as shown in Figure 1.13. The currently selected board and port appear in the status bar of the Arduino IDE and can be seen at the bottom right of the Arduino IDE in Figure 1.13.

1.5.2.2 Loading a Test Sketch

Loading the Blink example sketch to the Arduino MEGA 2560 is a first basic test to see if the board is working and the Arduino IDE is set up correctly. The Blink sketch comes with the Arduino IDE software and is available under the top File menu. It simply blinks or flashes the L LED on and off at a slow rate. If the Blink sketch runs, it proves that the Arduino IDE can "see" the board, that the board, processor and port are correctly set up, and that at least some of the Arduino hardware is working.

Open the Test Sketch

Open the Blink sketch using the top menu in the Arduino IDE. The sketch is found under File ▶ Examples ▶ 01.Basics ▶ Blink and will open as text in a new Arduino IDE window when clicked.

Upload the Sketch

Once opened, the sketch can be loaded to the Arduino MEGA 2560 board. Click the Upload button on the top toolbar (the second icon from the left that looks like a right pointing arrow, next to the tick mark icon), or use Sketch ▶ Upload from the top menu. If the correct Arduino board and port was selected, the sketch should compile and load to the Arduino, and then start running. The TX and RX LEDs will flash briefly during the upload.

Modify the Sketch

If the Blink sketch was already loaded to the Arduino MEGA 2560, such as with a new factory default board, no difference will be seen on the L LED when the Blink sketch is loaded again. In this case, changing the blink frequency of the LED in the sketch, and then loading the modified sketch to the Arduino, will show that a new sketch was indeed loaded properly to the Arduino, as the L LED will start blinking faster. The sketch that follows is a modified Blink sketch that has been changed to leave the L LED on and off for 200ms (0.2 second) periods instead of the normal 1s periods.

Arduino MEGA 2560 Hardware Manual

```
void setup() {
  pinMode(LED_BUILTIN, OUTPUT);     // Configure L LED pin as output
}
void loop() {
  digitalWrite(LED_BUILTIN, HIGH);  // Switch L LED ON
  delay(200);                       // Leave L LED ON for period
  digitalWrite(LED_BUILTIN, LOW);   // Switch L LED OFF
  delay(200);                       // Leave L LED OFF for period
}
```

To verify that this sketch is running on the Arduino, load it to the board and take note if the L LED is blinking faster than it does with the default Blink sketch.

1.5.2.3 Serial Port Demonstration

As already mentioned in this chapter, the USB link between the Arduino MEGA 2560 and the host computer can be used by a sketch to send and receive data between the computer and Arduino. This ability can be useful when debugging a board because diagnostic information in the form of text can be sent from the Arduino and displayed on the computer. The Arduino IDE has a utility called the Serial Monitor window that can display text sent from the Arduino board. Text can also be sent to the Arduino board using the Serial Monitor window.

Serial Port Sketch Example

Open the ASCIITable example sketch from the Arduino IDE by selecting File ▶ Examples ▶ 04.Communication ▶ ASCIITable from the top menu. Upload the sketch to the Arduino MEGA 2560 board. After uploading the sketch, nothing will be seen until the Serial Monitor window is opened.

Serial Monitor Window

In the Arduino IDE, open the Serial Monitor window by clicking the magnifying glass icon at the very right of the top toolbar, as can be seen in Figure 1.14. Alternatively, select Tools ▶ Serial Monitor from the top menu.

When the Serial Monitor window is opened, it connects to the Arduino from the host computer. This causes the USB bridge chip to issue a reset to the main microcontroller which restarts the sketch that is currently loaded in memory. With the ASCIITable example sketch loaded, it will start running and send text from the Arduino, which is then displayed in the Serial Monitor window as can be seen in Figure 1.14. Pressing the reset button on the Arduino MEGA 2560 will also restart the loaded sketch, and the text will be sent to the

Serial Monitor window again. Text will be seen scrolling up the Serial Monitor window. The ASCIITable sketch prints a certain number of lines of text and then stops, so the Arduino needs to be reset to run it again.

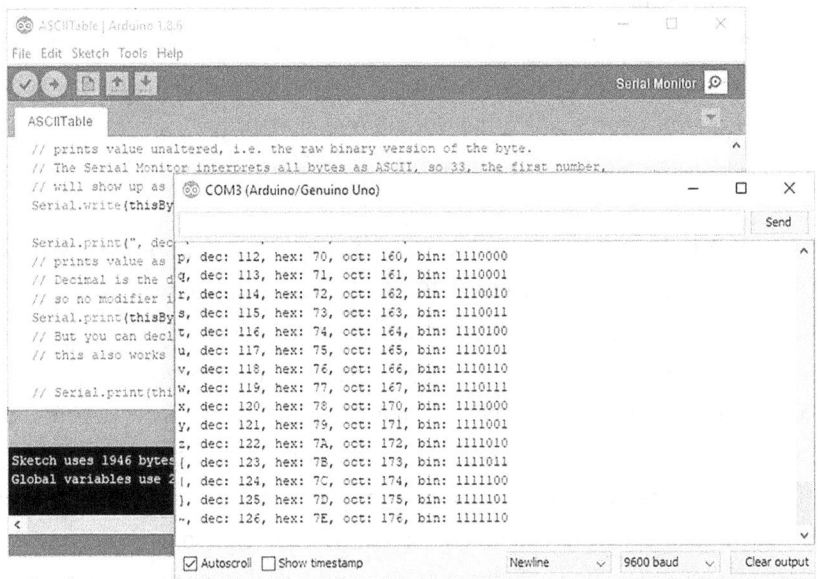

Figure 1.14: Opening the Serial Monitor Window in the Arduino IDE

When sending text or data to the Serial Monitor window from a sketch running on the Arduino board, it is important to make sure that the baud rate set in the Serial Monitor window matches the baud rate set in the sketch. The default baud rate of the Arduino IDE Serial Monitor window is 9600 baud. This setting can be seen at the bottom of the Serial Monitor window in Figure 1.14, where it can be changed by opening the drop-down list.

It is the serial port or UART in the ATmega2560 microcontroller chip that is sending and receiving serial data over the USB link via the USB bridge chip. This port is programmed using the Serial object in sketches. The baud rate of the port is set when the port is initialized at the start of the sketch with the following line of code.

```
Serial.begin(9600);
```

If the baud rate is changed here, the same baud rate must be selected in the drop-down list at the bottom of the Serial Monitor window.

In addition to being able to receive text, the Serial Monitor window can send text to the Arduino. Text typed into the text box at the top of the Serial Monitor window will be sent to the Arduino when the Send button at the right of the text box is clicked. The SerialEvent example sketch, found under File ▶ Examples ▶ 04.Communication ▶ SerialEvent on the top menu of the Arduino IDE, will echo back text that is sent using the Serial Monitor window. In other words, when text is typed into the top text box, and sent, it will appear in the big receive area of the Serial Monitor window because the Arduino simply sends back the text that it receives when running the SerialEvent sketch.

1.5.3 Basic Testing

Knowing how an Arduino MEGA 2560 board is supposed to behave greatly aids the testing of it. Section 1.5.1 – New Arduino MEGA 2560 Default Behavior, already provides good basic information on the board that helps with fault finding, whether testing a new Arduino MEGA 2560 that has just been bought to verify that it is working, or whether starting to do fault finding on a suspect or damaged board. If the board appears to be starting up correctly, and is recognized by the host computer (drivers are loaded and it can be seen in the operating system, for example in the Device Manager of Windows computers), the next step is to try to load a sketch as described in section 1.5.2 of this chapter – Loading a Sketch to an Arduino MEGA 2560. The Blink sketch is a good sketch to use for very basic testing. If an Arduino board that was known to be working becomes faulty, use the steps that follow to do some basic initial fault finding. More advanced fault finding requires a better understanding of the hardware which is explained in later chapters of this book.

1.5.3.1 Visually Inspect the Board

Check the board for mechanical damage such as broken tracks on the circuit board or obviously damaged components or bent connectors with pins that may be shorted together (ICSP headers). Also look for burned out components, which may contain burn marks or show burn marks on the circuit board around them. Don't power up the board if it shows obvious signs of damage. First repair the board or replace damaged components before powering up the board. It is better to first power a newly repaired board from external power to avoid the risk of damaging the host computer should anything go wrong.

1.5.3.2 Power LED and Voltages

If the board appears to be physically undamaged, power up the board and check that the ON LED lights up. The ON LED indicates that 5V is present on the board. If the LED does

Chapter 1 • Arduino MEGA 2560 Overview

not light up, use a multimeter set to the voltage scale to check if 5V is present between the GND and 5V pins. If 5V is present, it could indicate a blown ON LED, or possibly a broken circuit board track.

Check that the voltage on the 5V pin is actually 5V or a value near to it. Low voltage from a USB connection could be a possible problem. If 5V is not present when the board is powered from an external power supply, the on-board regulator could be faulty. Also check that the external voltage can be measured on the Vin pin to make sure that the external supply voltage is getting to the board.

1.5.3.3 Check Expected Default Behavior

See if the board shows the expected default behavior when powered up. If the bootloader was erased from the main microcontroller, or never factory programmed, it will not be possible to load a user sketch from the Arduino IDE. In this case, an external programmer is needed to load the bootloader to the main microcontroller by using the ICSP header.

1.5.3.4 Is the Board Recognized by the Host Computer?

Make sure that the board appears in the Port selection list of the Arduino IDE under the Tools menu, or that it can be found in the operating system, such as in the Device Manager on a Windows system. If the board is not found, it could indicate a problem with the USB bridge chip on the Arduino MEGA 2560, or a driver problem on the host computer.

On a Windows system the COM port number changes when changing boards – that is, if you have more than one Arduino MEGA 2560 and swap them on the computer's USB port. In this case a sketch won't upload to a new board if the old board was unplugged and a new or different board plugged into the USB port of the host computer, because the new port must first be selected in the Arduino IDE. Select the new COM port from the Port menu found under the top Tools menu before attempting to upload a sketch to the new board. Also make sure that the USB cable being used is not faulty.

1.5.3.5 Load a Test Sketch

If all of the tests in the previous sections pass, then the final test is to load a sketch to the Arduino to make sure that it uploads correctly and starts running. As already mentioned, the Blink example sketch is a good sketch to use for basic testing. If the Blink sketch does not work then try one of the serial port tests to see if the Arduino can send back text over the USB link to the Serial Monitor window, as described in section 1.5.2.3 of this chapter – Serial Port Demonstration.

1.6 Arduino MEGA 2560 References and Help

Several resources are available on the Arduino website to help new users get started with Arduino, as well as any Arduino users to get support. This section is mostly for the benefit of new Arduino users, to help them find all the basic information needed to get started with Arduino boards. Find the supporting website for this book at wspublishing.net and click the book name to go to its area on the website.

1.6.1 Installing Software

Help documentation on installing the Arduino IDE software is available for Windows, MAC OS X and Linux. Follow the links below for your operating system.

1.6.1.1 Windows

www.arduino.cc/en/Guide/Windows

1.6.1.2 MAC OS X

www.arduino.cc/en/Guide/MacOSX

1.6.1.3 Linux

www.arduino.cc/en/Guide/Linux

In Linux you need to add yourself to the dialout group to be able to program from the IDE. After adding yourself to the dialout group, the computer must be restarted, or you must log out and log back in again for the changes to take effect.

1.6.2 Getting Started, Examples and Reference

Getting started guides, examples and a software reference are all available on the Arduino website. Getting started guides and examples are a great way for new Arduino users to learn about building projects with Arduino and learning to write sketches.

1.6.2.1 Getting Started Guides

Links to getting started guides for any Arduino board can be found at:
www.arduino.cc/en/Guide

Arduino MEGA 2560 specific getting started guide:
www.arduino.cc/en/Guide/ArduinoMega2560

1.6.2.2 Arduino Examples and Tutorials

An index to tutorials and examples at www.arduino.cc/en/Tutorial/HomePage on the Arduino website provides links to various categories.

1.6.2.3 Building Breadboard Circuits

A tutorial series at startingelectronics.org/beginners/start-electronics-now/ shows how to build breadboard circuits with some Arduino examples.

1.6.2.4 Arduino Software Reference

Arduino language and library reference: www.arduino.cc/reference/en/

1.6.3 Getting Help

Find the **Arduino FAQ** (Frequently Asked Questions) at www.arduino.cc/en/Main/FAQ

Problems and solutions can be found on the **Arduino Troubleshooting** page at www.arduino.cc/en/Guide/Troubleshooting

The **Arduino wiki** at playground.arduino.cc/ is a user contributed collection of documentation and other useful information.

The **Arduino Forum** at forum.arduino.cc is a place where anyone can post a question that will be answered by community members. The forum can also be searched for other user's questions which may already have answers. It is also a place where more experienced Arduino users can help others by answering questions.

1.6.4 Related Open-Source Projects

Several open-source projects that are related to Arduino are used in education like Arduino is, and are useful to Arduino users. An overview of Arduino would not be complete without mentioning the projects in the sections that follow.

1.6.4.1 Fritzing

Fritzing, found at fritzing.org on the web, provide a software package that can be used to draw Arduino breadboard circuits and then turn them into custom made printed circuit boards or PCBs. Fritzing is available for Windows, Mac OS X and Linux. It is an easier way for beginners to create an Arduino shield or custom PCB without the need to learn a full-blown EDA CAD package.

The software has a drag-and-drop type of interface where common electronic components can be placed on a breadboard visually, and wired up to an Arduino MEGA 2560 or other board. In the Fritzing software there are three different views of the same circuit. A breadboard view shows the breadboard circuit as it is being drawn. A schematic or circuit diagram view of the same breadboard circuit can be seen under the schematic tab in the software. Under the PCB tab is a view of the shield PCB and the components placed on the breadboard. The PCB can be built by moving the components to the desired areas on the board and then joining them using tracks that will be the copper tracks of the PCB when it is manufactured. When laying out the PCB, lines show the electrical connections made on the breadboard so that joining the components correctly using PCB tracks is made easy.

1.6.4.2 Wiring

Wiring is the project that Arduino hardware and the Arduino IDE software is largely based on. Find the Wiring project at wiring.org.co on the web. Wiring was already mentioned in this chapter in section 1.1.3 – Uses of the Arduino MEGA 2560. The Arduino MEGA 2560 IDE is based on the Wiring IDE which in turn is based on the Processing IDE. Processing is described in the next section.

1.6.4.3 Processing

Processing, found at processing.org on the web, is a programming language based on Java, and a software package for developing applications that run on a computer. It was developed for use in the visual arts. Like the Arduino IDE, it uses the concept of sketches and looks very similar to the Arduino IDE software. As with Arduino it is available cross-platform for Windows, Mac OS X and Linux.

Processing is often used in conjunction with Arduino where a custom application is needed on a computer that communicates with an Arduino board via the USB cable. Some of the Arduino IDE example programs communicate with a Processing application. One such example is PhysicalPixel, found in the Arduino IDE under File ► Examples ► 04.Communication ► PhysicalPixel from the top Arduino IDE menu. Code at the bottom of this example sketch is commented out – meaning that it is made into one big comment so that the Arduino IDE and compile tools won't try to interpret or compile it. The idea is to copy this code from the bottom of the Arduino sketch and paste it into the Processing IDE, where it will be uncommented. Then load the Arduino sketch to the Arduino and run the Processing code sketch on the computer. When the Processing sketch runs, it displays a window with a small square in the middle of it. Moving the mouse cursor over the square switches the Arduino MEGA 2560 L LED on. Moving the mouse cursor off the square switches the Arduino L LED off. Find the PhysicalPixel tutorial on the Arduino website at www.arduino.cc/en/Tutorial/PhysicalPixel

1.6.5 Arduino MEGA 2560 on the Web

Find the Arduino MEGA 2560 web page at store.arduino.cc/arduino-mega-2560-rev3 which includes basic technical information and links to the circuit diagram (schematic) and board build files in electronic format. At the time of writing, the schematic, board size file, Eagle files and pinout diagram can be found under the DOCUMENTATION tab on this web page. The FAQ tab contains a lot of technical information about the board, however this information is not always correct, such as 50mA specified for the 3.3V pin.

1.7 Arduino MEGA 2560, DUE and MEGA ADK

Before closing this chapter, it is worth saying something about boards that look similar to the Arduino MEGA 2560, in that they have the same physical form factor and size, namely the Arduino DUE and the Arduino MEGA ADK. Both of these boards are briefly discussed and compared with the Arduino MEGA 2560 in the sections that follow.

1.7.1 Arduino DUE vs. Arduino MEGA 2560

Both the Arduino MEGA 2560 and Arduino DUE have identical board form factor and size, but there are some important differences between the two boards. Both are Arduino boards, but must not be confused with each other. Arduino MEGA 2560 boards are more closely related to the Arduino Uno: both of these boards operate from 5V and have an 8-bit AVR microcontroller as the main processor, although each have a different main microcontroller part from the same AVR family. On the other hand, Arduino DUE boards operate from 3.3V and have a main microcontroller that is a 32-bit ARM device. DUE boards also operate at a much higher clock speed than MEGA 2560 boards. Figure 1.15 on the next page shows an Arduino MEGA 2560 and Arduino DUE side by side.

Because the MEGA 2560 and Due operate at different voltages, it is important not to mix the two up. Connecting 5V circuits to an Arduino DUE could damage the board. This manual does not include any further information on the Arduino DUE, as it has specifically been written for the Arduino MEGA 2560. More information on the Arduino DUE can be found at store.arduino.cc/arduino-due

1.7.2 Arduino MEGA ADK vs. Arduino MEGA 2560

The Arduino MEGA ADK board is very similar to the Arduino MEGA 2560, having the same ATmega2560 microcontroller and also operating from 5V. Arduino MEGA ADK boards were specifically designed to work with Android and have the same form factor and size as MEGA 2560 boards. MEGA ADK boards have a USB host port in order to connect to Android phones. These boards are currently marked as *retired* on the Arduino website and will not be considered further in this book. For more information on the Arduino MEGA ADK, see store.arduino.cc/arduino-mega-adk-rev3

Figure 1.15: Arduino MEGA 2560 (top) and Arduino DUE (bottom)

Chapter 2 • Hardware Technical Information

A description of the Arduino MEGA 2560 hardware technical information is contained in this chapter, split up into various categories. This chapter and chapter 1 are the hardware user manual chapters of this book.

Whereas chapter 1 gave a broad overview of the Arduino MEGA 2560 hardware, this chapter gives more specific technical information on the hardware. It "zooms in" to the details of the Arduino MEGA 2560 and gives more information on the main microcontroller, memory types and sizes, power supply technical details and technical specifications on the programming and user headers, and other hardware on the board.

In this Chapter

- Arduino MEGA 2560 microcontroller and memory
- External and USB power specifications and connection
- Board operating frequency
- LED indicator and reset button information
- Header sockets pinout and detailed pin functions
- Programming headers pinout and functions

2.1 Microcontroller

The main microcontroller on an Arduino MEGA 2560 is an ATmega2560 8-bit AVR from Microchip that has the full part number ATmega2560-16AU. This part number shows that the Arduino MEGA 2560 was named after the ATmega2560 microcontroller that it uses.

At the time of writing, the full part number was incorrectly specified as ATMEGA2560-15AU in the MEGA2560_Rev3e version of the Arduino MEGA 2560 schematic or circuit diagram. As can be seen in the datasheet for the ATmega2560 microcontroller, there is no part ending with 15AU.

Table 2.1 shows a comparison between the Arduino MEGA 2560 and Arduino Uno with order codes, microcontroller part number and microcontroller chip packages.

Table 2.1: Arduino MEGA 2560 and Arduino Uno Microcontroller Part Numbers

Board	Board Code	Microcontroller	Chip Package
Arduino MEGA 2560	A000067	ATmega2560-16AU	TQFP (100 pin)
Arduino Uno	A000066	ATmega328P-PU	PDIP (28 pin)

On the Arduino MEGA 2560, the ATmega2560-16AU is housed in a 100-pin Thin Quad Flat Package (TQFP) which is surface mount soldered to the top of the board. Figure 2.1 shows a close-up of the microcontroller on an Arduino MEGA 2560 board.

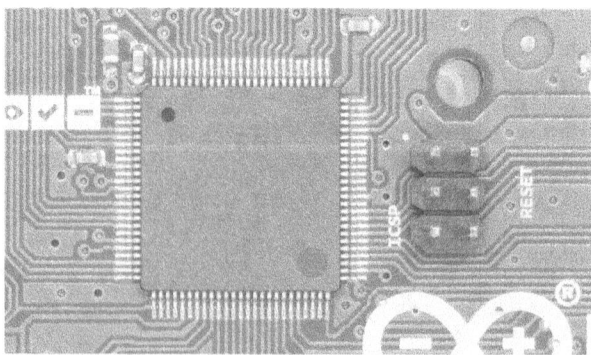

Figure 2.1: ATmega2560-16AU Microcontroller

2.2 Atmel, Microchip and AVR

Originally Atmel was the designer and manufacturer of AVR microcontrollers including the ATmega2560 found on Arduino MEGA 2560 boards. Microchip (www.microchip.com) bought the Atmel company in 2016 and is now the owner and manufacturer of AVR microcontrollers. At the time of writing, even new Arduino MEGA 2560 boards have AVR microcontrollers that still have the Atmel name on them. Many older books and internet sources still make reference to Atmel as the AVR microcontroller manufacturer and still link to the old Atmel website which redirects to the Microchip website. Note that AVR is the microcontroller family of which the ATmega2560 and ATmega16U2 (USB bridge chip on the Arduino MEGA 2560 REV3) are members. AVR refers to the internal processor architecture of these chips, which is 8-bit RISC (Reduced Instruction Set Computer).

2.3 Memory

All memory on the Arduino MEGA 2560 board is found in the ATmega2560 microcontroller chip and is summarized in Table 2.2, which includes a comparison with the ATmega328P microcontroller from Arduino Uno boards.

Table 2.2: Arduino MEGA 2560 (ATmega2560 Microcontroller) Memory Sizes Compared with Arduino Uno (Atmega328P Microcontroller) Memory Sizes

Board	Flash (Program)	SRAM (Data)	EEPROM (Data)
Arduino MEGA 2560	**256K bytes** (262,144 bytes) 248K available by default because of bootloader using an 8K segment	**8K bytes** (8,192 bytes)	**4K bytes** (4,096 bytes)
Arduino Uno	32K bytes (32,768 bytes) 31.5K bytes available by default because of bootloader using a 512 byte segment	2K bytes (2,048 bytes)	1K bytes (1,024 bytes)

As can be seen in Table 2.2, the Arduino MEGA 2560 has 8 times the amount of Flash program memory, 4 times the amount of SRAM data memory, and 4 times the amount of EEPROM data memory when compared to the Arduino Uno.

2.3.1 Flash Memory

Flash memory is non-volatile memory used to store the program instructions of an Arduino sketch or program. Non-volatile memory is memory that retains its contents even if the power is switched off. When an Arduino sketch is loaded to an Arduino, it is loaded to the Flash memory of the ATmega2560 microcontroller chip. Once a sketch is loaded to the Flash memory, every time the power to the Arduino is switched on, the program will start running.

2.3.1.1 Flash Memory Size

The ATmega2560 microcontroller, and therefore the Arduino MEGA 2560 board, has 256K bytes (256 × 1024 bytes) of Flash memory, where a byte is 8 bits wide and 1K = 1024 bytes. Because the bootloader software uses up 8K bytes, or 8192 bytes, of the Flash memory, 248K is available for user programs or sketches. Although the bootloader size is not exactly 8K bytes, an 8K byte sector of Flash is reserved for it.

2.3.1.2 Flash Wear

All Flash memory is subject to wear and has a certain lifetime determined by how many times it is erased and written to or programmed. The life of the Flash program memory of the ATmega2560 due to Flash wear is 10,000 Write/Erase cycles.

2.3.1.3 Data Retention

Data retention, or how long the program remains in the Flash memory before failure, is less than 1 PPM (Part Per Million) over 20 years at a temperature of 85 degrees Celsius, or 100 years at a temperature of 25 degrees Celsius.

2.3.2 SRAM

SRAM (Static Random Access Memory) is volatile memory that is used to store variables or data from an Arduino sketch or program. Part of the SRAM is used for special memory areas called the heap and the stack. Users or programmers need not worry about allocating memory as this is done automatically by the programming tools that are run when loading a sketch to the Arduino using the Arduino IDE.

2.3.2.1 Volatile Memory

Volatile memory is memory that loses its contents when its power is switched off. Part of the SRAM is initialized with data when the program in the main Flash memory starts running, depending on which data is allocated to this memory, for example global variables. Other parts of the SRAM are initialized with values while the sketch is running. All of these values are lost from SRAM memory when the Arduino is powered off.

2.3.2.2 SRAM Size

The ATmega2560 microcontroller, and therefore the Arduino MEGA 2560, has 8K bytes (8 × 1024 bytes) of SRAM, where a byte is 8 bits wide and 1K = 1024 bytes.

2.3.3 EEPROM

EEPROM (Electrically Erasable Programmable Read Only Memory) is non-volatile memory used for data storage. Data stored in EEPROM will not be lost if power to the Arduino is switched off.

2.3.3.1 EEPROM Programming

EEPROM is user programmable and is supported in the Arduino IDE by the EEPROM library, which includes such functions as *EEPROM.write()* and *EEPROM.read()* for writing data to and reading data from the EEPROM. www.arduino.cc/en/Reference/EEPROM is the library reference for using the EEPROM in sketches. EEPROM example sketches can be found in the Arduino IDE from the top menu under File ▶ Examples ▶ EEPROM where EEPROM is found near the bottom of the Examples menu.

2.3.3.2 EEPROM Size

The ATmega2560 microcontroller, and therefore the Arduino MEGA 2560, has 4K bytes (4 × 1024 bytes) of EEPROM, where a byte is 8 bits wide and 1K = 1024 bytes.

2.3.3.3 EEPROM Wear

As with Flash program memory on the ATmega2560 microcontroller, EEPROM is subject to wear as it is erased and programmed. EEPROM on the ATmega2560 has a lifetime of 100,000 Write/Erase cycles.

2.3.4 Adding External Memory

External data memory can be added to an Arduino MEGA 2560 in the form of Flash chips, EEPROM chips or SD cards. Although there are no options to directly add external memory to an Arduino MEGA 2560, external memory can be added using the header sockets or pins of the board. Connection of external memory can be in the form of a shield or breadboard circuit. Ready made shields such as data logging shields usually have an SD card or micro SD card socket. Some shields are combination shields, such as most Ethernet shields that have both an Ethernet connection and micro SD card socket.

2.3.4.1 SD Cards (SPI Interface)

SD cards or micro SD cards can be connected to an Arduino MEGA 2560 using a shield, such as already mentioned, or with an SD card socket breakout board, or module, with level shifters. Figure 2.2. shows both a data logger shield with micro SD card socket and a SD card module. SD cards interface to the SPI bus pins of an Arduino.

Figure 2.2: SD Card Module (left) and Data Logger Shield (right)

The shield at the right of Figure 2.2 has specifically been chosen to show one of the compatibility problems with some small form factor shields. The SD card of this particular shield does not work with the Arduino MEGA 2560, yet the SD card on the Ethernet shield shown in Figure 1.6 of section 1.1.6.1 in the previous chapter does work. The mystery of this incompatibility has to do with the position of the SPI pins on MEGA 2560 boards. Briefly put, the SPI bus pins are found on digital pins 10 to 13 on an Arduino Uno, but on digital pins 50 to 53 on an Arduino MEGA 2560. The only way to make a small form factor shield that uses the SPI bus, and works on both the Uno and MEGA, is to place a 6-pin (2 × 3) connector socket under the shield that connects to the ICSP header of the Arduino. On both the Uno and MEGA 2560, the SPI pins are routed to the ICSP header in addition to pins at the edges of the boards. This is fully explained and illustrated in the next chapter on pins and interfacing. Chapter 9 has more information on shield compatibility.

SD cards operate at 3.3V and are not 5V compatible, so it is important to make sure that the shield or SD card module used with an Arduino MEGA 2560 is specified to work with 5V Arduino boards. Although the voltage of an SD card is given as 3.3V, most SD cards operate over a range of voltages, usually between 2.7V and 3.6V. The SD card module

Chapter 2 • Hardware Technical Information

shown at the left of Figure 2.2 has a 3.3V regulator and a level shifting circuit for correct interfacing between a 5V Arduino and 3.3V SD card. The module is supplied with 5V from the Arduino which is stepped down to 3.3V by the regulator on the module, and then fed to the SD card. Level shifter and RTC (Real Time Clock) chips are found on the data logger shield of Figure 2.2. The shield uses 3.3V from the Arduino to power the SD card, so does not have a regulator on the shield. As already mentioned, this shield does not work by default with an Arduino MEGA 2560, although all the wiring is in place on the board for it to work. To get it to work with a MEGA 2560, the ICSP header on this board must be removed and replaced with a socket connector that connects to the Arduino ICSP header below it when plugged into an Arduino. There are several other design flaws in this shield that are fully discussed in section 9.5.1 of chapter 9.

SD cards have two operating modes, namely SD mode and SPI mode. SD cards will always use SPI mode when connected to an Arduino MEGA 2560. SD mode is patented and requires licensing for any equipment that uses it. SPI mode has no restrictions and can be used freely. To get the fastest data transfers from a standard SD card, SD mode would need to be used because it can transfer 4-bits in parallel at a time. An Arduino MEGA 2560 is not fast enough to get the full data transfer speed from an SD card, even if it were able to use the SD bus mode. www.arduino.cc/en/Reference/SDCardNotes contains more information from Arduino on using SD cards.

See www.arduino.cc/en/Reference/SD for more information on the Arduino SD card library. SD card examples can be found in the Arduino IDE from the top menu under File ▶ Examples ▶ SD where SD is below the middle of the Examples menu. The CardInfo sketch on the SD examples menu is a good sketch to use for testing an SD card and to check if an SD card is correctly wired to an Arduino. Note that when using the example sketches, it is necessary to first check which SD card pins are connected to which Arduino pins. For example, some shields may use Arduino pin 8, 9, or 10 for the CS (chip select) of the SD card, while Arduino Ethernet shields use pin 4 for CS. Modify the sketch to suit the shield being used. This is usually not a problem when using a module because the example sketch can first be opened and the module wired to the Arduino according to the pin information in the sketch. The CardInfo sketch uses pin 4 for CS, so when wiring the module from Figure 2.2 to an Arduino, simply connect the CS pin of the module to pin 4 of the Arduino. On the other hand, if a shield uses pin 9 for CS, update the example sketch to use this pin. In the CardInfo sketch, the following line of code sets the CS or chip select pin.

67

```
const int chipSelect = 4;
```
The above code is fine for the SD card on an Ethernet shield and a module wired with CS to pin 4, but must be changed if a different pin is used for CS, for example pin 9, as follows.
```
const int chipSelect = 9;
```

As we have seen, SD cards interface or connect to the Arduino MEGA 2560 using the SPI (Serial Peripheral Interface) pins of the board. See section 3.1.2 – Shared SPI Pins, in chapter 3 for more on the location of the SPI pins on the Arduino MEGA 2560. Section 3.3.5 – SPI Bus Pins, contains more information and an interfacing example on how to connect SD card modules to an Arduino MEGA 2560.

2.3.4.2 Flash and EEPROM Chips (SPI / TWI Interface)

Flash or EEPROM chips that use either the SPI (Serial Peripheral Interface) or TWI (Two Wire Interface) can be connected to the appropriate pins of an Arduino MEGA 2560. See sections 3.1.1 and 3.1.2 in the next chapter for TWI and SPI pinouts on the Arduino MEGA 2560. Section 3.3.4 contains a TWI interfacing example and section 3.3.5 contains a SPI interfacing example.

Both SPI and TWI are serial interface bus protocols that have software libraries available in the Arduino IDE. TWI is compatible with the I²C (Inter-Integrated Circuit) serial protocol, so I²C memory chips will also work with the Arduino MEGA 2560. I²C is pronounced "I squared C" (eye squared see) and may also be written as IIC or I2C.

The ATmega2560 microcontroller has built-in hardware that handles SPI and TWI serial communications. For this reason, SPI and TWI devices can only be connected to certain pins of the Arduino MEGA 2560, although an external library could be used to emulate SPI and TWI on other pins. SPI and TWI are not limited to only adding external memory to the Arduino MEGA 2560. Other devices that use SPI or TWI interfaces can also be connected to an Arduino, such as RTC (Real Time Clock) chips and I/O (Input/Output) expansion chips.

2.3.4.3 SPI Devices

SPI devices are supported in the Arduino IDE by the SPI library. See the library reference www.arduino.cc/en/Reference/SPI for more information on the SPI library. SPI examples can be found in the Arduino IDE from the top menu under File ▶ Examples ▶ SPI where SPI is found near the bottom of the Examples menu.

2.3.4.4 TWI and I²C Devices

TWI and I²C devices are supported in the Arduino IDE by the Wire library. See the library reference www.arduino.cc/en/Reference/Wire for more information on the Wire library. Find examples that use the Wire library in the Arduino IDE from the top menu under File ▶ Examples ▶ Wire where Wire is found at the bottom of the Examples menu.

2.4 Power and USB

An external DC power supply, battery or USB connection can be used to provide power to an Arduino MEGA 2560, as explained in the sections that follow.

2.4.1 USB Power

Power can be supplied to the Arduino MEGA 2560 from a computer via the USB connection, which supplies 5V. This is convenient for prototype and experimental use, but especially for a classroom environment where eliminating the need for an external power supply can save on costs.

A USB 2.0 computer port is specified to provide 5V ± 5% and is able to deliver up to 500mA of current. Arduino MEGA 2560 boards have a 500mA resettable fuse protecting the 5V supply from the USB port. A resettable fuse will break the circuit if more than its rated current is drawn by an overload or short circuit. The fuse will automatically reset after the overload or short circuit is removed. Bear in mind that a small amount of the USB 5V voltage will be dropped across the fuse. This voltage drop will increase as more current is drawn through the fuse, which means that as this voltage drop increases, the voltage measured on the Arduino 5V pin will decrease by the same amount.

2.4.2 USB Connection and Cable

An Arduino MEGA 2560 is a USB 2.0 full-speed device, which has a data throughput of 12Mbit/s and can have a USB cable length of up to 5m (16.4 feet), according to the USB 2.0 specification.

In addition to being able to power the Arduino MEGA 2560, the USB connection also allows the Arduino to be programmed from the Arduino IDE. An ordinary USB printer cable is used to connect the Arduino MEGA 2560 to a computer. This type of cable uses USB connectors of type A on the computer side and type B on the Arduino side. These cables are referred to as A-B USB cables. Figure 2.3 shows the type A and type B connectors of a USB cable and the end of an Arduino MEGA 2560 board showing the type B connector and external power jack.

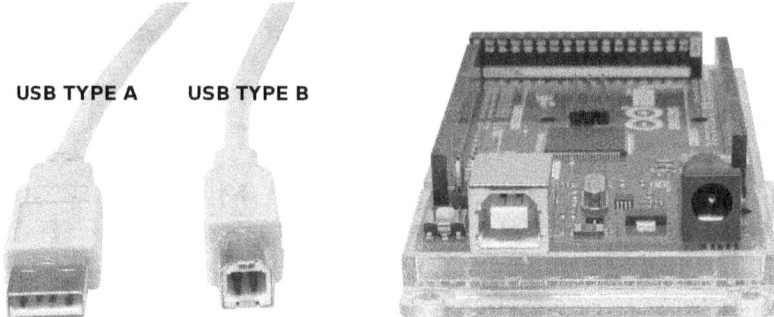

Figure 2.3: USB Type A-B Cable and Arduino MEGA 2560 Showing B Type Connector

2.4.3 External Power

External power can be supplied via the barrel connector jack on the Arduino MEGA 2560, allowing the board to run standalone without the need for a computer USB connection as shown in Figure 2.4.

An external DC (Direct Current) power supply with a voltage of 7V to 12V, capable of delivering at least 500mA is recommended. The center pin of the 2.1mm barrel connector must be connected to the positive connection from the external power supply. Actual current requirements for the Arduino depend on the project that it is used in. Current drawn will be a small amount from the Arduino itself and the remainder will be from the circuit or shield that is connected to it. Refer to chapter 4, section 4.1.4, for the pinout of the external power jack.

If the USB cable is plugged into the Arduino MEGA 2560 for programming and an external power supply is connected, the Arduino will automatically be powered from the external power supply. Power supply circuitry detects when external power is connected and automatically switches to it if found.

Chapter 2 • Hardware Technical Information

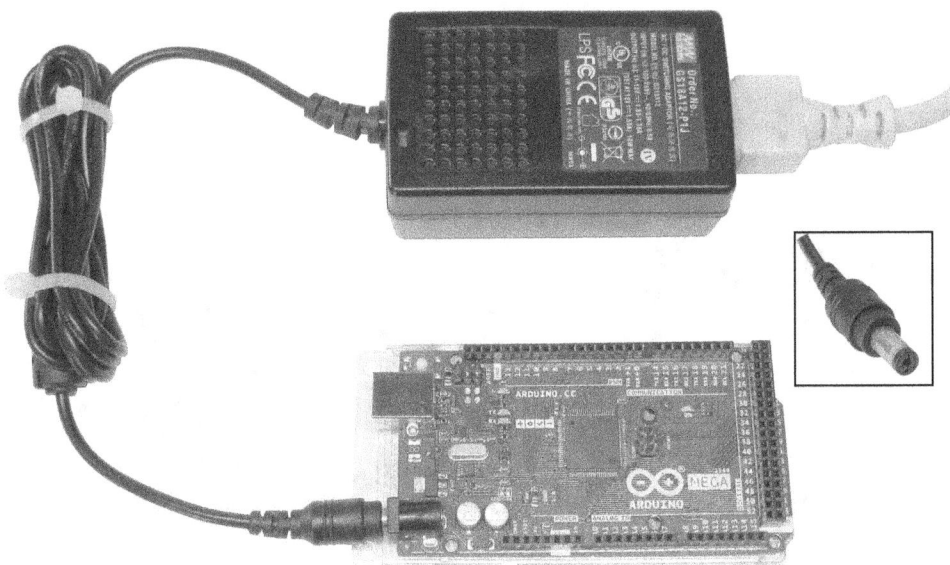

Figure 2.4: Arduino MEGA 2560 Powered by External DC Power Supply
Inset: Barrel Connector

2.4.4 Battery Power

A battery can be connected to either the external 2.1mm power jack or through the Vin pin of the Arduino MEGA 2560. Whenever connecting a battery, be sure to check the polarity of the connection – connect the center pin of the barrel power jack to positive of the battery and negative of the battery to GND. If connecting the battery to the Vin pin on the Arduino MEGA 2560 header socket, connect positive from the battery to the Vin pin and negative to a GND pin.

Common battery voltages that are safe to use with an Arduino MEGA 2560 through the power jack or Vin pin are 9V and 12V. Small 9V batteries of the PP3 or E-block size are not practical for powering an Arduino MEGA 2560 for long periods of time. They may be used for short periods, such as for a battery controlled robot car that is only operated intermittently. Other options are to use a battery holder that holds six 1.5V AA cells, making up 9V. This will be around 7.2V if rechargeable cells are used which usually supply 1.2V each. These holders have PP3 type battery terminals that connect to a PP3 type battery connector or clip. Rechargeable PP3 or E-block batteries have a voltage of 8.4V because internally they consist of seven 1.2V cells.

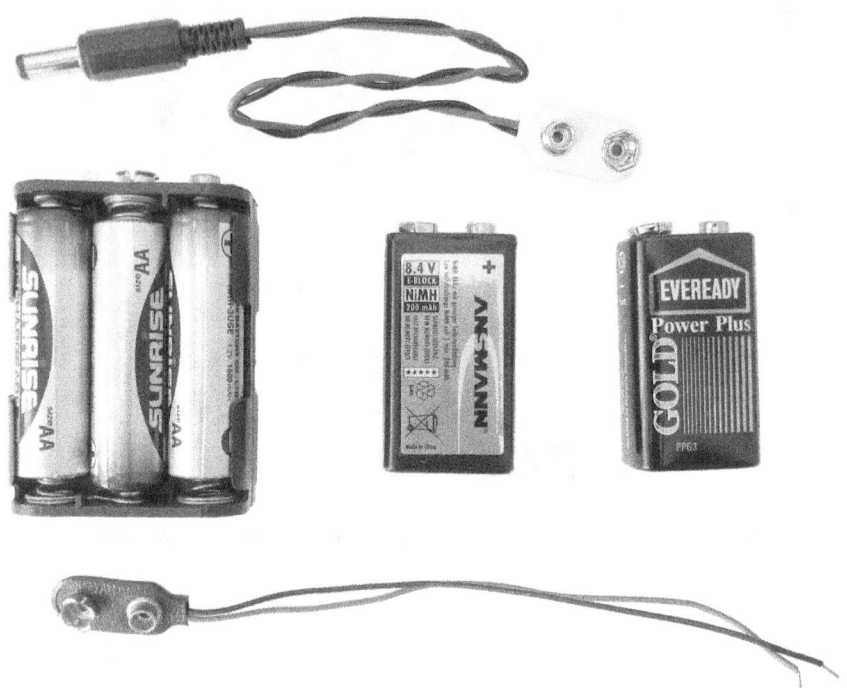

Figure 2.5: Battery Holder, Rechargeable Battery, 9V Battery and Battery Clips

Figure 2.5 shows a 6 cell holder, rechargeable battery, 9V PP3 battery and two battery clips. The battery clip at the top of the image has a barrel connector for connecting to the external power jack of an Arduino MEGA 2560. These battery cables can be bought ready assembled, or built from parts bought separately. The red wire on a battery clip is the positive lead and the black wire is the negative lead. Bigger 9V batteries are available, such as PP9. Sealed 12V gel type batteries that are commonly used in house alarm systems are available in several sizes and power ratings.

Consider storing batteries in plastic zip-lock bags to prevent the terminals from being shorted together by metal parts – don't just throw the battery into a spares box that may have other components in it that could short the battery.

Figure 2.6 shows the difference between connecting a battery to the external jack as opposed to using the Vin pin found on the POWER section of the header socket of the Arduino MEGA 2560. Vin is clearly labeled on the top layer of the Arduino MEGA 2560 board as well as silkscreened on both sides of the header socket on newer Arduino MEGA 2560 R3 boards. This circuit is essentially identical to the external power input circuit of an Arduino Uno, except that the Arduino MEGA 2560 has an extra 100n capacitor connected to Vin, not shown in the figure.

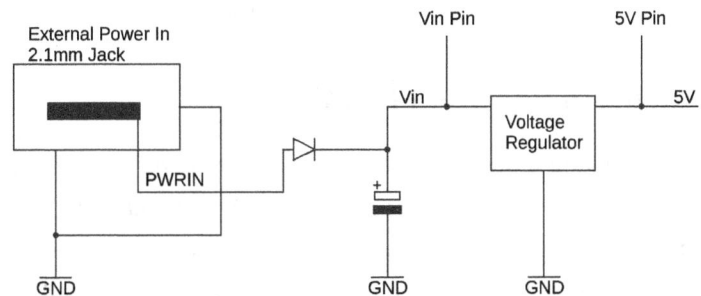

Figure 2.6: External Power In and Vin Circuit of an Arduino MEGA 2560

As can be seen in the figure, the positive connection from the 2.1mm jack (center pin) connects to the Vin pin via a diode. The diode offers some crude reverse polarity protection on the input jack, but does not protect the Vin input. If power is connected to the external jack, the voltage seen on the Vin pin will be the input voltage minus the voltage drop across the diode.

2.4.5 Operating Voltage

Because the internal circuitry and main microcontroller operate at a voltage of 5V, the Arduino MEGA 2560 is considered to be a 5V device. Input/output (I/O) or digital pins operate at 5V levels because the ATmega2560 microcontroller is supplied with 5V from either USB or from an external power supply, where the on-board voltage regulator drops the external power supply voltage to 5V. External devices connected to an Arduino MEGA 2560 must be rated at 5V, or have the necessary voltage regulator and level shifters for the pins to avoid damaging them. Watch out for some devices that may be rated at 3.3V. They may be available as a module or on a shield with the necessary regulator and level shifters built in. If not, they can still be interfaced to an Arduino MEGA 2560, but only through the correct voltage level adjusting circuit.

2.5 Operating Frequency

The main microcontroller (ATmega2560) of the Arduino MEGA 2560 runs at a frequency of 16MHz. A 16MHz ceramic resonator is connected to the oscillator pins of the ATmega2560, providing a 16MHz square wave clock pulse. A ceramic resonator is not as accurate as a quartz crystal. An Arduino Uno has the same 16MHz ceramic resonator for its main microcontroller, and therefore runs at the same speed as an Arduino MEGA 2560.

A 16MHz quartz crystal connected to the ATmega16U2 USB to serial bridge microcontroller allows this device to run at frequency of 16MHz.

2.6 LED Indicators and Reset Button

Four LEDs are found on the Arduino MEGA 2560 as summarized in Table 2.3. The LEDs are clearly marked on the top layer of the Arduino MEGA 2560 board and the same LED names are used in the left column of the table, as on the board. One reset button can be found next to the USB connector on new R3 boards, or next to the main ICSP header on older boards. The LEDs and reset button are described further in the sections that follow.

Arduino MEGA 2560 clone or compatible boards may use different colored LEDs than official Arduino boards. These boards may have different layouts as well, which means that the LEDs may be found in different locations on the boards when compared to official boards. Usually the LED names on clone boards are the same as on official boards.

Table 2.3: Arduino MEGA 2560 LED Names and Functions

LED Name	Purpose	Description
ON	Shows that the Arduino MEGA 2560 is powered and on.	This LED switches on if the Arduino is powered from USB or an external power supply. It indicates that the Arduino is getting 5V from USB or from an external power supply via the on-board 5V regulator.
TX	Shows Arduino is transmitting data.	Arduino is transmitting data over the serial UART to USB link.
RX	Shows Arduino is receiving data.	Arduino is receiving data over the serial UART to USB link.
L	User programmable LED.	User programmable LED connected to pin 13 of the Arduino MEGA 2560 via a unity gain op-amp.

2.6.1 ON LED

The green ON LED lights up if 5V is present on the board when the board is externally or USB powered.

Chapter 2 • Hardware Technical Information

2.6.2 L LED

The yellow L LED is connected to digital pin 13 of the Arduino MEGA 2560. It can be accessed in a sketch by setting pin 13 as an output and then using the digitalWrite() function to either set it HIGH (switches the LED on) or LOW (switches the LED off). The L LED can be accessed in sketches by referring to it as LED_BUILTIN. Open the Blink sketch in the Arduino IDE from the top menu under File ▶ Examples ▶ 01.Basics ▶ Blink for an example of how to program this LED.

The L LED is buffered through a unity gain op-amp circuit in revision 3 Arduino MEGA 2560 boards, so switching this LED on will draw virtually no current from Arduino MEGA 2560 pin 13. Pin 13 just supplies a signal to the op-amp, and current is supplied to the LED by the op-amp (only on revision 3 boards).

2.6.3 TX LED

TX = Transmit. The yellow TX LED will light up and flash or blink whenever data is sent or transmitted from the ATmega2560 serial or UART transmit line to the USB bridge chip. The TX LED lights up whether data being transmitted is from the bootloader or a user sketch. If data is transmitted continually, this LED will stay on rather than blink.

2.6.4 RX LED

RX = Receive. The yellow RX LED will light up and flash or blink whenever data is received by the ATmega2560 from the USB bridge chip. The RX LED lights up when data is received by the bootloader on the ATmega2560, from the Arduino IDE, when loading a new sketch. It will also light up if data is being sent over the USB to serial link from the computer and received by a user sketch. It will stay on if data is received continually.

2.6.5 Reset Button

Pressing the reset button next to the USB connector on an Arduino MEGA 2560 R3 board issues a manual reset to the ATmega2560 microcontroller which causes it to set internal registers to their default states and restart the microcontroller. This means that the bootloader will restart and then the sketch that is in memory will start running from the beginning. On Arduino MEGA 2560 boards before revision 3e, or the Rev3e schematic, the reset button was positioned near the ICSP header at the opposite side of the board from the USB connector. With the reset button next to the USB connector on new boards, it can easily be accessed and pressed, even with a shield plugged into the Arduino MEGA 2560. On older boards, a full sized shield completely blocks the reset button from access.

2.7 User Pin Headers

User pin headers are found on each side of the Arduino MEGA 2560 down the length of the Arduino. A double row pin header is found at one end of the board, on the opposite side to the USB connector. Although these "pins" are actually sockets, they are usually referred to as pins in the Arduino documentation. They provide power and ground connections, as well as access to the digital and analog pins of the ATmega2560 microcontroller. These header sockets allow external hardware to be connected to the Arduino in the form of shields, custom circuit boards or prototyping boards such as electronic breadboards. Each pin type is discussed in further detail in the sections that follow.

2.7.1 Power Pins

5V (five volts), 3.3V (three point three volts), Vin (voltage in) and GND (ground) are the four types of power pins found on the Arduino MEGA 2560.

2.7.1.1 GND Pins

GND pins are connected to 0V or negative from the power supply. All voltages are measured relative GND. In other words the negative lead of a voltmeter, multimeter set to voltage, or oscilloscope connects to GND when making voltage measurements.

2.7.1.2 5V Pins

The 5V pins get voltage from either the USB, or from the on-board 5V regulator if the board is powered from an external power supply. 5V can be used by a shield or other circuit that is interfaced to the Arduino MEGA 2560.

Both the Arduino MEGA 2560 and Arduino Uno use a fixed 5V Low-Dropout (LDO) regulator to drop an external input voltage of between 7V and 12V down to 5V. At the time of writing, the Arduino MEGA 2560 schematic specified a 5V regulator of part number LD1117S50CTR, which is manufactured by STMicroelectronics, while the Arduino Uno specified a 5V regulator of part number NCP1117ST50T3G from ON Semiconductor.

Regulators mentioned above are interchangeable, but the STMicroelectronics part specifies an output current up to 800mA, while the ON Semiconductor part specifies an output current in excess of 1.0A. This means that more current can be drawn by the Arduino and interfaced circuits when powered from an external power supply, compared to a maximum of 500mA that can be drawn from the USB connection.

Chapter 2 • Hardware Technical Information

2.7.1.3 3.3V Pin

3.3V on the Arduino MEGA 2560 is derived from 5V through a 3.3V regulator. The 3.3V regulator is able to supply a recommended maximum output current of 150mA. Older Arduino boards were able to supply only 50mA on the 3.3V pin which was derived from a 3.3V output pin on the FT232RL chip. This chip is replaced by an ATmega16U2 and separate 3.3V regulator (part number LP2985-33DBVR) on an Arduino MEGA 2560. At the time of writing, Arduino still incorrectly specify the DC current for the 3.3V pin as only 50mA for both the Arduino MEGA 2560 and Arduino Uno. Both these boards have the same 3.3V regulator which can deliver an output current of 150mA under normal operating conditions. The datasheet for the regulator does not specify an absolute maximum output current because the regulator has internal current limiting and short circuit protection.

2.7.1.4 Vin Pin

Vin is the voltage from an external power supply connected to the barrel connector, but after it has been fed through a protection diode (see Figure 2.6), so the voltage of Vin will be slightly lower than the actual input voltage from the power supply. Subtract around 0.7V to 0.8V from the input voltage to get the value of Vin. This is because the diode has approximately 0.7 to 0.8V forward voltage drop. Refer to section 2.4.4 for more information on battery powering the Arduino through this pin. Vin is available to any shield plugged in.

2.7.2 IOREF Pin and Unconnected Pin

The IOREF pin was added to revision 3 Arduino MEGA 2560 boards. IOREF is 5V on an Arduino MEGA 2560 – it simply connects to the on-board 5V supply. The idea of this pin is that it is set to the voltage that the Arduino operates at. This means that it is 3.3V on Arduino boards that operate at 3.3V and 5V on Arduino boards that operate at 5V. It is intended as a reference voltage for shields so that they can determine whether they are connected to a 3.3V or 5V Arduino. This allows the shield to enable voltage level shifters or translators if necessary. Clone or compatible Arduino boards may not have this pin available. It is not present on Arduino MEGA 2560 R1 and Arduino MEGA 2560 R2 boards. The IOREF pin was added to both Arduino MEGA 2560 and Arduino Uno revision 3, or R3 boards. Immediately next to the IOREF pin is an unused pin that is unconnected and reserved for future purposes. The Arduino header that the IOREF and unused pin are connected to increased pin count from 6 pins to 8 pins in the Arduino MEGA 2560 R3 as a result of these two pins being added to revision 3 boards. Revision 1 and 2 boards have a 6 pin header in this position on the board.

2.7.3 RESET Pin

The Arduino reset pin connects to the ATmega2560 microcontroller reset pin. This pin is active low and enables shields to have a reset button placed on them that can reset the main microcontroller. In cases where a shield blocks access to the reset button on the Arduino MEGA 2560, a reset button on the shield enables easy manual resetting of the Arduino. Bringing the voltage level on this pin LOW (to GND) resets the main microcontroller. It does not reset the ATmega16U2 USB to serial bridge microcontroller.

2.7.4 Digital, PWM and Communication Pins

Digital pins are clearly marked as such on the Arduino MEGA 2560 board and are numbered from 0 to 53 which means that there are 54 digital pins – 1 to 53 would be 53 pins, but because the pins are numbered starting from 0, 0 to 53 means there are 54 pins. Digital pins are highly configurable and can individually be set up as input pins or output pins from within a sketch. Some of the digital pins have special functions available on them and can be set up as PWM (Pulse Width Modulation) pins, and communication pins. Each digital pin configuration is described in more details in the sections that follow.

2.7.4.1 Output Pins

When a digital pin is configured as an output pin, it can drive a load such as an LED with a series resistor or other low current devices such as some buzzers. Driving a load means switching power to the load on. A load can be connected in either a current sourcing or current sinking configuration as described in section 3.3.1.1, under the Current Sourcing and Current Sinking headings, in the next chapter. To avoid destroying, or partially destroying the microcontroller, it is important not to connect a load to any of the digital pins that will draw more current from the pin than the pin can safely deliver. More on this in the next section.

To set up a digital pin as an output, call the pinMode() function in the setup() part of the sketch as shown in the code listing that follows. To switch the digital pin that is configured as an output on or high, which will make the voltage of the pin change to 5V, call the function digitalWrite() with the second argument set to HIGH. To switch the voltage level on the pin to low, also called GND, 0V or off, call digitalWrite() with the second argument set to LOW as shown in the sketch that follows. Whether the load on the pin switches on or off depends on whether it is wired in a current sourcing or current sinking configuration.

```
void setup() {
  pinMode(12, OUTPUT);     // Configure digital pin 12 as an output pin
}

void loop() {
  digitalWrite(12, HIGH);  // Set pin 12 voltage to 5V on a MEGA 2560
  delay(500);
  digitalWrite(12, LOW);   // Set pin 12 voltage to 0V or GND
  delay(500);
}
```

The above sketch is a simple variation on the Blink example sketch that has already been described in chapter 1. This sketch configures digital pin 12 as an output pin instead of pin 13 that the Blink sketch uses. It then drives pin 12 high and low which will switch an LED on and off if it is attached to pin 12 using a series resistor. In the Blink sketch, digital pin 13 for an Arduino MEGA 2560 is defined as LED_BUILTIN. LED_BUILTIN is just a name that is defined for the on-board L LED on Arduino boards. On other Arduino boards the L LED may be connected to a pin other than pin 13. LED_BUILTIN will then be defined as the correct pin for the L LED on that board. In other words, LED_BUILTIN is defined as the L LED pin for each different Arduino board so that any sketch that uses the L LED will work on any Arduino board, irrespective of which pin the L LED is connected to, so long as the L LED is referred to as LED_BUILTIN in the sketch.

LED_BUILTIN is defined within source code in the Arduino IDE in a similar way that is described here, which is illustrated with an example sketch that follows. The correct source code file with the correct definition, or pin number, for LED_BUILTIN is linked to an Arduino sketch project for the board that is selected in the Arduino IDE. The sketch that follows is an alternative to the above sketch that gives the digital pin a user friendly name, instead of referring to it by its pin number – this is how LED_BUILTIN is defined in source code included with the Arduino IDE. The advantage of this method is that if the pin number needs to be changed, it can be changed in one place, at the top of the sketch. In the previous sketch, changing the pin number would mean that each place that the pin is used in the sketch would need to be found and modified – three places in the previous sketch. In bigger sketches with many lines of code, this could be difficult and prone to error. As can be seen in the sketch that follows, #define is used to give a meaningful name to a digital pin. The text MY_LED can be any name that is more meaningful than using the pin number. By convention, names defined this way are always written using uppercase letters and underscore characters are used to separate words.

```
#define MY_LED   12

void setup() {
  pinMode(MY_LED, OUTPUT);    // Configure digital pin as an output pin
}

void loop() {
  digitalWrite(MY_LED, HIGH); // Set pin voltage to 5V on a MEGA 2560
  delay(500);
  digitalWrite(MY_LED, LOW);  // Set pin voltage to 0V or GND
  delay(500);
}
```

An alternative to using #define is to use the const keyword which allows the type of data to be specified. Some of the example sketches in the Arduino IDE use this method of defining pins, but don't use the uppercase naming convention. For example, the code below can be used in place of the #define statement in the above sketch.

```
const int MY_LED = 12;
```

But examples in the Arduino IDE may use camel case instead of upper case, such as the following code.

```
const int myLed = 12;
```

2.7.4.2 Pin Current Rating

There is a limit to the amount of current that can be drawn by a load connected to a digital pin configured as an output. This limit is determined by the electrical characteristics of the ATmega2560 microcontroller on an Arduino MEGA 2560 and is given in the datasheet of the microcontroller manufacturer. Online documentation for Arduino boards is notorious for promoting bad engineering practice by quoting the absolute maximum rating of components as the normal or usable maximum ratings. On the Arduino MEGA 2560 page on the Arduino website, DC current per I/O pin (digital pin) was quoted as being 40mA. At some stage this was changed to 20mA which is better, and is the value given on the website at the time of writing this book.

Quoting the maximum current per pin is actually more complex than just quoting a value. The reason for this is that there is an absolute maximum total current of 200mA that can be drawn by the ATmega2560 microcontroller. Note that this is the same maximum total current for the ATmega328P microcontroller found on Arduino Uno boards. If 20mA was

Chapter 2 • Hardware Technical Information

drawn from each of the digital pins, a total of 54 × 20mA = 1080mA or 1.08A, plus the current that the microcontroller core is using, which is way over the 200mA absolute maximum rating. Further to this, certain groups of pins have their own maximum current ratings. What this means is that some pins can be used to draw 20mA from, but not all of them at the same time, and not too many in a group. This is explained further in the next chapter in section 3.3.1.1, under the Current Limitation Per Pin heading and the sections that follow it. Good design practice dictates that current drawn must not come too close to an absolute maximum rating, but within a certain percentage of it, say 60% to 80% for better reliability – this is usually called overrating.

When a load that draws more current than an output pin can deliver is to be interfaced to an Arduino MEGA 2560, a transistor can be used to interface the heavier load to the Arduino. For even bigger electrical loads, a transistor can be used to switch a relay. Refer to section 3.3.1.1, under the heading "Switching Heavier Loads with Transistors and Relays", in the next chapter.

2.7.4.3 Input Pins

Digital pins can be configured as input pins in a sketch. An input pin can be used to test whether the voltage applied to it is high (5V) or low (at 0V or GND). This can be used, for example, to see whether a switch that is attached to a pin is open or closed.

By default, when an Arduino is powered up, its pins are configured as input pins. Most sketches that use pins as inputs will explicitly configure the pins as inputs, even though this is not entirely necessary. The ATmega2560 microcontroller has internal pull-up resistors attached to each pin that can individually be enabled or disabled. These pull-up resistors are relatively weak, meaning that they have high resistance values and are rated at between 20kΩ and 50kΩ, so have a wide tolerance range. The internal pull-up resistor can be enabled on a pin by passing INPUT_PULLUP to the pinMode() function.

Alternatively pinMode() can be passed INPUT to enable a pin as an input without a pull-up resistor. In this case an external pull-up or pull-down resistor may be needed, depending on what is being interfaced to the pin. See section 3.3.1.2 in the next chapter for examples of interfacing to an input pin. For an example sketch that uses an input pin to test the state of an attached button or switch, select File ▶ Examples ▶ 02.Digital ▶ Button from the top menu of the Arduino IDE.

2.7.4.4 PWM Pins

Some of the digital pins of an Arduino MEGA 2560 have PWM (Pulse Width Modulation) capabilities and are marked by a PWM section on the board, from pin 2 to pin 13. Pins 44, 45 and 46 also have PWM, bringing the total number of PWM pins to 15. These PWM capabilities are available on certain Arduino MEGA 2560 pins because the ATmega2560 microcontroller has built-in PWM hardware on these pins.

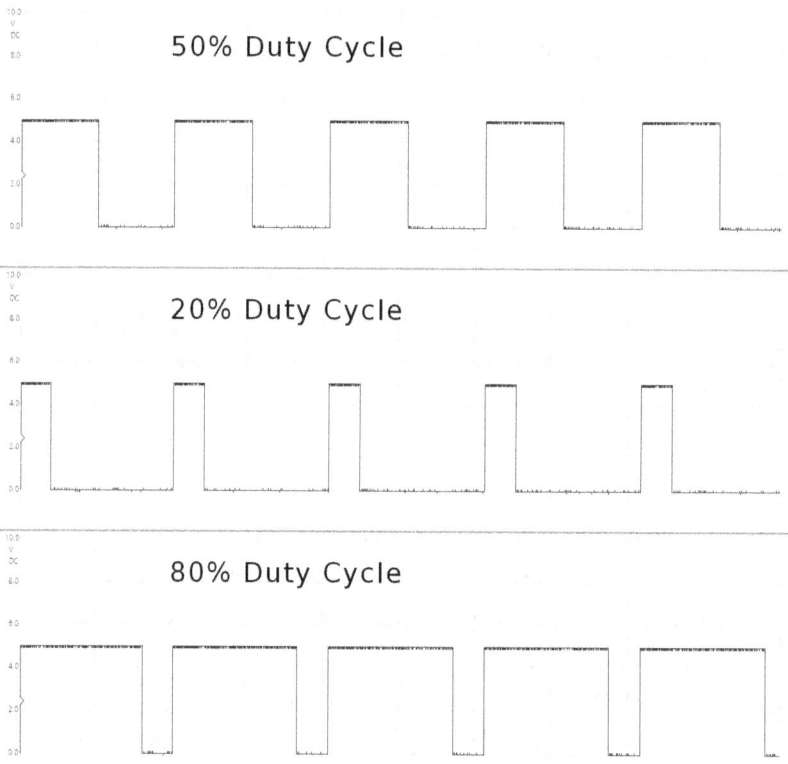

Figure 2.7: PWM Waveforms from an Arduino MEGA 2560 PWM Pin

PWM allows the brightness of an LED, or the speed of a DC motor to be controlled. PWM is just a square wave output on a pin that can have its duty cycle changed. Duty cycle is the ratio of on time to off time of the square wave, usually expressed as a percentage.

Chapter 2 • Hardware Technical Information

Figure 2.7 shows an example of the same square wave with its duty cycle adjusted to 50%, 20% and 80%. In each case the frequency of the square wave is exactly the same. A square wave with a 50% duty cycle is created by switching a pin to 5V for a period of time and to GND for the same period of time. Although this is an alternating current waveform, it has an average direct current value. Pulse width modulation works by altering the time that the wave is at 5V to the time that the wave is at GND. If the time that 5V is present is for 80% of the time and GND for only 20% of the time, a higher average voltage will be present on the pin and an attached LED will burn brighter – in this case the duty cycle is said to be 80% because the voltage is at 5V, on, or high for 80% of the time. When compared to the same wave at the same frequency, but with the wave at 5V for only 20% of the time and at GND for 80% of the time, a lower average voltage will be present on the pin, and an attached LED will burn more dimly – the duty cycle is said to be 20% for this example because the square wave is on for 20% of the time and off, or at GND, for the remainder of the time.

PWM Example Sketch

In an Arduino sketch, the analogWrite() function is used to control the duty cycle of PWM pins on an Arduino. An example sketch that sets the PWM duty cycle of pin 3 of an Arduino MEGA 2560 to approximately 50% is shown in the code listing that follows.

```
void setup() {
  pinMode(3, OUTPUT);

  analogWrite(3, 127);
}

void loop() {
}
```

Notice that PWM is set up on the pin in the setup() part of the sketch when analogWrite() is called. The sketch then starts executing the main loop(), which does nothing. At this stage, the PWM waveform set up on the PWM pin will still be present because the internal hardware of the ATmega2560 microcontroller is set up to continually output the PWM waveform.

Strictly speaking, pinMode() does not need to be called to set the pin as an output before calling analogWrite(). The first parameter passed to analogWrite() is the digital pin number to produce the PWM waveform on. In the example sketch it is set to 3, which means that the PWM waveform will appear on digital pin 3. At the time of writing, the Arduino IDE does not issue a warning or error message if a digital pin that does not have PWM capabilities is passed to analogWrite(). In this case, a sketch will build and load, but nothing will happen on a non-PWM pin.

Calculating PWM Duty Cycle

The second parameter passed to analogWrite() sets its duty cycle and can be a value between 0 and 255. When set to 0, the output of the PWM pin will be off or at GND level. When set to 255, the PWM pin will be on, or set to 5V. To calculate the value to pass to analogWrite() to set a certain duty cycle as a percentage, divide 255 by 100, and then multiply the result by the desired percentage. For example, to work out the value for a 20% duty cycle, divide 255 by 100 and then multiply by 20: 255 ÷ 100 × 20 = 51. Pass 51 as the second parameter to analogWrite() to set the duty cycle of a PWM pin to 20%, as shown in the code below for pin 3.

```
analogWrite(3, 51);
```

If the result of a duty cycle calculation has a fractional part, then round off to the nearest integer (whole number) value. For example, a 50% duty cycle is calculated as follows: 255 ÷ 100 × 50 = 127.5 which can be rounded to either 127 which would make the duty cycle slightly less than a round 50%, or it can be rounded up to 128 which would make the duty cycle slightly above 50%.

PWM Frequency

On an Arduino MEGA 2560, all PWM pins produce a square wave at a frequency of 490Hz, except for pin 4 and pin 13 which operate at a frequency of 980Hz.

PWM LED Control Example

One of the example sketches found in the Arduino IDE, called Fade, demonstrates how to use PWM to continuously change the brightness of an LED. The LED changes from dim to bright and back to dim continually by continually changing the duty cycle of the PWM wave on pin 9 of an Arduino. Find this sketch under File ▶ Examples ▶ 0.1Basics ▶ Fade using the top menu in the Arduino IDE.

2.7.4.5 Communication Pins

Pins 0, 1 and 14 to 21 are marked as COMMUNICATION pins on Arduino MEGA 2560 boards. These pins can be used as normal digital input and output pins, but can also be used as special pins for various communication ports, such as TWI and UART.

Chapter 2 • Hardware Technical Information

Serial Port / UART Pins to USB

Arduino MEGA 2560 pin 0 (RX0 or receive 0) and pin 1 (TX0 or transmit 0) are internally connected to a serial port or UART of the ATmega2560 microcontroller and are routed to the ATmega16U2 USB to serial bridge chip. Data that is sent and received over the serial port appears on these two pins. This includes data that is sent to the ATmega2560 when a new sketch is being loaded to the Arduino from the Arduino IDE. A 1k resistor between each of these pins and the ATmega16U2 USB to serial bridge chip protect both microcontrollers in case these pins are set up as outputs and data is transmitted from the USB bridge chip, which can cause a short circuit that may otherwise damage these devices. It is not recommended to use these pins as normal digital input or output pins, as this could result in interference with any circuit attached to them, or voltage levels read from them in an Arduino sketch. When using these pins as digital pins, the serial port on the Arduino can not be used to send and receive data over the USB link from a sketch. Figure 2.8 shows how these pins are connected on an Arduino MEGA 2560.

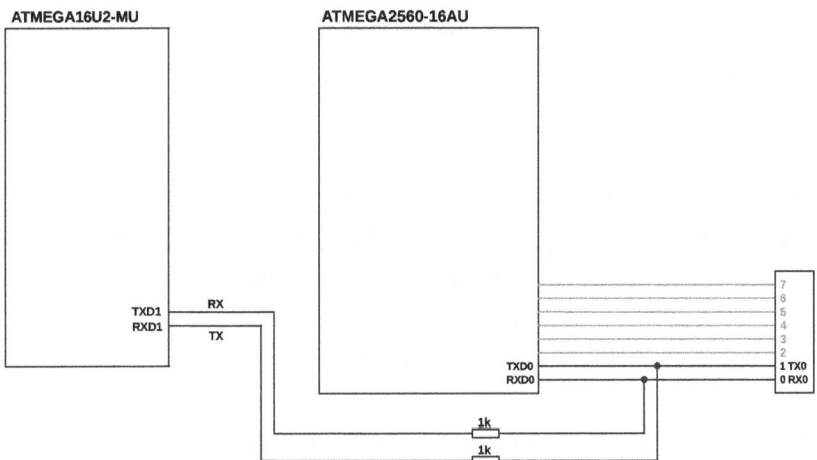

Figure 2.8: Arduino MEGA 2560 Pin 0 and Pin 1 Connections on the Board

As can be seen in the figure, pin 0 or RX0 is connected to the ATmega2560 RXD0 pin which is also routed through a 1k resistor to the TXD1 pin of the ATmega16U2. This is so that anything received from a host computer via USB will be transmitted from the ATmega16U2 TXD1 pin and received by the ATmega2560 RXD0 pin. Similarly, pin 1 or TX0 of the Arduino MEGA 2560 connects to the TXD0 pin of the ATmega2560 which is routed through a 1k resistor to RXD1 of the ATmega16U2. Anything transmitted from the ATmega2560 TXD pin will be received on the ATmega16U2 RXD1 pin and then sent out over USB.

These two pins are associated with the main serial port of the Arduino MEGA 2560 and commonly used in sketches that communicate with the Serial Monitor window in the Arduino IDE. Calling such functions as Serial.begin() and Serial.println() initializes these pins as serial port pins and sends data out of the USB connection, typically to be received by the Serial Monitor window. Example sketches, such as the ASCIITable sketch that we have already looked at in section 1.5.2.3 of chapter 1, use this serial port to send data to the Serial Monitor window via USB. It is best to never use these pins for any other purpose.

Serial Port / USART Pins

ATmega2560 microcontrollers found on Arduino MEGA 2560 boards have four hardware devices built into the microcontroller chip called USARTs and named USART 0, USART 1, USART 2 and USART 3. USART stands for Universal Synchronous/Asynchronous Receiver/Transmitter. A USART is a serial communication device that can be used for both synchronous communications (uses a separate clock line to synchronize communications) and asynchronous communications (no separate clock line is used, only transmit and receive lines).

On Arduino MEGA 2560 boards, one USART (USART 0) is configured as a UART (for asynchronous communications) and connected to pins 0 and 1, as discussed in the previous section. Transmit and receive pins from the remaining three USARTs are found on pins 14 to 19. This arrangement suggests that they are intended to mainly be used as UARTs, as their corresponding clock lines are not located next to their transmit and receive pins and are not labeled on the Arduino board.

Having three available USARTs means that an Arduino MEGA 2560 can communicate serially with various hardware devices. This includes serial TTL devices, such as TTL serial to USB adapters, RS-232 and RS-485 interface chips, and various serial to parallel conversion chips and circuits. Note that the Arduino Uno has only one USART that is dedicated to serial USB communications on pins 0 and 1, as on the MEGA 2560.

TWI or I²C Pins

Two communication pins on Arduino MEGA 2560 boards can be used for the TWI serial bus of the ATmega2560 microcontroller. These pins can be used either as digital pins 20 and 21, or as TWI pins. TWI or I²C compatible devices can be interfaced to pin 20 (TWI SDA pin) and 21 (TWI SCL pin). TWI and I²C devices are supported by the Wire library in the Arduino IDE. For more information on TWI, see section 3.3.4 in next chapter.

SPI Pins

Although not found on the connector marked COMMUNICATION on MEGA 2560 boards, SPI pins are also serial communication pins. SPI stands for Serial Peripheral Interface and is a type of synchronous serial communication interface. We already briefly looked at the SPI bus in this chapter, starting from section 2.3.4.1 which deals with SD cards. Section 2.9.4 near the end of this chapter looks at how the SPI pins are shared on the main ICSP header of the Arduino MEGA 2560. The location of SPI pins is one of the big differences between Arduino MEGA 2560 boards and Arduino Uno boards. On Arduino Uno boards, SPI pins are found on digital pins 10 to 13 and the ICSP header. On Arduino MEGA 2560 boards, SPI pins are found on digital pins 50 to 53 and the ICSP header.

2.7.5 Analog In Pins

Arduino MEGA 2560 boards have sixteen analog input pins labeled A0 to A15. As with the digital pins, numbering starts at 0 and not 1, which means that A0 to A15 are 16 pins and not 15. Analog pins can read an analog voltage applied to them that can be between 0V to 5V by default.

In the ATmega2560 microcontroller the analog pins connect to an ADC (Analog to Digital Converter) that uses a 5V reference voltage to determine the voltage level on the analog pins. It is a 10-bit ADC which means that it will calculate a value between 0 to 1023 that is a representation of the voltage level on one of the analog input pins. Knowing that the reference voltage is 5V and that the resolution of the ADC is 10 bits allows the voltage applied to an analog input pin to be calculated, as explained in section 2.7.5.3 – Calculating Analog In Voltage, that follows in this chapter.

2.7.5.1 Analog In Example Sketch

A good example sketch that demonstrates how to read an analog value from analog input pin A0 is found under File ▶ Examples ▶ 01.Basics ▶ AnalogReadSerial on the top menu of the Arduino IDE. The corresponding tutorial page for the AnalogReadSerial example sketch can be found at www.arduino.cc/en/Tutorial/AnalogReadSerial on the Arduino website, which shows how to connect a potentiometer to A0 to vary the voltage on this pin. With the potentiometer connected and the AnalogReadSerial sketch loaded, open the Serial Monitor window from the Arduino IDE to see the values that the Arduino is reading from the A0 pin and sending across the serial to USB link. The values will be between 0 and 1023. The serial monitor window is covered in section 1.5.2.3 – Serial Port Demonstration, in chapter 1.

As can be seen in the AnalogReadSerial sketch, analogRead() is called to get the ADC value from one of the analog inputs. Pass A0 to A15 to this function to select the analog pin to read from.

2.7.5.2 Floating Analog Input Pin

If nothing is attached to an analog pin, in other words no stable voltage level is applied to the pin, it will be 'floating'. When the ADC value is read from a floating pin, the value read will be random and depend on what noise the pin is picking up. If a floating pin is continually read and the value displayed, the value usually keeps changing and appears to randomly jump around.

2.7.5.3 Calculating Analog In Voltage

The analog voltage on an analog pin is calculated by dividing the reference voltage by 1024 (for a 10-bit ADC) and then multiplying the result by the value read on the analog input pin. On the Arduino MEGA 2560 we know that the default reference voltage is 5V, so the calculation becomes *5 ÷ 1024 × <analog value read on pin> = voltage*. The sketch that follows is a modified version of the AnalogReadSerial example sketch that reads the analog value on pin A0, but this time converts the value to voltage.

```
void setup() {
  Serial.begin(9600);
}

void loop() {
  int sensorValue = analogRead(A0);                        // Read ADC value
  float voltage = (5.0 / 1024.0) * (float)sensorValue;     // Calculate voltage
  Serial.print(voltage);                                   // Display voltage
  Serial.println(" V");
  delay(1);
}
```

In the code listing above, the analog input A0 is read as an integer value, which can be any value between 0 and 1023. The voltage is then calculated using floating point mathematics so that a decimal voltage value will be displayed. If integer mathematics were used, the voltage would be displayed as whole numbers only, 0, 1, 2, 3, 4 and 5 with no decimal point.

2.7.5.4 Analog In Pins Used as Digital I/O

Analog pins on the Arduino MEGA 2560 are connected to pins of the ATmega2560 that are multiplexed pins. This means that they can be configured as digital input pins, or digital output pins, or can be configured as analog pins attached to the internal ADC. To

Chapter 2 • Hardware Technical Information

use analog pins as digital output pins, use the same pin functions as used for digital pins, but reference the pins by their analog pin names. To set up analog pin A0 as a digital output, call pinMode() and pass it A0 as the pin to configure as an output, as shown in the following line of code.

```
pinMode(A0, OUTPUT);
```

To set the voltage level on the pin to either high or low, call digitalWrite(), using A0 as the target pin again, as shown in the code that follows.

```
digitalWrite(A0, HIGH);
```

In this way the Blink example sketch can be rewritten to flash an LED connected to the A0 pin with a series resistor, as shown in the code listing that follows.

```
void setup() {
  pinMode(A0, OUTPUT);
}

void loop() {
  digitalWrite(A0, HIGH);
  delay(500);
  digitalWrite(A0, LOW);
  delay(500);
}
```

As can be seen in the sketch, the analog pin is simply referenced by its pin name and is used as a digital pin that is driven high and low. To use the pin as a digital input, use pinMode() to set the pin up as an input pin in the same way, again referencing it by its analog pin name.

2.7.6 AREF Pin and Internal ADC Reference Voltages

An external reference voltage can be applied to the AREF pin that will be used by the ADC when doing analog to digital conversions. This can be used in place of the default 5V analog reference, but must be enabled by calling the analogReference() function which must have EXTERNAL passed to it as shown in the following line of code.

```
analogReference(EXTERNAL);
```

The AREF pin can have a reference voltage in the range of 1V to 5V applied to it. If using an external reference voltage on AREF, the above line of code must be called before reading an analog value by calling analogRead(). If analogRead() is called first, the default reference voltage will be shorted to the voltage that is applied to the AREF pin, possibly damaging the main microcontroller on the Arduino.

89

There is an option of using a 1.1V or 2.56V internal reference for the ADC by passing INTERNAL1V1 for 1.1V, or INTERNAL2V56 for 2.56V to analogReference(). Passing DEFAULT to this function uses the 5V reference which is the default value at power up. For more information on the analogReference() function, see
www.arduino.cc/reference/en/language/functions/analog-io/analogreference/

For an example of connecting an external reference voltage to the AREF pin, see section 3.3.10 in the next chapter.

2.8 Programming Headers

Two 6 pin (3 × 2) ICSP programming headers are found on the Arduino MEGA 2560. One connects to the main microcontroller and the other to the ATmega16U2 USB bridge microcontroller.

2.8.1 MEGA 2560 with External Programmer on ICSP

To program a sketch to the Arduino MEGA 2560 (main microcontroller) using an external programmer, such as the Atmel-ICE seen in Figure 2.9, from the Arduino IDE, first connect the programmer to the ICSP header near the middle of the board, as can be seen in the figure. In the Arduino IDE, select Tools ▶ Programmer and then select the correct programmer from the list. A list of all the supported programmers can be seen on this menu, and is shown in Figure 2.10 on page 92.

Figure 2.9: Atmel-ICE Connected to the ICSP Header of an Arduino MEGA 2560

To load a sketch to the Arduino MEGA 2560 using the programmer instead of the USB connection, select Sketch ▶ Upload Using Programmer from the top menu in the Arduino IDE. This will erase the bootloader from memory making the full 256k of memory available to the sketch.

Note that if Atmel Studio is installed on the computer, as is described in chapter 5, this method of programming will not work from the Arduino IDE because of a driver clash.

Atmel Studio is an example of a full featured C and C++ IDE, that can be used for advanced programming of an Arduino MEGA 2560 using an external programmer connected to the ICSP header. This is an alternative to using the Arduino IDE.

2.8.2 Restore Bootloader with IDE and External Programmer

If the bootloader is erased by programming the Arduino MEGA 2560 using an external programmer, as is described in the previous section, the bootloader can be restored using an external programmer and the Arduino IDE. Connect the programmer to the ICSP header, as is described in the previous section, and as shown in Figure 2.9. In the Arduino IDE, select the correct programmer under Tools ▶ Programmer from the top menu. Make sure that the correct Arduino is selected under Tools ▶ Board in the Arduino IDE, and that the correct processor is selected under Tools ▶ Processor. Select Tools ▶ Burn Bootloader from the top menu to load the bootloader to the main microcontroller. This will also set the fuses in the main microcontroller to the correct values. Again, this will not work if Atmel Studio is installed on the computer because of a driver clash. This is not a problem, because Atmel Studio can be used to restore the bootloader. See chapter 5 for more information on programming the bootloader using Atmel Studio.

2.8.3 ATmega16U2 ICSP Header

The second ICSP header, found near the USB connector, can be used to program the ATmega16U2 microcontroller using an external USB programmer. It can be used to update the firmware on this chip, however there is a method called DFU that allows the firmware to be upgraded using the Arduino MEGA 2560 USB connection and some additional software.

More information on DFU programming can be found on the Arduino website at www.arduino.cc/en/Hacking/DFUProgramming8U2 and in section 5.1 of chapter 5 of this book.

2.8.4 ICSP Programming Resources

Out of several external USB programmers for AVR microcontrollers that use the ICSP header and were originally from Atmel, but now from Microchip, only the Atmel-ICE is currently available. All other former Atmel or Microchip AVR programmers are currently marked as no longer for sale on the Microchip website, which includes the AVRISP mkII. The Atmel-ICE replaces all other previous programmers, but some of these programmers still work with the Arduino IDE, and clones of some of these programmers may be available.

There are also several USB programmers that can be home built or purchased from third parties. Figure 2.10 shows a list of external programming tools supported by the Arduino IDE, that include official Microchip programmers, both redundant and new, as well as programmers from other sources.

Figure 2.10: External Programmers Supported by the Arduino IDE

The links that follow provide more information on the Atmel-ICE, Atmel Studio and C programming of Arduino boards using Atmel Studio. Also see chapter 5. Links to older Atmel/Microchip programmers that are now redundant are also listed for interest.

Atmel-ICE   – www.microchip.com/DevelopmentTools/ProductDetails/atatmel-ice
Atmel Studio   – www.microchip.com/mplab/avr-support/atmel-studio-7
C Programming – wspublishing.net/avr-c/

Redundant no longer for sale programmers:

AVRISP mkII – www.microchip.com/developmenttools/ProductDetails/atavrisp2
JTAGICE3 – www.microchip.com/DevelopmentTools/ProductDetails/PartNO/ATJTAGICE3

2.8.5 Using an Arduino as an In-System Programmer

One of the external programmers that can be found under Tools ▶ Programmer in the Arduino IDE is "Arduino as ISP". This option means that an Arduino can be used to program the bootloader to a second Arduino. Find more information on the Arduino website at www.arduino.cc/en/Tutorial/BuiltInExamples/ArduinoISP

2.9 Shared Pins

Several pins are shared between connectors and functions on Arduino MEGA 2560 boards. Some of these have already been covered in this chapter, but are included here again to make this section complete and to provide additional details.

2.9.1 Serial Port Pins

Digital pins 0 and 1 are shared with the serial port or UART. RX0, or receive, is found on digital pin 0. TX0, or transmit, is found on digital pin 1. For more information on the serial / UART pins, see section 3.3.6.

2.9.2 L LED Pin

The on-board L LED is connected to digital pin 13. On revision 3 Arduino MEGA 2560 boards, this LED is buffered through a unity gain op-amp, which means that it will not interfere with any circuit connected to pin 13. On Arduino MEGA 2560 boards before R3, a 1k resistor in series with the L LED was connected directly between pin 13 and GND. On these boards, the resistor and LED load may interfere with connected circuits. See section 6.1.2 – Main Microcontroller Circuit, for the circuit diagram of the unity gain op-amp and L LED found in Figure 6.2 of chapter 6.

On Arduino Uno boards pin 13 is the SCK (Serial Clock) pin for the SPI bus and does not have PWM capabilities. Arduino MEGA 2560 boards do not have the SPI SCK on pin 13, but this pin does have PWM capabilities. This means that the L LED can be PWM controlled from a sketch on an Arduino MEGA 2560, but not on an Arduino Uno.

2.9.3 TWI or I²C Pins

TWI is a serial bus protocol that uses a clock and data line called SCL (Serial Clock) and SDA (Serial Data) and is compatible with the I²C protocol. On an Arduino MEGA 2560, these pins are found on pin 20 (SDA) and pin 21 (SCL). When using the Wire library to access TWI devices, the default serial clock frequency is 100kHz which can be changed by calling Wire.setClock().

Arduino MEGA 2560 revision 3 boards route pin 20 and pin 21 to the last two pins at the end of the edge connector near the USB connector, where they are called SDA1 and SCL1 on the labels on the connector. The names are silkscreened on the header on newer R3 boards only. This means that there is only one TWI controller available on the ATmega2560 chip, and the same SCL and SDA pins are found in two places on the edge connectors. Pins labeled SDA1 and SCL1 line up with the SDA and SCL pins in the same position on Arduino Uno boards.

2.9.4 ICSP SPI Pins and Reset

The ICSP header near the middle of the board that connects to the main microcontroller shares its pins with digital pins on the double row header socket at the end of the board. These are the pins used for the SPI bus protocol as well as the reset pin. The six pins of the ICSP header are connected as shown in Table 2.4.

Table 2.4: ICSP Pin Functions and Connections

ICSP Pin	Pin Function	Connects To
1	MISO – Master In Slave Out for SPI	Digital Pin 50
2	5V	5V Supply
3	SCK – Serial Clock for SPI	Digital Pin 52
4	MOSI – Master Out Slave In for SPI	Digital Pin 51
5	RESET	Reset Pin and Button
6	GND	GND

In addition to MISO, MOSI and SCK, SPI has a slave select pin (SS) which is available on digital pin 53. When using the SPI bus, the SS pin (pin 53) must be kept as an output or the SPI interface will not work, as specified at www.arduino.cc/en/Reference/Ethernet for use with the Ethernet shield. Figure 2.11 shows a schematic of the pin numbering of the ICSP header and Figure 2.12 shows the same header on the Arduino MEGA 2560 board.

Chapter 2 • Hardware Technical Information

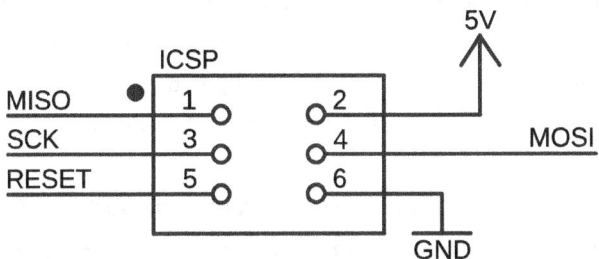

Figure 2.11: ICSP Header Pin Numbers

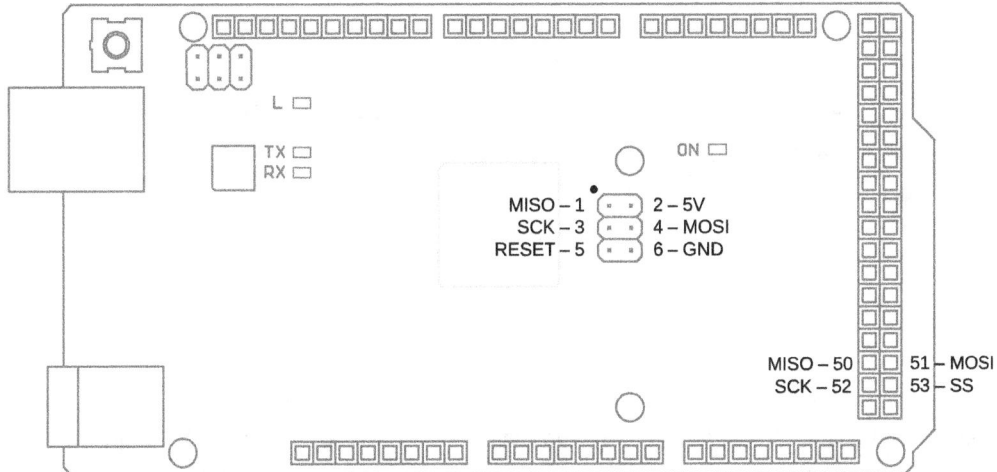

Figure 2.12: ICSP Header Pin Numbers on the Arduino MEGA 2560 Board

2.9.5 JTAG Pins

Four pins on the Arduino MEGA 2560 allow access to the JTAG functionality of the ATmega2560 microcontroller, namely A4, A5, A6 and A7. JTAG (Joint Test Action Group) on the ATmega2560 microcontroller is a IEEE standard 1149.1 compliant interface that provides on-chip debug support, programming of Flash, EEPROM, fuses and lock bits, as well as boundary-scan capabilities. This functionality is advanced and not supported by the Arduino IDE. As with the ICSP header, an external USB programmer/debugger device such as an Atmel-ICE is needed to use JTAG. The external programmer must be used in conjunction with software, such as Atmel Studio.

JTAG is a more advanced way of programming and debugging the ATmega2560, and is available in addition to the ISP/ICSP interface, that also has programming and debugging capabilities through the ICSP header. Single-step debugging can be performed through the ISP/ICSP header by putting the ATmega2560 into debugWIRE mode. If this interface is needed for use with the SPI bus, then JTAG debugging can be used instead. This is useful for software development and debugging of SPI bus devices.

As JTAG is an advanced feature that is not supported by the Arduino IDE, it is not discussed further in this manual, except to provide pin information in Table 2.5 below, and to provide pinout information in section 3.7 of Chapter 3. Note that JTAG functionality is not available on the ATmega328P microcontroller used on Arduino Uno boards.

Table 2.5: Arduino Pins with JTAG Functionality

Arduino Pin	JTAG Pin	I/O Port Pin	Alternate Function
A4 (58)	TCK	PF4	ADC4
A5 (59)	TMS	PF5	ADC5
A6 (60)	TDO	PF6	ADC6
A7 (61)	TDI	PF7	ADC7

JTAG pins are TCK (Test Clock), TMS (Test Mode Select), TDO (Test Data Out) and TDI (Test Data In). RESET is also usually connected to a JTAG programmer/debugger device, in addition to GND, and the target voltage which is 5V on the Arduino MEGA 2560.

Chapter 3 • Pin Reference and Interfacing

The reference part of this book starts with this chapter which is an Arduino MEGA 2560 pin reference with interfacing examples.

Use this chapter as a quick reference to find pin names, alternate pin functions and the mapping of the ATmega2560 pins to the Arduino headers.

Although this book is a hardware manual for the Arduino MEGA 2560 and not a book that teaches basic electronics, it does include basic interfacing examples to help users with connecting various electronic components to an Arduino. The interfacing examples are used to illustrate various interfacing techniques and principles.

In this Chapter

- Arduino MEGA 2560 pin names, functions and alternate functions
- Arduino MEGA 2560 to main microcontroller (ATmega2560) mapping
- Why an LED must be interfaced using a series resistor
- Current sourcing and sinking configurations
- Pull-up and pull-down resistors on inputs
- TWI and SPI serial buses
- Serial ports / USARTs
- Various interfacing examples

3.1 Pin Default and Alternate Functions

Figure 3.1 on the next page shows the default Arduino MEGA 2560 pin functions as well as the alternate functions such as pins used for TWI and SPI serial buses. This figure is very revealing in that it shows what is really happening with the pins, especially the TWI and SPI pins, where the same pins appear on more than one connector.

3.1.1 Shared TWI Pins

Notice in Figure 3.1 that the TWI pins, SCL (on pin 21) and SDA (on pin 20), are routed to SCL1 and SDA1 found at the other end of the connector near the USB port (on Arduino MEGA 2560 R3 boards, not present on earlier revision boards). In other words there are no additional SCL and SDA TWI pins on Arduino MEGA 2560 R3 boards, these pins are electrically connected or wired to SCL1 and SDA1. SCL1 and SDA1 line up with the SCL and SDA pins found in the same position on Arduino Uno R3 boards.

When making an Arduino Uno sized shield that is to be compatible with both Arduino Uno and Arduino MEGA 2560 boards that uses TWI, always use the pins positioned at SCL1 and SDA1, so that TWI devices on the shield connect to TWI pins on both Arduino boards. On Arduino Uno boards, the TWI pins are also available on two analog pins, A4 and A5, but this is not the case on Arduino MEGA 2560 boards.

3.1.2 Shared SPI Pins

SPI bus pins on Arduino MEGA 2560 boards appear on digital input / output pins 50 to 53, so don't line up with SPI pins on Arduino Uno boards. If these pins are used for SPI, then they can no longer be used as input / output pins.

Notice in Figure 3.1 that three of these pins appear on the ICSP header, namely pins 50, 51 and 52. When an external programmer is connected to the ICSP header, it will also be electrically connected to whatever circuit is connected to pins 50, 51 and 52.

Avoid using pins 50 to 53 for any other purpose except for SPI when designing a shield so that the shield will be compatible with other shields that use these pins for SPI. Start designing a shield by using pins that are not multiplexed with other pin functions first. If there are not enough pins, then the SPI or TWI pins can be used, but compatibility with other shields may be lost. To make a shield that uses SPI and is compatible with Arduino Uno sized boards, SPI connections must be taken off the ICSP header.

Chapter 3 • Pin Reference and Interfacing

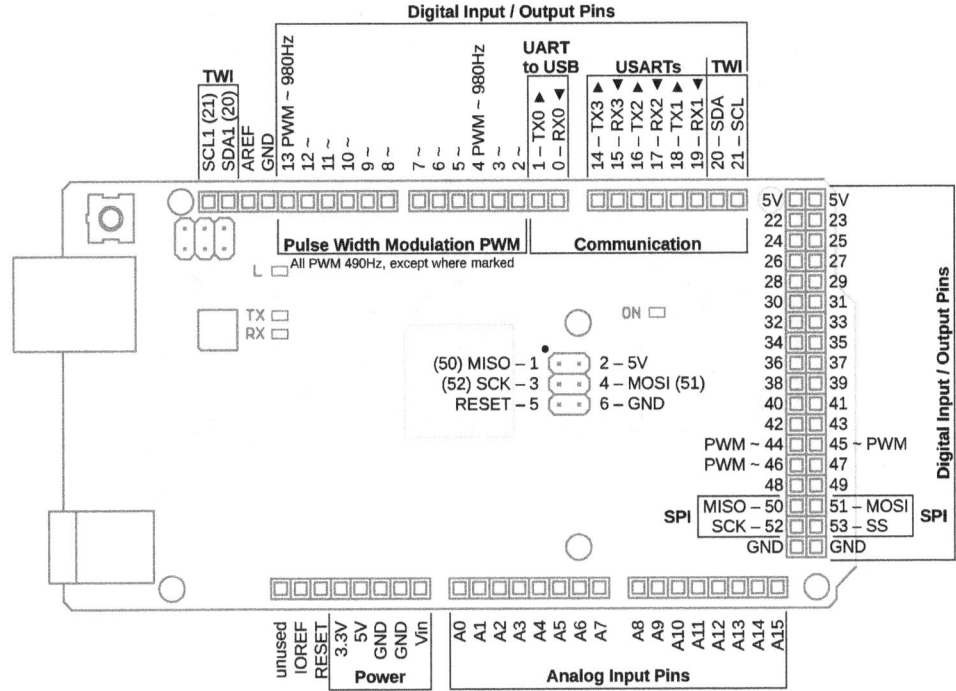

Figure 3.1: Arduino MEGA 2560 R3 Default Pins and Alternate Pin Functions

3.2 ATmega2560 to Arduino MEGA 2560 Pin Mapping

Figure 3.2 shows the ATmega2560 microcontroller chip (not to scale) with its pin functions and alternate pin functions on the outer most labels. The Arduino MEGA 2560 pins that these microcontroller pins are connected to are shown on the inner most labels. Labels down the left and right sides of the image on the inside of the microcontroller body are the Arduino names found on the MEGA 2560 board. Labels closest to the ATmega2560 pins on the top and bottom of the image are the names found on the MEGA 2560 board. This arrangement is simply to prevent labels at the top and bottom clashing with labels on the left and right, if they had all been placed inside the ATmega2560 microcontroller body.

Arduino Pins 0 to 53 are the digital pins, and A0 to A15 the analog inputs which also have digital pin numbers from 54 to 69. This means that analog pins A0 to A15 can be accessed as digital pins 54 to 69 in a sketch. RESET, AREF, 5V and GND are as labeled on the Arduino MEGA 2560 board. XTAL1 and XTAL2 are not connected to external Arduino pins, but are connected to the on-board ceramic resonator. The circle at the top left of the body of the image represents the marking that is normally found on the body of the chip, at the top left to mark where pin 1 is. It is placed outside the body in the image to prevent obscuring the labels inside the body. Pins on the ATmega2560 chip not connected to anything on the Arduino and are grayed out and marked with n.c. for "not connected".

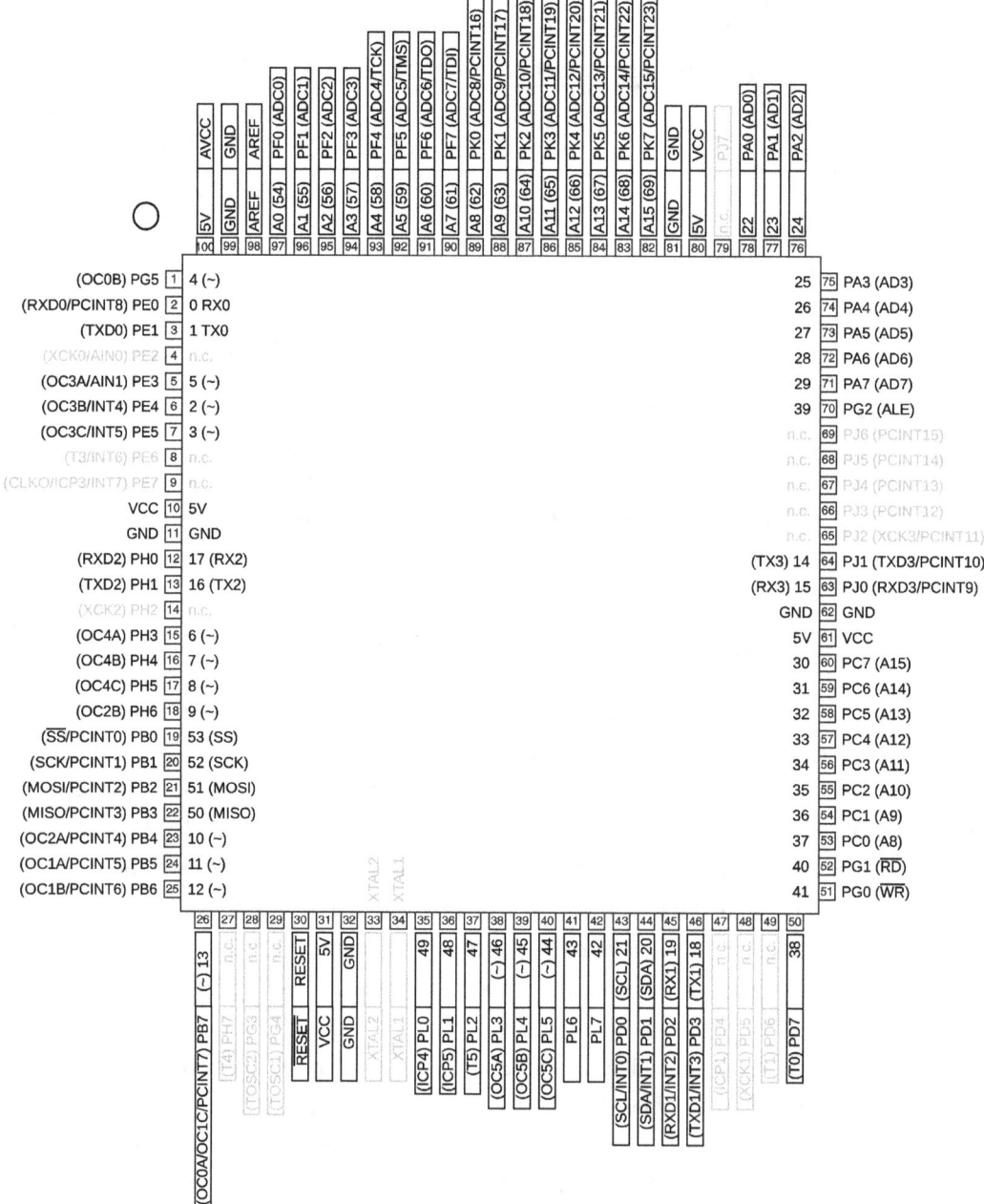

Figure 3.2: ATmega2560 to Arduino Pin Mapping

Chapter 3 • Pin Reference and Interfacing

ATmega2560 to Arduino pin mapping of Figure 3.2 is generally only needed by advanced Arduino users. For those who want to use alternate hardware functions available on certain pins, and those directly programming the hardware in plain C, the figure is useful to find out which functionality is available on which pin. Figure 3.3 provides the same information, but from the point of view of the Arduino MEGA 2560 pins.

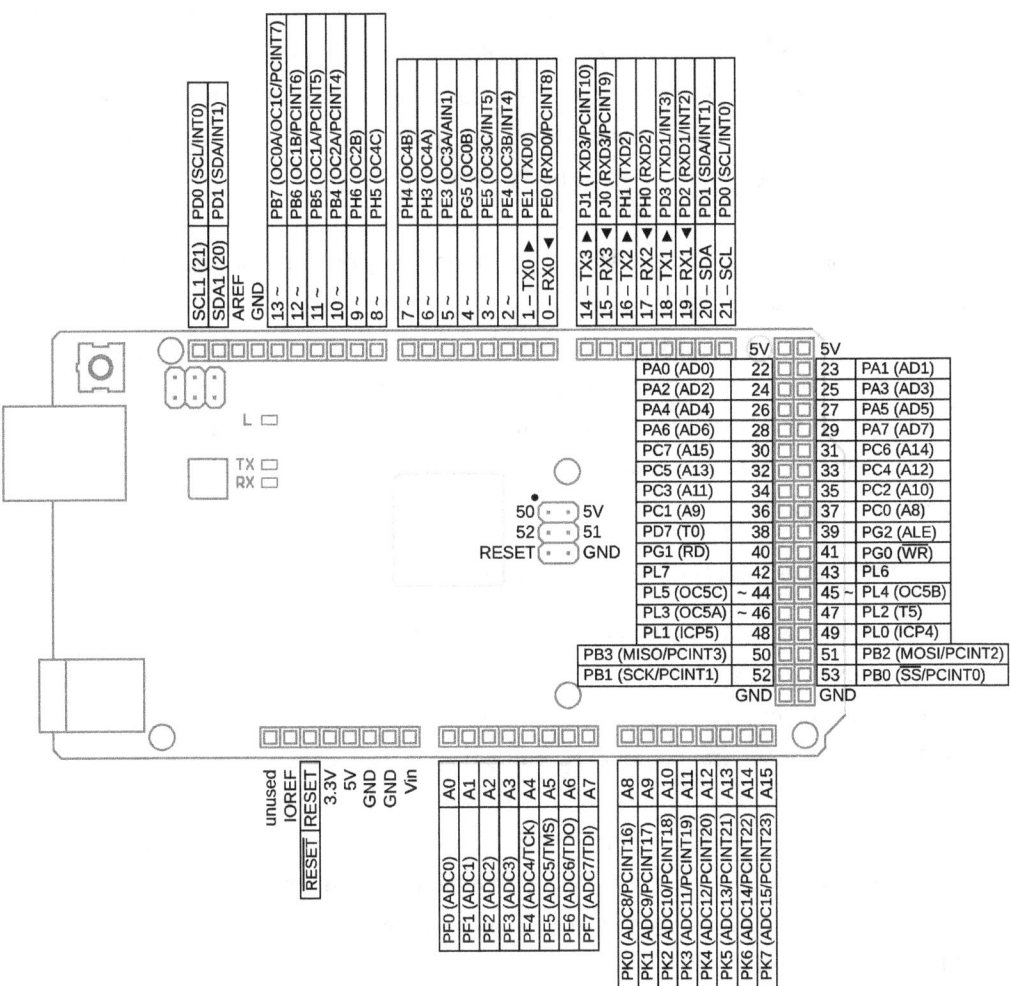

Figure 3.3: Arduino MEGA 2560 to ATmega2560 Microcontroller Pin Mapping

3.2.1 ATmega2560 Ports

ATmega2560 microcontroller I/O, or input/output pins, are grouped into 8-bit ports that are each labeled with a letter of the alphabet. Ten ports are available on the ATmega2560,

101

namely port A (PAx pins), port B (PBx pins), port C (PCx pins), port D (PDx pins), port E (PEx pins), port F (PFx pins), port G (PGx pins), port H (PHx pins), port J (PJx pins), and port K (PKx pins), where x is a number from 0 to 7. Notice that there is no port I. Skipping a letter such as I when labeling items in engineering is common, because the letter I can look too much like the number 1, depending on the font used. Port pin numbers seen in the previous two figures map to Arduino pins, for example PB4, or port B pin 4, maps to Arduino MEGA 2560 digital I/O pin 10. When programming in plain C, ports or individual pins on ports can be programmed by knowing their port and pin names. When programming using the Arduino IDE with the Arduino library functions, these same port pins are accessed using their Arduino MEGA 2560 pin names. The real microcontroller pin names are hidden by software when using the Arduino IDE.

Although the ports are 8 bits wide, all bits from a port may not be available on pins of the microcontroller, because there may not be enough pins on the microcontroller. An example is port G that only has pins PG0 to PG5. There are no PG6 and PG7 pins on the ATmega2560 microcontroller. All other ports on this microcontroller are full 8-bit wide ports with none of the pins missing. Not all microcontroller pins are brought out to Arduino pins because there are too many pins on the ATmega2560, so some of these pins are left unconnected to anything.

3.2.2 ATmega2560 Alternate Pin Functions

Each additional label next to each pin in figures 3.2 and 3.3 denotes an alternate function that is multiplexed on the pin. Multiplexed means that the pin can be configured in software to use one of the alternative pin functions. For example Arduino MEGA 2560 pin 21 can be used as a general purpose I/O port pin PD0. The same pin can be used as the TWI serial clock (SCL) pin, or as external interrupt pin INT0. Using an alternative pin function essentially connects the pin to a hardware device inside the microcontroller that performs the function, such as the hardware that handles TWI serial communications. This hardware is configurable by software, which is usually handled by Arduino libraries used in the Arduino IDE.

Official Arduino libraries don't support all possible ATmega2560 pin functions. These pin functions can still be used by programming them in C or C++, typically by more advanced users or hackers. More information on each pin function can be found in the ATmega2560 datasheet from the page www.microchip.com/wwwproducts/en/ATmega2560 on the Microchip website. A link to the datasheet can be found on this web page.

Chapter 3 • Pin Reference and Interfacing

3.3 Pin Types and Interfacing

In this section pins are grouped by types or functions, such as digital, analog, PWM, TWI, and so on. Basic interfacing circuits and principles are presented in each section where appropriate.

3.3.1 Digital Input / Output Pins

Arduino MEGA 2560 pins 0 to 53 are digital Input/Output or I/O pins and can individually be configured as input pins or output pins in an Arduino sketch. Pins 0 and 1 are connected to the USB to serial bridge chip via two 1k resistors, so may not be suitable as I/O pins, depending on the application. Although analog input pins A0 to A15 are labeled as ANALOG IN pins on an Arduino MEGA 2560, they can be used as digital input and output pins as well. As was already mentioned, analog pins A0 to A15 can be accessed as digital pins 54 to 69. This means that if analog input pins are not needed in a project, 70 digital I/O pins are effectively available, numbered from 0 to 69.

3.3.1.1 Pins as Outputs

Pins are configured as outputs in the setup() part of an Arduino sketch. Call the pinMode() function to set an Arduino pin up as an output that can be used to switch an attached device on and off. This function has the following format when setting up a pin as an output.

```
pinMode(<pin number>, OUTPUT);
```

Where *<pin number>* can be one of the following.
0 to 53 — for digital pins.
A0 to A15 — to set up an analog pin as a digital output (or 54 to 69).
LED_BUILTIN — set up the default L LED pin as an output.

Examples:

```
pinMode(48, OUTPUT);    // Set up digital pin 48 as an output

pinMode(A8, OUTPUT);    // Set up analog input pin A8 as a digital output

pinMode(LED_BUILTIN, OUTPUT);  // Set up pin attached to L LED as an output
```

Why an LED Needs a Series Resistor

LEDs are diodes that have a certain forward voltage rating and maximum forward current. If a voltage higher than the maximum forward voltage is applied directly between the leads or pins of an LED, it will try to draw more than its maximum rated forward current. This can cause the LED to burn out, and/or the device that is driving it, such as the microcontroller on an Arduino. Putting a resistor in series with an LED limits the current that the LED can draw, preventing it from burning out and damaging the microcontroller.

Figure 3.4 shows an LED with a series resistor. If the forward voltage, V_F, across the LED is 2V, then the voltage across the resistor will be the supply voltage minus the LED voltage. In this example it is 5V – 2V = 3V dropped across the resistor, where 5V can be directly supplied from a power supply or switched onto the circuit from an Arduino pin. As can be seen in this figure, excess voltage is dropped across resistor R1, preventing too much voltage being applied directly across the LED.

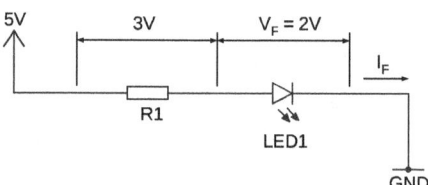

Figure 3.4: LED and Series Current Limiting Resistor

The actual LED forward voltage depends on the type and color of the LED, and can also differ between manufacturers. A red diffused LED typically has a forward voltage of around 2V, while some blue and white LEDs can have forward voltages of 3V or higher, up to around 4V. Forward voltage (V_F) of an LED is also affected by the forward current, I_F, flowing through the LED – forward voltage will typically increase slightly as forward current is increased. Table 3.1 contains sample parameters taken from LED datasheets for various sized LEDs from various different manufacturers, and is explained on the next page. As an example, the red 5mm LED from the top of Table 3.1 has the following characteristics.

Forward Voltage (V_F):   1.9V to 2.6V (@ 20mA forward current)
Forward Current (I_F):   20mA
Maximum Forward Current: 30mA
Maximum Reverse Voltage: 5V (not shown in Table 3.1)

Table 3.1: Sample Parameters for Various Through-hole Mounting Round LEDs

LED Color	Diameter	Typical V_F	Maximum V_F	Test Conditions (I_F)	Absolute Maximum I_F
Red	5mm	1.9V	2.6V	20mA	30mA
Bright Red	5mm	2.25V	2.5V	20mA	25mA
Red, Clear	5mm	2.1V	2.7V	50mA	50mA
Green	5mm	2.2V	2.5V	20mA	25mA
Green	5mm	3.4V	3.6V	20mA	30mA
Yellow	5mm	2.1V	2.5V	20mA	30mA
Super Bright Yellow	5mm	2V	2.5V	20mA	30mA
Orange	5mm	2V	2.5V	20mA	30mA
Blue	5mm	3.3V	4V	20mA	30mA
Blue	5mm	2.7V	3.6V	20mA	30mA
White	5mm	3.2V	4V	20mA	30mA
Red	3mm	2V	2.6V	20mA	30mA
High Efficiency Red	3mm	1.7V	2.5V	2mA	30mA
Yellow	3mm	2.1V	2.6V	20mA	20mA
Green	3mm	2.1V	2.6V	20mA	30mA
Green	3mm	1.9V	2.5V	2mA	25mA
Pure Orange	3mm	2.05V	2.5V	20mA	25mA
Blue	3mm	2.8V	3.6V	20mA	30mA
Super Bright Red	8mm	1.85V	2.5V	20mA	30mA
Yellow	8mm	2.1V	2.5V	20mA	30mA
Green	8mm	2.2V	2.5V	20mA	25mA

LEDs have a typical and maximum forward voltage which is written as V_F in datasheets. These forward voltages are always specified as being measured under certain test conditions, which is usually for a forward current of 20mA. Table 3.1 shows that most, but not all forward voltages are specified for a 20mA forward current. The exceptions in this table are one LED that has its forward voltages specified at 50mA, and two LEDs that have forward voltages specified for a 2mA forward current.

As can be seen in Table 3.1, some LEDs that have the same color, but are supplied by different manufacturers, have different forward voltages. For example, there are two green LEDs that are both 5mm, but have rather different forward voltages. Two 3mm green LEDs are another example. These 3mm green LEDs have similar forward voltages, but these forward voltages are specified for different forward currents. The point of the table is to show that similar LEDs can have different electrical parameters, and the only reliable way to find the exact electrical parameters is to consult the manufacturer's datasheet for the particular LED. Alternatively the voltage and current of an LED can be measured in a circuit.

Figure 3.5 shows an example of a graph that is found in many LED datasheets. It is a graph of the forward voltage of a particular LED from a particular manufacturer, plotted against the forward current of the LED. Each type of LED will have a slightly different graph, again depending on the LED color, type and manufacturer. This graph reveals the full picture of how an increase in forward current results in an increase in forward voltage of the LED. With a forward current of 5mA, the forward voltage is about 1.9V, taken from Figure 3.5 in this example. When the forward current is increased to 20mA, the forward voltage increases to 2V.

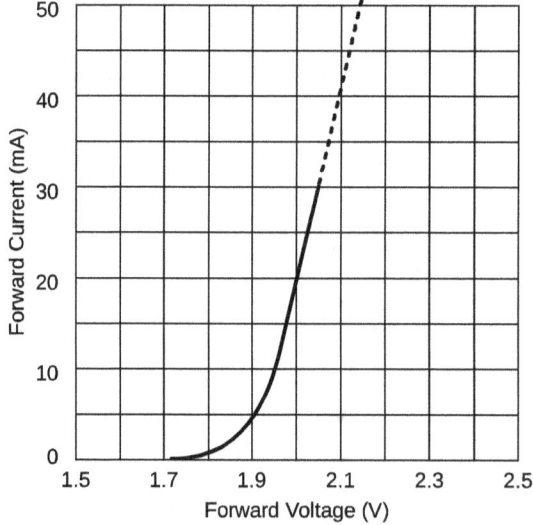

Figure 3.5: Forward Current vs. Forward Voltage of an LED

How to Calculate a LED Current Limiting Series Resistor

Before calculating the value of a series current limiting resistor for an LED, forward current must be selected, which will typically be a value in milliamps (mA). The more current that flows through the LED, the brighter it will burn. Limiting factors are the maximum forward current of the LED and the amount of current that the device driving the

Chapter 3 • Pin Reference and Interfacing

LED can deliver. If the maximum forward current of an LED is 20mA and the maximum current that an Arduino MEGA 2560 pin can deliver is also 20mA, then for good design practice, a value less than 20mA must be selected. Forward voltage of the LED must also be known before it is possible to calculate the series resistor value. Two examples follow that show how to calculate the series resistor value. A third and fourth example show how to calculate the current flowing through the LED and series resistor if the value of the resistor is known.

Example 1

It is decided to calculate the series resistor value using a forward current of 10mA, which is well within the 20mA limit, and a forward LED voltage of 2V. To do the calculation, we use Ohm's law, but first calculate the voltage drop across the resistor.

An Arduino MEGA 2560 operates at 5V, and switching a digital pin high switches 5V onto the pin. The voltage dropped across the resistor will then be 5V minus the 2V voltage drop across the LED:

5V − 2V = 3V

To calculate the resistance of the series resistor, divide the resistor voltage drop by the desired forward current. In this example it is 3V divided by 10mA:

3V ÷ 10mA = 300Ω

OR

3V ÷ 0.01A = 300Ω
(10mA = 0.01A)

A 300Ω series resistor will limit the LED current to 10mA.

Example 2

It is decided that the LED from the previous example is not bright enough for the application, so the LED forward current is changed to 16mA, which is still within the 20mA limit. The same LED with a forward voltage of 2V is used, so the voltage drop across the series resistor is still 3V. The resistor is calculated as follows:

3V ÷ 16mA = 187.5Ω
OR
3V ÷ 0.016A = 187.5Ω

As 187.5Ω is not a standard resistor value, use 180Ω, 200Ω or 220Ω instead.

Example 3
From the previous example, if a 220Ω resistor is the only value close to 187.5Ω that is immediately available, the current flowing through the 220Ω series resistor and LED can be calculated as follows, if the voltage drop across the resistor is 3V:

I = V ÷ R (Current equals Voltage divided by Resistance)

I = 3V ÷ 220Ω
I = 0.0136A OR 13.6mA

Example 4
In a circuit diagram, an LED and 470Ω resistor are connected in series. Assuming the LED forward voltage is 2V and the supply voltage is 5V, the current through the LED can be calculated as follows:

Voltage across resistor = 5V – 2V = 3V

I = V ÷ R
I = 3V ÷ 470Ω
I = 0.0064A OR 6.4mA

All of the series resistor current calculations are approximate, because resistors have certain tolerances, such as 5% or 1%. This means that the resistance values of these resistors could be higher or lower by their given tolerance.

LED voltages are also not exact values, as we saw they have a typical and maximum forward voltage. This means their forward voltages could be higher or lower than the values used in calculations. Finally power supply values may not be exactly 5V. The main point is that calculated current values must be below the maximum LED and Arduino pin current ratings for safety.

Current Sourcing and Current Sinking

There are two ways that an LED and series resistor, or other load such as a buzzer, can be connected to an Arduino or other electronic system, namely current sourcing and current sinking. How they are wired determines how they are turned on and off in software sketches. In a current sourcing configuration, an Arduino pin is switched high to switch the load on and low to switch the load off. For a current sinking configuration, the opposite is true – the pin is switched high to switch the load off and low to switch the load on. Both configurations are explained in the sections that follow. In the figures that follow, it does not matter if the LED and series resistor are swapped. It does matter that the LED is connected the correct way around, as current can only flow one way through an LED.

Current Sourcing

Figure 3.6 shows an LED and series resistor connected to an Arduino MEGA 2560 in a current sourcing configuration. When Arduino MEGA 2560 pin 2 is switched high, the Arduino sources current that flows through the series resistor and LED, switching the LED on. When the pin is switched low, the LED switches off.

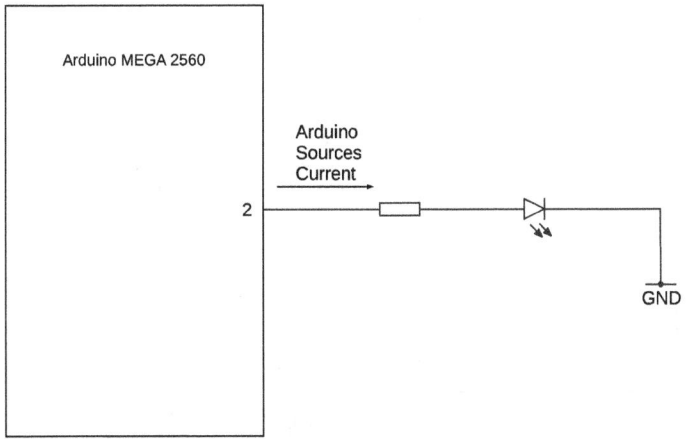

Figure 3.6: Arduino MEGA 2560 and LED in Current Sourcing Configuration

In a sketch, pin 2 is first set up as an output pin as follows.

```
pinMode(2, OUTPUT);
```

To switch the LED on, the pin is switched high as shown in the following line of code.

```
digitalWrite(2, HIGH);    // Switch LED on (current sourcing)
```

To switch the LED off, the pin is switched low as follows.

```
digitalWrite(2, LOW);     // Switch LED off (current sourcing)
```

The built-in L LED on Arduino MEGA 2560 boards is wired to pin 13 of the Arduino in a current sourcing configuration and should be the most familiar way of switching an LED on and off for most users. This is the same configuration as on an Arduino Uno.

Current Sinking

Figure 3.7 shows an Arduino MEGA 2560 and LED connected in a current sinking configuration. The anode of the LED is connected to 5V, this means that it can only switch on if the other side of the LED, or cathode is connected to GND through the series resistor. When connected to an Arduino, as shown in the figure, the Arduino pin can be switched to either 5V or GND. Switching the pin to 5V, or high, switches the LED off because both sides of the LED series resistor circuit are at this same potential. The only way to switch the LED on is to switch the Arduino pin low, which provides GND to the other side of the circuit. Current then flows from the 5V supply, through the LED and series resistor to GND that is supplied by the microcontroller on Arduino pin 2.

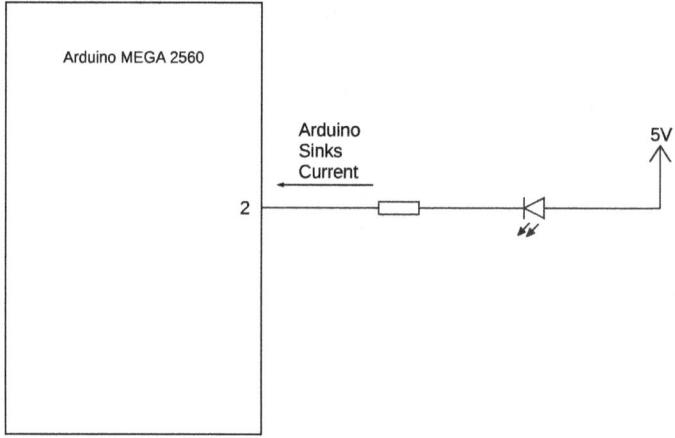

Figure 3.7: Arduino MEGA 2560 and LED in Current Sinking Configuration

As with current sourcing, current sinking requires the Arduino pin to be set up as an output. In a sketch, pin 2 is first set up as an output pin as follows.

```
pinMode(2, OUTPUT);
```

To switch the LED on, the pin is switched low as shown in the following line of code.

```
digitalWrite(2, LOW);    // Switch LED on (current sinking)
```

To switch the LED off, the pin is switched high as shown below.

```
digitalWrite(2, HIGH);   // Switch LED off (current sinking)
```

Chapter 3 • Pin Reference and Interfacing

Current sinking may seem strange at first, but is a legitimate way to wire a load to an Arduino or other electronic device. Users are usually accustomed to high being on and low being off, current sinking reverses this logic. Bear this in mind if ever coming across a circuit or shield that has an LED or other device connected in a current sinking configuration.

Current Limitation Per Pin

On the Arduino MEGA 2560 R3 page on the Arduino website, the technical specifications give the current limit per pin as 20mA. The ATmega2560 datasheet gives the absolute maximum current per pin as 40mA. Further to this, the datasheet gives the absolute maximum total current that can be drawn from the device as 200mA. No device should be operated at its absolute maximum values, but rather well below them to avoid destroying the device and for long term reliability. It is put this way in the datasheet: *"Stresses beyond those listed under "Absolute Maximum Ratings" may cause permanent damage to the device. This is a stress rating only and functional operation of the device at these or other conditions beyond those indicated in the operational sections of this specification is not implied. Exposure to absolute maximum rating conditions for extended periods may affect device reliability."* In addition to these operating conditions, there is a limit of 100mA or 200mA that certain groups of pins can source and sink as shown in the following section.

I/O Port Current Source and Sink Limits

I/O port current source limits and current sink limits for the ATmega2560 are identical. Below are the current source limits taken from the ATmega2560 datasheet and are exactly the same for the current sink limits.

Although each I/O port can source more than the test conditions (20mA at VCC = 5V) under steady state conditions (non-transient), the following must be observed:

(1) *The sum of all IOH, for ports J0-J7, G2, A0-A7 should not exceed 200mA.*

(2) *The sum of all IOH, for ports C0-C7, G0-G1, D0-D7, L0-L7 should not exceed 200mA.*

(3) *The sum of all IOH, for ports G3-G4, B0-B7, H0-H7 should not exceed 200mA.*

(4) *The sum of all IOH, for ports E0-E7, G5 should not exceed 100mA.*

(5) *The sum of all IOH, for ports F0-F7, K0-K7 should not exceed 100mA.*

Arduino MEGA 2560 Hardware Manual

Figure 3.8 shows the five groups of pins that can source or sink either 100mA or 200mA per group. Remember that the datasheet gives the absolute maximum total current that can be drawn from the device as 200mA. This is found in the datasheet under the absolute maximum ratings and is given as DC current for V_{CC} and GND pins.

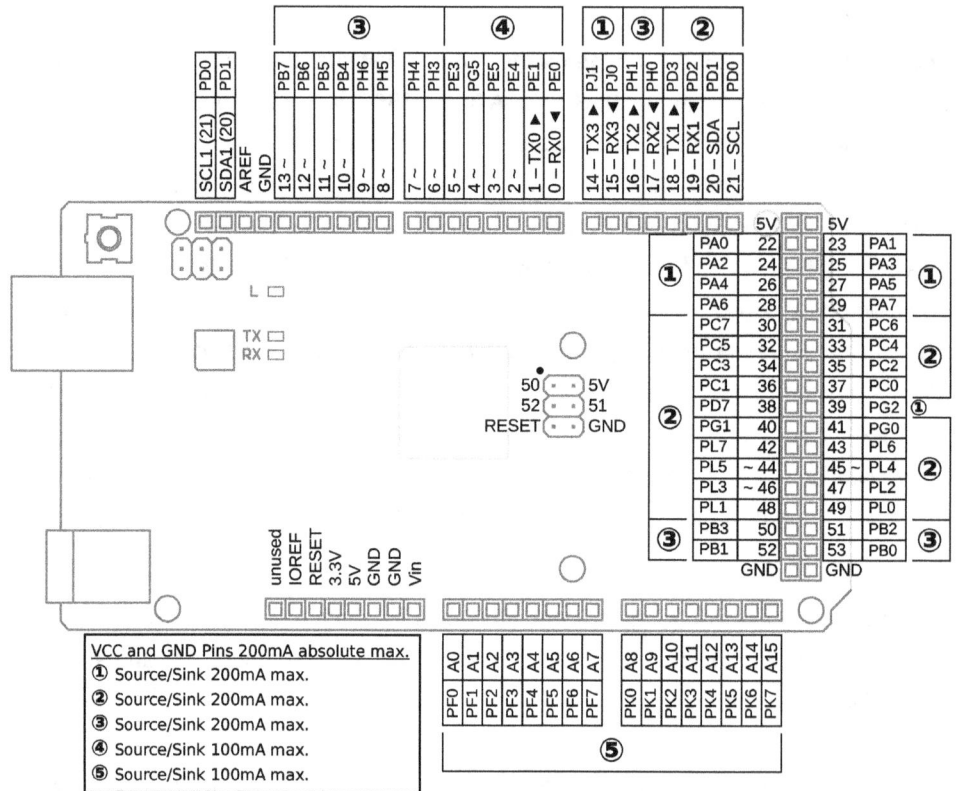

Figure 3.8: Arduino MEGA 2560 Current Source/Sink Limits for Pin Groups

In Figure 3.8, it can be seen that the first three groups of port pins can source or sink a maximum of 200mA each, and that group 4 and 5 can source or sink a maximum of 100mA each. Because there is an absolute maximum current limit of 200mA for the ATmega2560 microcontroller, we can't operate all of these ports at their maximum current ratings simultaneously. If we did, this would give a total current consumption of 200mA × 3 for the first three port groups, plus 100mA × 2 for the last two port groups, resulting in a total current consumption of 800mA, which is way above the 200mA absolute maximum. Note in the figure that Arduino pins 20 and 21, or PD1 and PD0 occur at the top left of the figure, as well as at the top right, so are only included in a group once, at the top right.

Chapter 3 • Pin Reference and Interfacing

Getting back to the stated 20mA DC current per I/O pin, we can now see that it is not possible to source or sink this current from all Arduino MEGA 2560 pins at the same time, due to the total absolute maximum current that can be drawn from the ATmega2560 device, as well as the pin group limits, as shown in Figure 3.8. Drawing 20mA from 10 pins simultaneously would already bring us to the 200mA absolute maximum current. This in itself would be bad because as we saw, operating at the 200mA absolute maximum is not recommended. In addition to this, the core of the ATmega2560 is using some current, and there is bound to be some other current usage from pins that are used as outputs from the UART/USART, TWI bus and SPI bus. The datasheet gives the maximum active current of the ATmega2560, when running at only 8MHz, as 14mA. On an Arduino MEGA 2560 operating at 16MHz, this current is even higher. From the "active supply current versus frequency" graph in the ATmega2560 datasheet, it is seen that the supply current can be over 20mA for an ATmega2560 powered from 5V and operating at 16MHz.

Because not all I/O pins on the ATmega2560 microcontroller are connected to I/O pins on the Arduino MEGA 2560, there are fewer pins per current limit group in most cases, when comparing the Arduino MEGA 2560 with the ATmega2560 microcontroller – remember that some of the I/O pins on the ATmega2560 are not connected on the Arduino MEGA 2560. Table 3.2 summarizes the current limit pin groups from the Arduino MEGA 2560 in Figure 3.8, and compares them with all available current limit pin groups of the ATmega2560.

Table 3.2: Pin Groups on Arduino MEGA 2560 and ATmega2560

Pin Group	Arduino MEGA 2560 Pins	Number of Pins	ATmega2560 Microcontroller Pins	Number of Pins	Current Limit
①	J0-J1, G2, A0-A7	11	J0-J7, G2, A0-A7	17	200mA
②	C0-C7, G0-G1, D0-D3, D7, L0-L7	23	C0-C7, G0-G1, D0-D7, L0-L7	26	200mA
③	B0-B7, H0-H1, H3-H6	14	G3-G4, B0-B7, H0-H7	18	200mA
④	E0-E1, E3-E5, G5	6	E0-E7, G5	9	100mA
⑤	F0-F7, K0-K7	16	F0-F7, K0-K7	16	100mA

In each case, except for pin group 5 (which by default are analog inputs anyway), the Arduino MEGA 2560 has fewer pins per group than the ATmega2560 microcontroller, simply because some of the pins in a group from the ATmega2560 are not connected to anything on the Arduino MEGA 2560, so current will never be drawn from these pins.

Arduino MEGA 2560 Hardware Manual

Note when looking at the pin names in Figure 3.8 and in Table 3.2, that pin names in the figure are preceded with the letter 'P', while this letter is left off in the table. For example, pins C0 to C7 in the table correspond to pins PC0 to PC7 in the figure. This follows the convention used in the datasheet.

Taking all of the previous information into consideration, we can calculate an average current limit for all digital I/O pins as follows. To operate the ATmega2560 microcontroller far enough away from its absolute maximum total current of 200mA, choosing to operate this device within 80% of its absolute maximum is a reasonable choice. 80% of 200mA is calculated as 0.8 × 200mA = 160mA. We know that the active current of the ATmega2560 can be over 20mA at 16MHz, so taking this value as 22mA is reasonable. Subtract this value from 160mA to get the total I/O pin source or sink current left: 160mA − 22mA = **138mA**. If we consider the number of pins that are marked as digital pins on the Arduino MEGA 2560, we get 54 digital pins minus 10 communication pins, leaving 44 pins. The average source or sink current for 44 pins is now 138mA ÷ 44 ≈ **3.14mA** per pin.

Of course, if we decided to use the communication pins and analog input pins as digital output pins as well, we would have 44 pins + 10 communication pins + 16 analog input pins, giving a total of 70 pins. The average source or sink current is now 138mA ÷ 70 ≈ **2mA** per pin.

The above calculations are of course calculating an average current if all pins were to be used as output pins. Practically this would seldom if ever be done, but has been included to give some understanding of current limits for the Arduino MEGA 2560. As there is an absolute maximum current limit of 40mA per pin, some pins could be used to draw up to **30mA** of current each, which is 75% of 40mA, but each pin current must then be subtracted from the 138mA total that we calculated as a reasonable value available for current sourcing or sinking. For example, two pins used to supply 30mA each leaves 138mA − (2 × 30mA) = 78mA for all other pins. We must also make sure that we do not draw too much current from a pin group. If we took the pins from pin group 4, which have a current limit of 100mA, and used 4 pins from this group to supply 30mA each, we would be drawing 120mA from a 100mA group, which over draws 20mA from this group, while still remaining within the 138mA total limit. In this case it would be better to use only two pins from this group to draw 30mA each, and choose the other two pins from a different group.

Chapter 3 • Pin Reference and Interfacing

From the previous calculations, it can be seen that when designing a circuit that connects to an Arduino MEGA 2560, first consider the total maximum current that is available for current sourcing or sinking from I/O pins. We saw that **138mA** is not a bad choice for this value. Using Figure 3.8 and Table 3.2, make sure that current drawn from pins does not exceed any pin group limit. If a circuit or project requires many pins to supply enough current so that total current exceeds 138mA, then it will be necessary to supply the extra current with an interface circuit that uses transistors, op-amps, buffer chips, or similar devices to limit that amount of current drawn from the ATmega2560 pins. Table 3.3 is a quick reference that summarizes the calculations from this section of the chapter.

Table 3.3: Summary of Arduino MEGA 2560 Current Limits for Digital Output Pins

Condition	Current	Notes
Available Source/Sink Current for I/O Pins	138mA	80% of 200mA absolute max. minus 22mA for ATmega2560 active supply current at 16MHz. See text for details.
Average Current Available for 44 Digital Pins	3.14mA	Average source or sink current for pins marked as digital only, excludes communication and analog in pins.
Maximum Current per Pin (Only 4 pins simultaneously)	30mA	75% of the 40mA absolute maximum current per pin. Number of pins that can supply 30mA is limited by the 138mA total current and pin group current limits.
Arduino Specified Pin Current	20mA	Can only be drawn from 6 or 7 pins simultaneously and must take into consideration the pin group limits.

Switching Heavier Loads with Transistors and Relays

When it is required to use an Arduino to switch a heavier load than an Arduino pin can handle, two basic options are to use a transistor, or a transistor and a relay. Other options are available such as optocouplers or opto-isolators, solid state relays, thyristors, and similar devices. This book looks only at basic interfacing and does not cover more advanced devices.

Figure 3.9 shows two basic transistor interface circuits using NPN BJTs (Bipolar Junction Transistors). A transistor can be used not only to switch on a device that draws more current than an Arduino MEGA 2560 pin can deliver, but also to switch on a device that operates at a higher voltage than the Arduino. At the left of the figure, a buzzer is powered from a 12V external supply and switched on by transistor T1 that is controlled by the Arduino. This circuit can safely drive a buzzer that draws a current of up to about 400mA, or 0.4A. The circuit at the right of the figure uses transistor T1 to switch on higher power transistor T2, which can safely drive a 12V siren that draws current up to about 1A. Transistor T2 may need to be bolted to a heatsink, depending on how much current the siren draws.

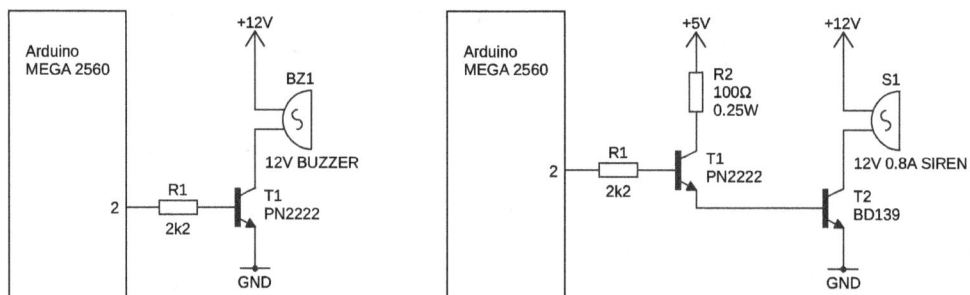

Figure 3.9: Driving a 12V Buzzer (left) and 12V Siren (right) from an Arduino MEGA 2560

In the circuit at the left of Figure 3.9, when the Arduino MEGA 2560 pin is set to a high level in a sketch, current flows from the pin through resistor R1, into the base of transistor T1 and out the emitter pin of the transistor to GND. This switches the transistor on causing current to flow from the 12V supply through the buzzer, into the collector pin of the transistor, out of the emitter of the transistor and finally to GND. Switching the Arduino pin to a low level stops current flowing into the base of the transistor which switches the transistor, and therefore the buzzer off. The positive lead of the external 12V power supply must be connected to the positive pin of the buzzer and the negative or GND of the power supply must be connected to the GND of the Arduino. The ON Semiconductor (www.onsemi.com) datasheet for a PN2222 shows the absolute maximum collector current of this device to be 600mA which means that it can safely and reliably switch a load of between 100mA to about 400mA, which enables it to be used with a number of small DC devices. It could even be used to drive a device that draws up to 500mA if needed.

In the circuit at the right of Figure 3.9, when the Arduino MEGA 2560 pin is set to a high level, current flows through resistor R1, into the base of transistor T2, then out of its emitter and into the base of transistor T2, and finally from the emitter of T2 to GND. Current flowing though the base emitter junction of T1 causes T1 to switch on, causing

Chapter 3 • Pin Reference and Interfacing

about 38mA to flow from the 5V power supply through R2, then through the collector and emitter of T1, and finally through the base and emitter of T2, switching T2 on. When T2 switches on, current flows from the 12V power supply through the siren, into the collector of T2, and out of its emitter to GND, causing the siren to sound. In the ON Semiconductor datasheet for a BD139 transistor, the absolute maximum collector current is 1.5A. This means that a DC device, such as a siren that draws up to about 1A can safely be driven by this transistor.

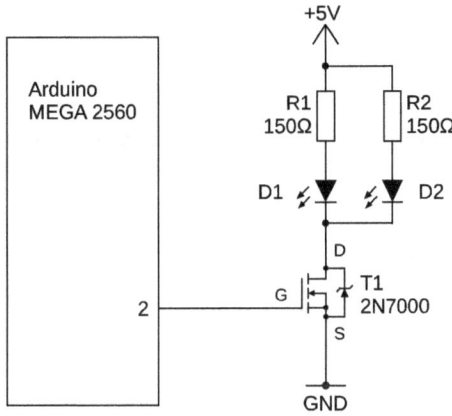

Figure 3.10: Driving LEDs from an Arduino using an N-Channel MOSFET

Another type of transistor is a MOSFET (Metal Oxide Semiconductor Field Effect Transistor). While a BJT transistor is a current controlled device, a MOSFET is a voltage controlled device. Figure 3.10 shows an N-Channel MOSFET used to drive two LEDs with an approximate current of 20mA each. When the Arduino pin is driven high, the voltage between the G (gate) and S (source) pins switches the transistor on, hence it is voltage controlled. This causes current to flow from the D (drain) pin to the source pin, switching the LEDs on. Only a very small and insignificant leakage current flows into the gate pin, so no resistor is needed between the Arduino pin and the MOSFET gate. The leakage current can effectively be ignored. Switching the Arduino pin low, connects the gate pin to GND, switching the N-Channel MOSFET, and therefore the LEDs off. MOSFETs are sensitive to static electricity or ESD, so precautions must be taken when handling them. The 2N7000 MOSFET shown in Figure 3.10, can drive an absolute maximum current of 200mA.

When an Arduino MEGA 2560 is required to switch more current than a simple transistor circuit can handle, or if it needs to switch an AC load, then a relay is an option. A relay will usually be driven by a transistor as shown in Figure 3.11.

Arduino MEGA 2560 Hardware Manual

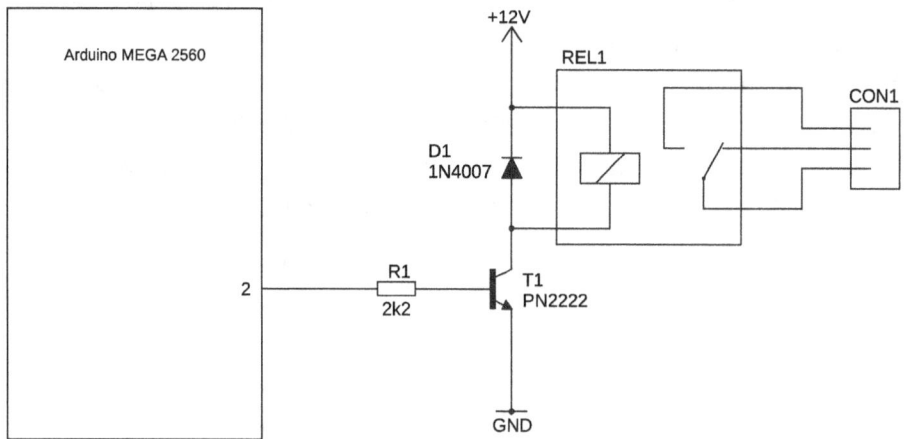

Figure 3.11: Using an Arduino MEGA 2560 to Switch a Relay On

A relay has an electromagnetic coil, that when activated switches a set of contacts. A simple relay may have one set of normally open contacts that can be used as a switch in an external circuit, for example to switch an AC bulb on. Other relays may have a normally open and normally closed set of contacts, or even more than one set of contacts.

The coil of a relay is an electromagnet that consists of wire wound many times around a metal core. When a DC voltage is applied across the coil, the metal core magnetizes enough to close the set of relay contacts. When the voltage is removed from the coil, the magnetic field that exists in the core breaks down, inducing a high voltage back into the coil. For this reason a protection diode is placed between the relay coil pins as can be seen in Figure 3.11. This prevents the high voltage produced from the decaying magnetic field from destroying the transistor and Arduino.

As mentioned before, this book is an Arduino MEGA 2560 reference manual and so does not go into a lot of detail on interfacing, but rather just uses some simple examples to show interfacing principles. For more details on interfacing Arduino boards and microcontrollers, refer to the appropriate texts or other sources such as the Interfacing With Hardware page playground.arduino.cc/Main/InterfacingWithHardware in the playground area on the Arduino website.

3.3.1.2 Pins as Inputs

Pins are configured as inputs in the setup() part of an Arduino sketch. Call the pinMode() function to set an Arduino pin up as an input that can be used to read the logical state of a pin (high or low, on or off), or the state of a device attached to a pin. Input pins can be set up to use internal pull-up resistors that are internal to the ATmega2560 microcontroller, or they can be set up not to use internal pull-up resistors. Pull-up and pull-down resistors are explained further in this section.

The pinMode() function has the following format when setting up a pin as an input.

```
pinMode(<pin number>, <input type>);
```

Where **<pin number>** can be one of the following:

0 to 53 — for digital pins.
A0 to A15 — to set up an analog pin as a digital input (or 54 to 69).

<input type> can be one of the following:

INPUT — input without internal pull-up resistor.
INPUT_PULLUP — input with internal pull-up resistor enabled.

Examples:

```
pinMode(2, INPUT);   // Set up digital pin 2 as an input (no internal pull-up)

pinMode(A9, INPUT);  // Set up analog input pin A9 as a digital input

pinMode(7, INPUT_PULLUP);  // Digital pin 7 as an input with internal pull-up
```

An Arduino pin that is interfaced to a switch needs either a pull-up or pull-down resistor connected to it. If no resistor is used, the pin will be "floating" which means that the state of the switch (on or off) can not be reliably read by the Arduino.

Pull-down Resistor

A pull-down resistor pulls an Arduino MEGA 2560 digital pin down to GND, as shown in Figure 3.12. A switch attached to the pin will connect the pin to 5V when it is closed. When the switch is open and the state of the pin is read in a sketch, it will be low because the pull-down resistor is pulling it low, or to GND. When the switch is closed, and the state of the switch is read by the Arduino, the state of the switch will be high. The switch does not short 5V to GND when it is closed because of the pull-down resistor.

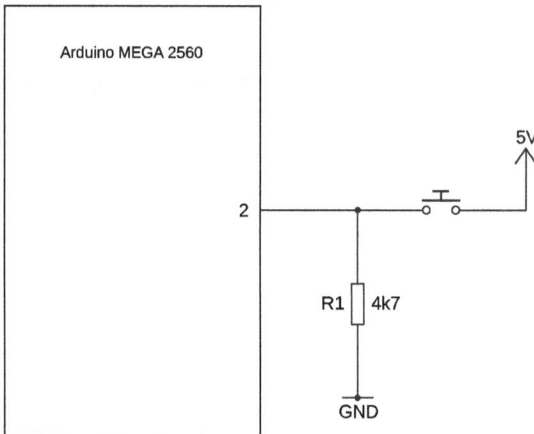

Figure 3.12: Switch Interfaced to an Arduino MEGA 2560 with a Pull-down Resistor

In the sketch code listing that follows, the state of Arduino MEGA 2560 digital pin 2 is read and the on-board L LED is switched on if the switch is closed, or off if the switch is open.

```
void setup() {
  pinMode(LED_BUILTIN, OUTPUT);
  pinMode(2, INPUT);
}

void loop() {
  if (digitalRead(2)) {
    // Pin state is high or 1, switch is closed (pull-down resistor)
    digitalWrite(LED_BUILTIN, HIGH);  // Switch L LED on
  }
  else {
    // Pin state is low or 0, switch is open (pull-down resistor)
    digitalWrite(LED_BUILTIN, LOW);   // Switch L LED off
  }
}
```

As can be seen in the code listing, digitalRead() is used to read the state of the switch, or pin that the switch is connected to, and is passed the pin number to read. This function returns 0 (LOW) if the logic level on the pin is low (switch is open) or 1 (HIGH) if the logic level on the pin is high (switch is closed). The *if* statement could also be written as:

```
if (digitalRead(2) == HIGH) {
```

For a similar sketch, open the DigitalReadSerial example sketch found under File ▶ Examples ▶ 01.Basics ▶ DigitalReadSerial from the top menu of the Arduino IDE. Find the tutorial page at www.arduino.cc/en/Tutorial/BuiltInExamples/DigitalReadSerial on the Arduino website. When running this example, open the Serial Monitor window in the Arduino IDE to see the state of the switch.

Chapter 3 • Pin Reference and Interfacing

Pull-up Resistor

An alternative to using a pull-down resistor when interfacing a switch to an Arduino MEGA 2560 is to use a pull-up resistor as shown in Figure 3.13. When the switch is open and the state of the pin is read in a sketch, it will be high or 1. This is because the resistor is pulling the pin up to 5V or high. When the switch is closed, it connects the pin to GND or low – in a sketch the state of the switch will now be read as low or 0. When the switch is closed, it does not short 5V to GND because of the pull-up resistor.

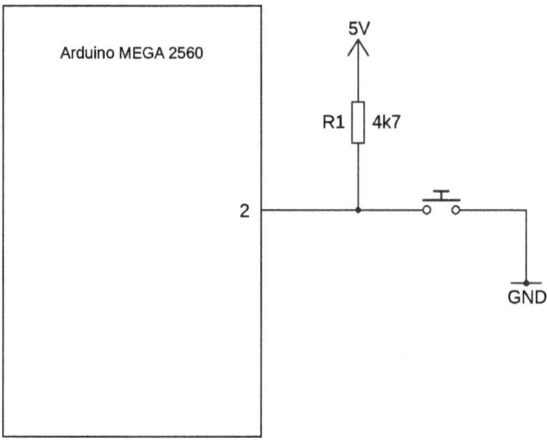

Figure 3.13: Switch Interfaced to an Arduino MEGA 2560 with a Pull-up Resistor

In the sketch code listing that follows, it can be seen that the logic is reversed when using a pull-up resistor with a switch instead of a pull-down resistor. This means that when a value of 1 or high is read from pin 2, the switch is open and not closed. When a value of 0 or low is read, the switch is closed, because the input pin is pulled down to GND.

```
void setup() {
  pinMode(LED_BUILTIN, OUTPUT);
  pinMode(2, INPUT);
}

void loop() {
  if (digitalRead(2)) {
    // Pin state is high or 1, switch is open (pull-up resistor)
    digitalWrite(LED_BUILTIN, LOW);    // Switch L LED off
  }
  else {
    // Pin state is low or 0, switch is closed (pull-up resistor)
    digitalWrite(LED_BUILTIN, HIGH);   // Switch L LED on
  }
}
```

As can be seen in the sketch, digitalRead() returns 1 when the switch is open, so the L LED is switched off. When the switch is closed, digitalRead() returns 0, so the L LED is switched on. When this pull-up configuration is used with the DigitalReadSerial example sketch mentioned in the previous section, the logic is reversed. 1 is displayed in the Serial Monitor window when the switch is open, it then changes to 0 when the switch is closed.

Internal Pull-up Resistors

The internal resistor on a pin can be enabled in a sketch, in which case a switch can be interfaced to the pin by connecting it between the pin and GND as shown in Figure 3.14.

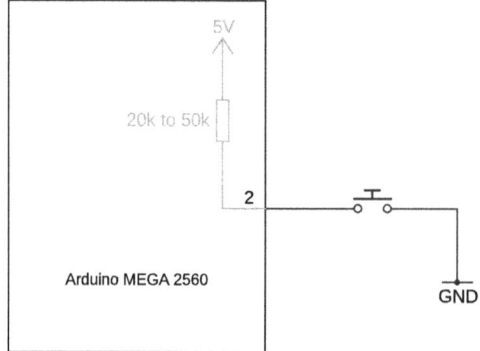

Figure 3.14: Switch Interfaced to an Arduino MEGA 2560 with Internal Pull-up Resistor

Internal pull-up resistors are fairly weak which means that they have high resistance values. They also have a very wide tolerance range, and can be between 20kΩ to 50kΩ. A weak pull-up resistor will be more susceptible to electrical noise, so should only be used in environments that are not excessively electrically noisy.

```
void setup() {
  pinMode(LED_BUILTIN, OUTPUT);
  pinMode(2, INPUT_PULLUP);
}

void loop() {
  if (digitalRead(2)) {
    // Pin state is high or 1, switch is open (pull-up resistor)
    digitalWrite(LED_BUILTIN, LOW);    // Switch L LED off
  }
  else {
    // Pin state is low or 0, switch is closed (pull-up resistor)
    digitalWrite(LED_BUILTIN, HIGH);   // Switch L LED on
  }
}
```

Chapter 3 • Pin Reference and Interfacing

The sketch listing on the previous page is exactly the same as the sketch used with the external pull-up resistor, except that pin 2 is set up using INPUT_PULLUP as the second parameter passed to pinMode() which enables the internal pull-up resistor. The logic of the sketch works exactly the same as the previous sketch that was used with the external pull-up resistor.

3.3.2 PWM Pins

Pulse Width Modulation (PWM) and PWM pins are explained in section 2.7.4.4 of the previous chapter. PWM is available on the Arduino MEGA 2560 pins marked "PWM" on the silkscreen of the board (pins 2 to 13), as well as on three pins on the double row connector at the end of the board (pins 44 to 46) as shown in Figure 3.15. PWM pins are marked with the tilde symbol (~) in figures in this book. The total number of PWM pins in the Arduino MEGA 2560 technical specification is 15 pins. This total is the sum of 12 pins from digital pins 2 to 13 and 3 pins from digital pins 44 to 46.

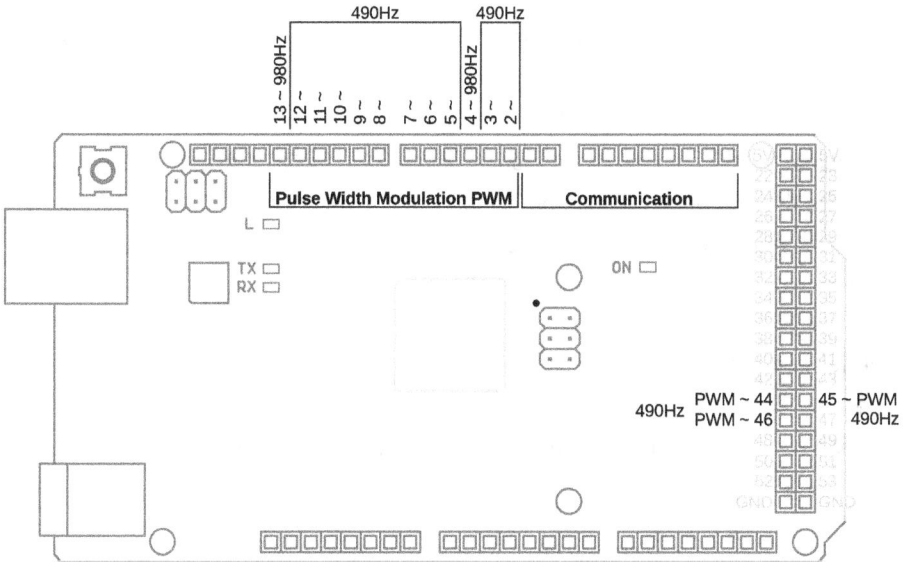

Figure 3.15: Arduino MEGA 2560 PWM Pins and Frequencies

The analogWrite() function is used to generate a PWM waveform and change the PWM duty cycle on the selected PWM pin. A good example that demonstrates PWM is the Fade example sketch found under File ▶ Examples ▶ 01.Basics ▶ Fade on the top menu of the Arduino IDE. Unlike the Arduino Uno, the Arduino MEGA 2560 has PWM capabilities on pin 13, which drives the L LED. This means that the on-board L LED can be operated using the Fade sketch by changing the pin number in the sketch. Simply change the following line of code in the sketch:

```
int led = 9;            // The PWM pin the LED is attached to
```

To use pin 13, as follows:

```
int led = 13;           // The PWM pin the LED is attached to
```

After making this change, load the sketch to the Arduino MEGA 2560 and the on-board LED will start fading from dim to bright and back to dim again continuously.

PWM can also be used to control an external LED. Interfacing an external LED to a PWM pin is the same as interfacing an LED to a digital output pin, it must be connected using a current limiting series resistor, as has already been explained in this chapter. Figures 3.6 and 3.7 show the current sourcing and current sinking configurations – use the same circuits for PWM control of an LED, and make sure that the circuit is connected to one of the PWM pins.

The Arduino reference has the following to say about Arduino MEGA 2560 pins 5 and 6 when being used as PWM pins: *"The PWM outputs generated on pins 5 and 6 will have higher-than-expected duty cycles. This is because of interactions with the millis() and delay() functions, which share the same internal timer used to generate those PWM outputs. This will be noticed mostly on low duty-cycle settings (e.g. 0 – 10) and may result in a value of 0 not fully turning off the output on pins 5 and 6."*
(Taken from: www.arduino.cc/reference/en/language/functions/analog-io/analogwrite/)

Note the following, also taken from the above reference: *"You do not need to call pinMode() to set the pin as an output before calling analogWrite(). The analogWrite function has nothing to do with the analog pins or the analogRead function."*

3.3.3 Analog Pins

Analog input pins A0 to A15 can read analog voltage values between 0V and 5V by default. Whatever device is interfaced to any of these pins must keep the voltage in this range to avoid damaging the Arduino or ATmega2560 microcontroller. Not much more can be said in this section than has already been said about analog input pins in section 2.7.5 from the previous chapter. Refer to that section for information on using the analog input pins and refer to sub-section 2.7.5.1 – Analog In Example Sketch for an example of interfacing a potentiometer to an analog input. Sub-section 2.7.5.3 – Calculating Analog In

Chapter 3 • Pin Reference and Interfacing

Voltage shows how to calculate the voltage that is present on an analog input pin. When interfacing a device such as a thermometer, that represents temperature on one of its pins by voltage levels, a similar calculation will be needed to convert the value read on the analog pin to a temperature. The exact calculation depends on the characteristics of the thermometer.

Refer to www.arduino.cc/reference/en/language/functions/analog-io/analogread/ for information on using the analogRead() function to read values from the analog input pins. Also refer to section 3.3.10 – AREF Pin for information on changing the voltage reference used by the analog pins or ADC.

3.3.4 TWI Bus Pins

TWI bus pins allow one or more TWI compatible device to be connected to an Arduino MEGA 2560. TWI devices share the SCL (Serial Clock) and SDA (Serial Data) pins. Each TWI device must have a unique TWI address which is set by the manufacturer of the device. Some devices allow the address to be changed by connecting certain of its pins to high or low logic levels (5V or GND voltage levels). The Arduino MEGA 2560 acts as a master on the TWI bus and devices connected to it are slave devices that are controlled by the master. TWI is compatible with I²C devices and the I²C bus protocol.

Examples of TWI slave devices are EEPROM memory chips, I/O expansion chips, ADC (Analog to Digital Converter) and DAC (Digital to Analog Converter) devices, and temperature sensors or thermometers.

3.3.4.1 TWI Interfacing Example

Figure 3.16 shows two TWI devices connected to an Arduino MEGA 2560. When data is sent to a device on the TWI bus, or when data is requested from the TWI device, the address of the device is part of the request so that the correct device is accessed. The AT24C16C device shown in the figure is a TWI EEPROM chip with a fixed address. This means that only one of these devices can be connected to a TWI bus because all of these devices have the same address. Other TWI devices can be attached to the same TWI bus as long as they have different addresses from all other devices attached to the bus. The second device in the figure represents any other TWI device on the TWI bus. As can be seen in the figure, the SDA and SCL lines are shared between the two devices. The WP pin of the EEPROM chip is a write protect feature. This pin must be connected to GND in order to be able to write to the device. NC pins are pins that are not connected or unused.

Arduino MEGA 2560 Hardware Manual

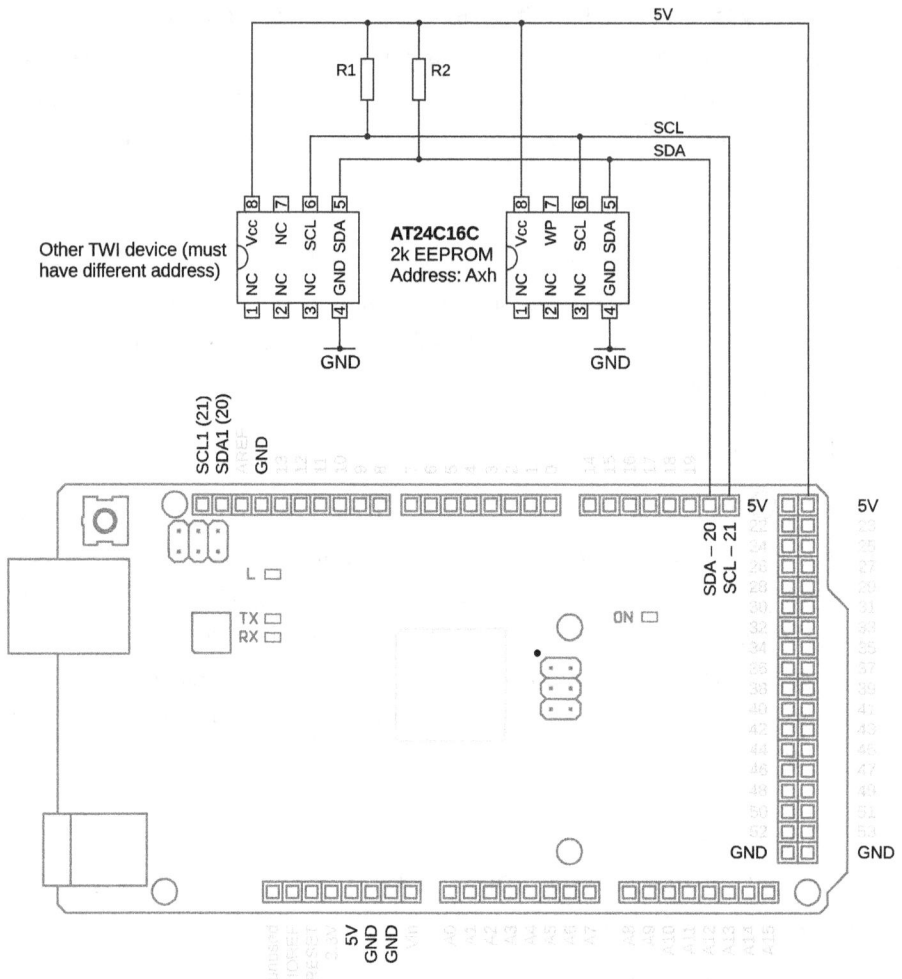

Figure 3.16: Arduino MEGA 2560 Interfaced to Two TWI Devices

TWI Pull-up Resistors

Manufacturers of TWI devices usually recommend pulling up the SDA and SCL lines to 5V using external resistors of between 2k2 to 4k7, as shown by R1 and R2 in Figure 3.16. This is important when more than one device is connected to the TWI bus and for longer connecting wires. Arduino MEGA 2560 boards already have two external 10k resistors pulling up the SDA and SCL lines to 5V. These external pull-up resistors are not present on Arduino Uno boards. The Wire library drivers also enable the internal pull-up resistors on the TWI pins. As the Arduino MEGA 2560 already has external pull-up resistors, it is less likely that additional external pull-up resistors will be needed on the TWI bus. If stronger pull-up resistors are needed, adding an additional 10k resistor to both SCL and

SDA, as represented by R1 and R2 in Figure 3.16, will bring the total pull up resistance of these two lines close to 4k7.

3.3.4.2 Accessing TWI Devices in Software

Use the Wire library in a sketch to access TWI bus devices by including the Wire.h header file in a sketch, and using the Wire library object and functions found in the reference www.arduino.cc/en/Reference/Wire on the Arduino website. Find Wire example sketches in the Arduino IDE under File ▶ Examples ▶ Wire from the top menu.

The actual commands and sequence of bytes that must be sent in order to access a particular TWI device is found in the datasheet for the device and varies from device to device, although the actual TWI bus protocol is common to all devices. EEPROM devices need to receive their TWI address as well as the address of the byte in the EEPROM to access. Number of address bits and address byte order can be different for different devices, hence the necessity of referring to the correct datasheet. The EEPROM Arduino library is for accessing the on-chip EEPROM of the ATmega2560 microcontroller on Arduino MEGA 2560 boards and not for accessing EEPROM chips on the TWI or SPI bus.

```
// Reads a single byte from a AT24C16C EEPROM on the TWI or I2C bus
#include <Wire.h>

void setup() {
  Wire.begin();            // Join TWI bus as a master
  Serial.begin(9600);      // For displaying results in Serial Monitor window

  // *** Perform Random Read ***
  // Address byte 0 of EEPROM
  Wire.beginTransmission((0xA0 >> 1));
  Wire.write(0x00);
  Wire.endTransmission();
  // Read 1 byte from EEPROM at address 0
  Wire.requestFrom((0xA0 >> 1), 1);
  // *** End Perform Random Read ***

  while (Wire.available()) {          // Check for response from EEPROM
    byte data8 = Wire.read();         // Read byte from the EEPROM
    Serial.print("Byte read is: ");
    Serial.println(data8, HEX);       // Display the byte
  }
}

void loop() {
}
```

In the above sketch, a single byte is read from address 0 of a AT24C16C EEPROM TWI device connected to the TWI pins of an Arduino MEGA 2560 as shown in Figure 3.16. The value read from EEPROM address 0 is sent out of the serial USB port and can be seen in the Serial Monitor window of the Arduino IDE. In a new EEPROM, this value is expected to be 0xFF, rather than 0x00. 0xFF is the default value of an erased byte in an EEPROM. In the code, the address of the EEPROM must first be sent and is 0xA0. This address includes 3 bits that are used to address a byte within the EEPROM. The next byte that is sent forms the lower 8 bits of the 11 bit address of the byte being accessed. After the EEPROM and byte have been addressed in this way, a single byte is requested from the device which is then read from the EEPROM and sent to the serial USB port. The address of the EEPROM is right shifted by 1, to convert it to a 7-bit address which is required by the Wire library. The sequence of sending the TWI device address and byte address to the EEPROM before reading the value of the addressed byte is obtained directly from the EEPROM datasheet, where it is called a random read – which means that this method can be used to address and read any byte in the EEPROM. In an EEPROM with a bigger storage capacity, two or more bytes may be used to address each data byte in the device. In the case of a two byte address, the EEPROM would be accessed by first sending its TWI address, followed by two bytes that make up the address of the data byte to access.

3.3.5 SPI Bus Pins

SPI bus pins allow one or more SPI device to be connected to the Arduino MEGA 2560. Devices connected to the SPI bus share the MOSI (Master Out Slave In), MISO (Master In Slave Out) and SCK (Serial Clock) pins. The Arduino MEGA 2560 acts as the SPI bus master and controls the slave devices connected to the bus.

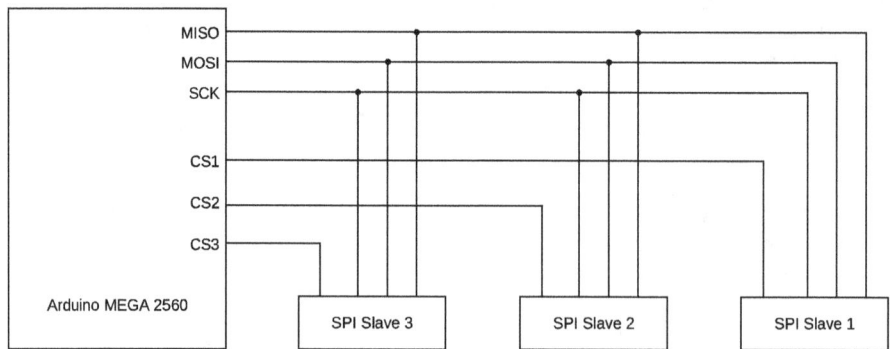

Figure 3.17: How Slave Devices are Connected to a SPI Bus

Each slave device must have a separate slave select (SS) or chip select (CS) pin connected to a pin on the Arduino for addressing or selecting it. Figure 3.17 shows the

Chapter 3 • Pin Reference and Interfacing

concept of how SPI slave devices share the MOSI, MISO and SCK SPI bus pins, but each have a separate chip select line.

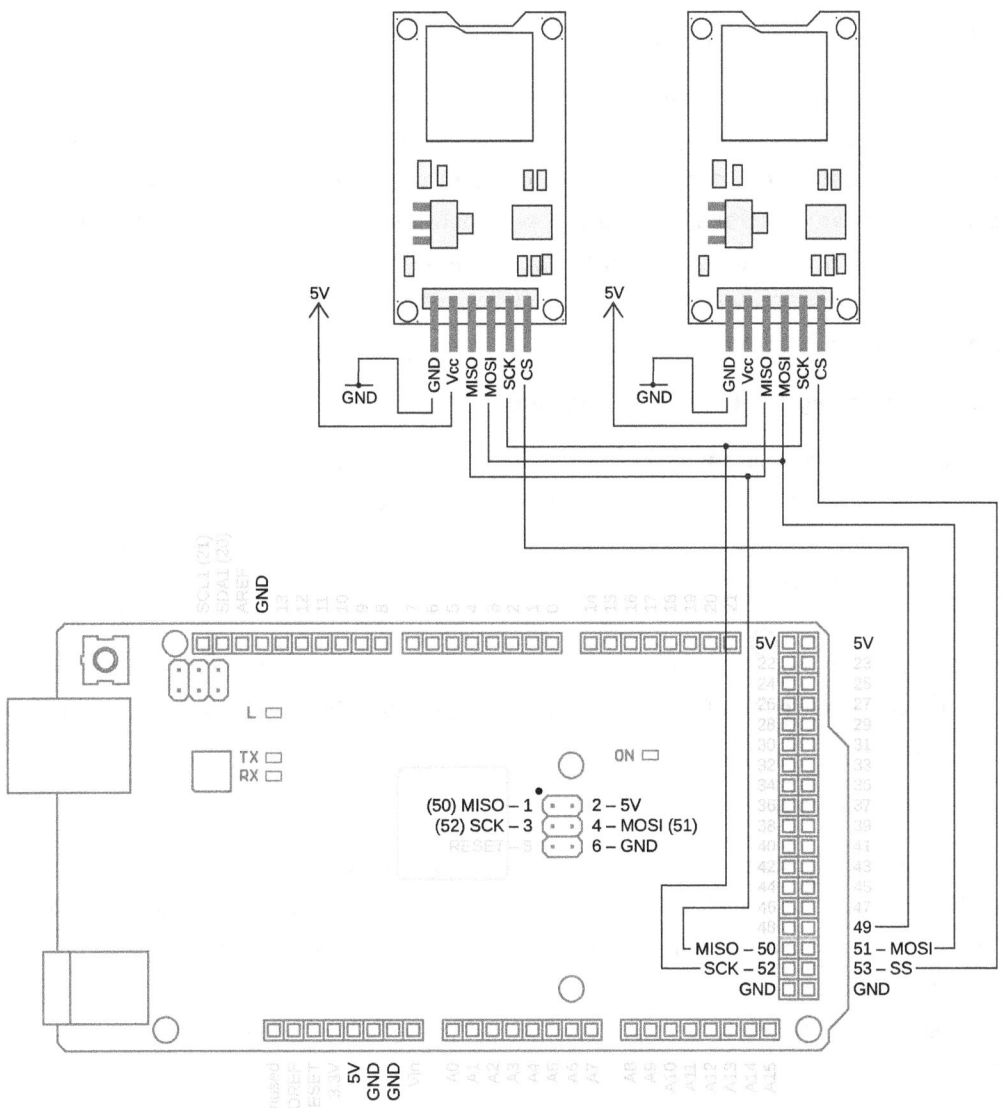

Figure 3.18: Arduino MEGA 2560 Interfaced to Two SPI Devices

Although the SPI hardware in the ATmega2560 microcontroller has one SS pin, it is not necessary to use this pin – any digital I/O pin can be used as the slave select pin. This pin is more useful if the Arduino were to be set up as a slave on the SPI bus as it would then be used by the SPI master to select the Arduino. An example of a shield that puts two devices on the SPI bus is the Ethernet shield that has an Ethernet chip and an SD card connected to the SPI bus. The Ethernet shield uses digital pin 4 for the chip select of the SD card and digital pin 10 for the chip select of the Ethernet chip.

3.3.5.1 SPI Bus Interfacing Example

Figure 3.18 on the previous page shows two micro SD card adapters connected to the common SPI bus pins and digital pin 49 used to select the adapter on the left. Digital pin 53 is used to select the adapter on the right. Note that these SD card adapters each have a circuit on-board that translates voltage levels between the 5V Arduino MEGA 2560 and 3.3V SD card. A 3.3V voltage regulator on the board steps down the 5V Arduino voltage to 3.3V to power the SD card. Refer back to section 2.3.4.1 – SD Cards (SPI Interface) for more information on SD cards.

3.3.5.2 Accessing SPI Devices in Software

Use the Arduino SPI library to access SPI devices in a sketch. This means that the SPI.h header file must be included at the top of sketches that use the SPI library. Use the SPI object and functions from www.arduino.cc/en/Reference/SPI – the SPI reference page on the Arduino website.

SPI examples can be found in the Arduino IDE under File ▶ Examples ▶ SPI from the top menu. SD cards use the SD library which in turn uses the SPI library and is covered in the next section.

3.3.5.3 Accessing SD Cards in Software

The SD library is a layer of software that sits on top of the SPI drivers and handles access to the file system on the SD card. Go to www.arduino.cc/en/Reference/SD to find the SD card reference on the Arduino website. The library supports FAT16 and FAT32 file systems and short file names (8.3 format – file name of 8 characters maximum and file extension of 3 characters maximum, for example *filename.txt* is a name that is 8 letters long and has a 3 letter file extension).

SD card example sketches are very useful and can be found under File ▶ Examples ▶ SD from the top menu in the Arduino IDE. The CardInfo example is particularly useful when testing if a new SD card works with the Arduino MEGA 2560, as it displays information about the SD card in the Serial Monitor window of the Arduino IDE. The ReadWrite example writes a simple text file to the SD card, reads the contents of the file and displays it in the Serial Monitor window. Both of these examples use digital pin 4 as the chip select pin by default. Refer back to section 2.3.4.1 SD Cards (SPI Interface), in

Chapter 3 • Pin Reference and Interfacing

chapter 2 which has an example of how to change the chip select pin number to access an SD card.

3.3.6 Serial / UART Pins

A serial port or Universal Asynchronous Receiver Transmitter (UART) sends and receives serial data asynchronously, which means without a separate square wave clock line for synchronization.

Although the ATmega2560 microcontroller contains four USART (Universal Synchronous and Asynchronous Receiver Transmitter) devices in the form of internal USART hardware, these devices are intended to be configured in UART mode on the Arduino MEGA 2560, so are referred to as UARTs in this book. In the ATmega2560 datasheet, information on the internal USARTs can be found in the USART section. The USARTs in the ATmega2560 can be configured to operate in either synchronous mode (with a separate clock pin), or asynchronous mode. They are only ever used in an asynchronous configuration with the Arduino MEGA 2560 and Arduino libraries.

Arduino MEGA 2560 boards output serial data and receive data at 5V levels, also known as 5V TTL levels. To connect these pins to an RS-232 device, an interface chip is needed to convert the Arduino 5V levels to the RS-232 voltage levels which can be between ±3V to ±15V. UART pins can also be connected to RS-485 and RS-422 chips to communicate over these types of buses.

3.3.6.1 Hardware Serial Ports

The Arduino MEGA 2560 uses one of the four hardware serial ports, or USARTs, to connect to the receive or RX line called RX0 on digital pin 0, and the transmit or TX line called TX0 on pin 1. These same lines connect to the ATmega16U2 serial to USB bridge via 1k resistors, which allows data sent and received on the serial port to be relayed across the USB connection. Hardware serial port means that the USART or UART hardware inside the ATmega2560 microcontroller connects to these pins on the Arduino MEGA 2560. Serial port pins 0 and 1 line up with the same pins on an Arduino Uno, and are connected to the ATmega16U2 for the same serial to USB functionality. An Arduino MEGA 2560 has an additional three serial ports that Arduino Uno boards don't have.

If any of the serial port pins marked as COMMUNICATION on the Arduino MEGA 2560 (serial ports pins 0, 1, and 14 to 19) are used as digital input or output pins, then the

Arduino MEGA 2560 Hardware Manual

corresponding hardware serial ports can not be used. If a serial device is connected to pins 0 and 1, the communications between the connected serial device and the Arduino MEGA 2560 will also appear on the USB port.

Using the USB Port / Serial Port 0

An example of a sketch that uses serial port 0, to communicate with the Serial Monitor Window can be seen below. After loading this sketch to an Arduino MEGA 2560, open the Serial Monitor window in the Arduino IDE. Send a character from the Serial Monitor window and it will be echoed back with the text "Received: ". This sketch is a simple way to test the transmit and receive functionality of the Arduino default serial port.

serial_echo sketch on USB Port / Serial Port 0 (TX0 and RX0)

```
void setup() {
  Serial.begin(9600);            // Initialize serial port 0
}

void loop() {
  if (Serial.available()) {      // Check if character received
    char rx_char = Serial.read();  // Read the character
    Serial.print("Received: ");    // Transmit a string
    Serial.println(rx_char);       // Transmit the received character
  }
}
```

Using Serial Port 1, Serial Port 2 and Serial Port 3

The same sketch as above can be used to test serial ports 1 to 3 with a small modification as shown below. In the sketch below, the Serial1 object is used to access serial port 1, rather than the Serial object that was used in the previous sketch to access serial port 0.

serial_echo_1 sketch on Serial Port 1 (TX1 and RX1)

```
void setup() {
  Serial1.begin(9600);           // Initialize serial port 1
}

void loop() {
  if (Serial1.available()) {     // Check if character received
    char rx_char = Serial1.read();  // Read the character
    Serial1.print("Received: ");    // Transmit a string
    Serial1.println(rx_char);       // Transmit the received character
  }
}
```

Serial port 2 and serial port 3 are accessed in the same way, but using the Serial2 and Serial3 objects in a sketch, as shown in the following code snippet.

Chapter 3 • Pin Reference and Interfacing

```
void setup() {
  Serial2.begin(9600);      // Initialize serial port 2
  Serial3.begin(9600);      // Initialize serial port 3
}
```

One way to test serial ports 1 to 3 with the previous sketch is to attach a USB to TTL adapter to the transmit and receive pins of a serial port of the Arduino, and then use a terminal emulator program to communicate with the Arduino over the serial/USB port. Figure 3.19 shows the concept of connecting any type of TTL adapter to an Arduino on the left. Notice that the TX or transmit pin of the Arduino connects to the RX or receive pin of the adapter, and the RX pin of the Arduino connects to the TX pin of the adapter. Crossing over the TX and RX lines in this way is necessary so that the adapter receives what the Arduino is transmitting, and the Arduino receives what the adapter transmits. The adapter at the left of Figure 3.19 could be any adapter or device that converts TTL serial data to any other format, such as USB, RS-232, RS-485, TTL serial fingerprint scanner, etc.

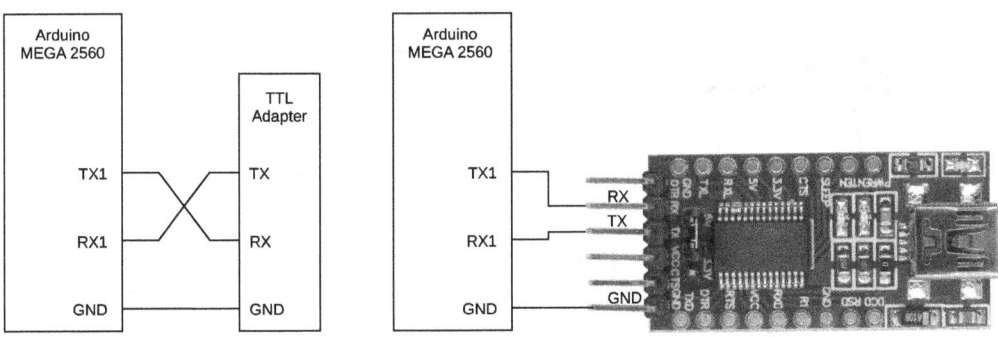

Figure 3.19: Interfacing a TTL Adapter to an Arduino

At the right of Figure 3.19 is an example of a USB to TTL adapter that is based on a FT232RL chip from FTDI. This adapter has a jumper that can be used to select either 5V or 3.3V settings, which enable it to be connected to any 5V or 3.3V device. It is set to 5V for connecting to an Arduino MEGA 2560. There are many different types and brands of USB to TTL adapter, so make sure that the adapter you use is compatible with the 5V Arduino MEGA 2560. Also check the pin configuration, or pinout, of the adapter that you are using, they will not all be the same as the one in Figure 3.19. At the right of Figure 3.19 it can be seen that TX1 from the Arduino MEGA 2560 connects to the RX pin of the USB to TTL adapter. RX1 of the Arduino connects to TX of the adapter. In both images in the figure, GND is common and connected between the two devices. Figure 3.20 on the next page shows an adapter, also based on the FTDI FT232RL chip, connected to an Arduino MEGA 2560. This adapter is from SparkFun and is called the SparkFun FTDI

Basic Breakout (www.sparkfun.com/products/9716). Again, TX and RX are crossed, and GND is connected between the Arduino and adapter boards.

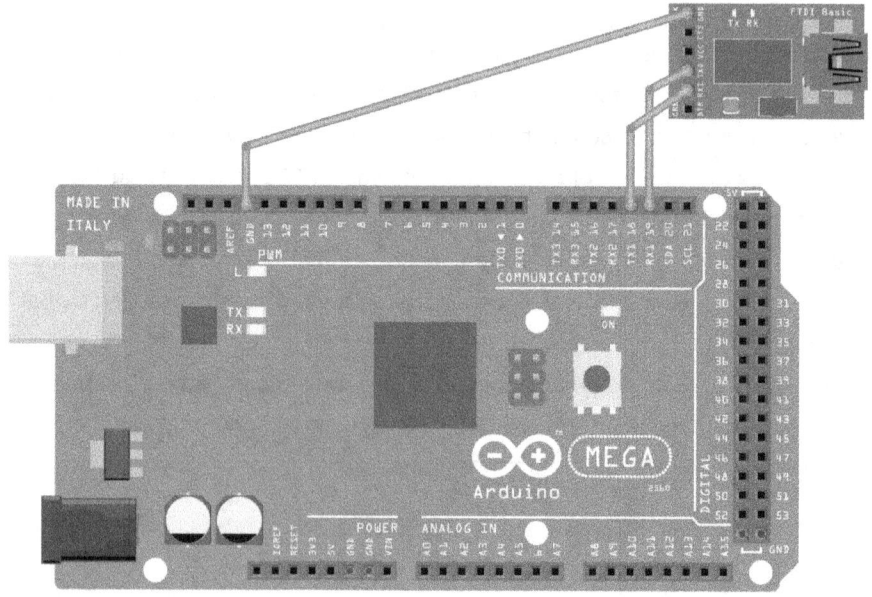

Figure 3.20: FTDI Basic Breakout Interfaced to Arduino MEGA 2560 Serial Port 1

After connecting a USB to TTL adapter to an Arduino MEGA 2560 and loading the serial_echo_1 sketch to the Arduino, a terminal emulator program is needed to connect to the USB to TTL adapter from a PC. On a Windows 10 computer, a terminal emulator program called Tera Term can be used. Click the download link on the Tera Term home page at ttssh2.osdn.jp/index.html.en which will take you to a page with a link to the latest version of Tera Term. Click the zip file, e.g. teraterm-4.105.zip, to download Tera Term. Using the zip file means that it is not necessary to install Tera Term on the host computer. Simply unzip or extract the folder from the downloaded zip file to a convenient place, such as the desktop.

After extracting the folder, e.g. a folder called teraterm-4.105, to the desktop or other location, open the folder and double-click **ttermpro.exe** to start Tera Term. If you have not enabled file name extensions to be shown in Windows file explorer, then the Tera Term program will just appear as **ttermpro** in the folder.

When Tera Term starts, a "New connection" dialog box opens. Click the Serial radio button in the dialog box, and then select the correct COM port in the Port: drop-down box. Figure

3.21 shows the dialog box with the correct COM port selected. The COM port number on your computer may differ from the one in the figure.

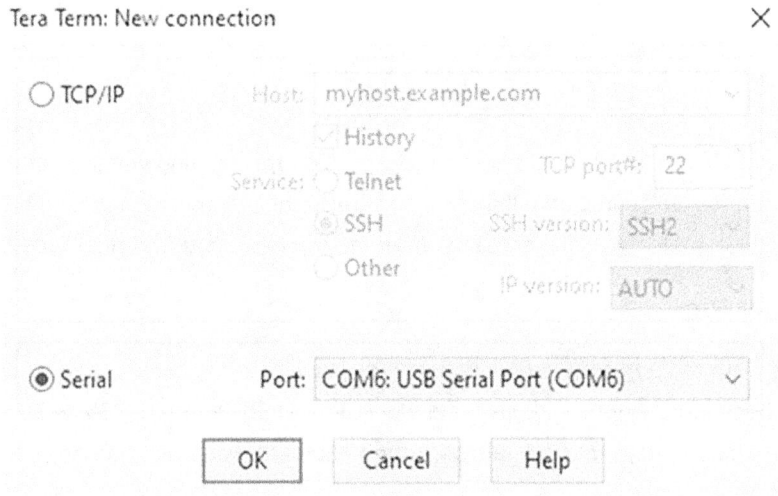

Figure 3.21: Tera Term New Connection Dialog Box

After selecting the COM port for the USB to TTL adapter, click the OK button. Tera Term connects with a baud rate of 9600, 1 stop bit and no parity. If the baud rate set in the sketch is also 9600, then pressing a keyboard key in Tera Term should return the echo message from the Arduino sketch. If the baud rate or other communication parameters need to be changed, then select Setup ▶ Serial port... from the top menu in Tera Term. A dialog box opens that allows the baud rate to be changed as well as other serial port communication settings.

Serial Port Reference

Go to www.arduino.cc/reference/en/language/functions/communication/serial/ for the serial port library reference. Serial example sketches can be found under File ▶ Examples ▶ 04.Communication from the top menu of the Arduino IDE.

3.3.6.2 Software Serial Port

Additional serial ports can be added to the Arduino MEGA 2560 by using the library called SoftwareSerial. Using the software serial library allows additional serial ports to be simulated in software by using the so-called "bit banging" method. From a hardware point of view this entails just selecting any digital pins for the serial transmit or receive pins and then configuring these pins in the SoftwareSerial driver in an Arduino sketch. There are some limitations when using a software serial port. Not all pins on the Arduino MEGA 2560 support pin change interrupts, so only the following can be used for RX: 10, 11, 12, 13, 14, 15, 50, 51, 52, 53, A8 (62), A9 (63), A10 (64), A11 (65), A12 (66), A13 (67), A14 (68), A15 (69). If using multiple software serial ports, only one can receive data at a time. It is always better to use a hardware serial port if possible and only use software serial ports as a last resort.

Go to www.arduino.cc/en/Reference/SoftwareSerial on the Arduino website for more information on the SoftwareSerial library. SoftwareSerial example sketches can be found under File ▶ Examples ▶ SoftwareSerial from the top menu of the Arduino IDE.

3.3.7 Power Pins

Power pins were already covered in section 2.7.1, however this section has a few more details on these pins. Figure 3.22 shows a block diagram of where the 5V, 3.3V and Vin voltages are derived from that are found on the header socket pins of an Arduino MEGA 2560.

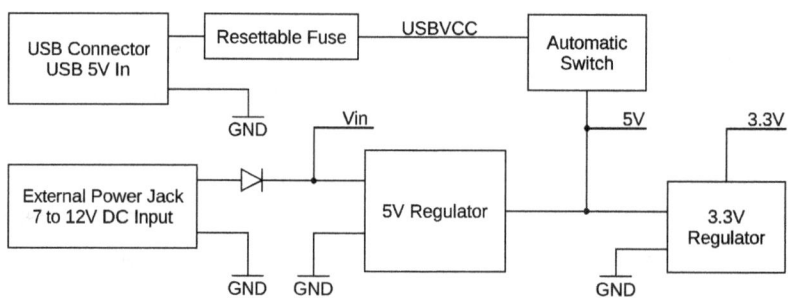

Figure 3.22: Block Diagram of the Arduino MEGA 2560 Power Sources

3.3.7.1 GND Pins

GND is the common level of all of the power sources and is found on five of the socketed header pins, down the sides and at the end of an Arduino MEGA 2560. GND is the negative or 0V connection of any power source.

3.3.7.2 5V Pins

5V DC found on the Arduino MEGA 2560 5V pins can be derived from either the USB 5V or from an external power supply connected to the power jack on the board, which is then stepped down to 5V by a regulator on the Arduino. An Arduino MEGA 2560 has an extra two 5V pins that an Arduino Uno does not have, totaling 3 pins. The extra two 5V pins are

Chapter 3 • Pin Reference and Interfacing

found on the double row connector at the end of the board. In the section of the connector marked POWER, is one 5V pin which lines up with the same pin on an Arduino Uno.

USB 5V

When powered from the USB connector, the circuitry on the Arduino MEGA 2560 that makes up an automatic switch, as shown in Figure 3.22, switches the USB 5V onto the Arduino 5V pins. The same 5V is also fed into the 3.3V regulator. The voltage from a USB 2.0 port is specified as 5V ± 5% and up to 500mA current.

External Power to 5V Regulator

With an external power supply of 7 to 12V DC voltage plugged into the external power jack on an Arduino MEGA 2560, the 5V on the Arduino 5V pins is derived from this external power source after it is fed through a 5V regulator. The automatic switch circuitry shown in the block diagram of Figure 3.22 will block the USB 5V if external power is present.

The 5V regulator is able to deliver an output current of 0.8A to 1A, depending on which regulator is fitted (see Table 4.1 in section 4.1.1 of chapter 4), however the more current that is drawn through the regulator, the hotter the regulator will get. The 5V regulator has an absolute maximum input voltage of 15V to 20V (see Table 4.1). The higher the external input voltage, the more power will be dissipated in the 5V regulator, and the hotter it will get. Be aware that a fully charged 12V lead acid battery has a voltage of 13.8V. The main restriction on the amount of current that can be drawn from the regulator is thermal because this regulator does not have adequate heat sinking on an Arduino MEGA 2560.

3.3.7.3 3.3V Pin

3.3V DC found on the Arduino 3.3V pin is derived from a 3.3V regulator that is fed with 5V from either USB, through the automatic switch (Figure 3.22), or the 5V regulator when the Arduino MEGA 2560 is externally powered. The regulator, and therefore pin can deliver up to 150mA.

3.3.7.4 Vin Pin

The Vin pin voltage is derived from an external power supply connected to the power jack of the Arduino MEGA 2560. This external DC voltage is fed through a diode before arriving at the Vin pin (See Figure 3.22), which means that the voltage on the Vin pin will be around 0.7 to 0.8V lower than the external power supply voltage because of the forward voltage drop across the diode. Also see section 2.4.4 for information on battery powering the Arduino MEGA 2560 through this pin. Vin is available to any shield that is plugged into the Arduino MEGA 2560.

The power supply circuit of a MEGA 2560 is essentially identical to that of an Arduino Uno, except for extra capacitors on the MEGA 2560, and some other minor differences. See section 4.2.7 for details on the differences between these power circuits.

3.3.8 Reset Pin

A reset pin is found on the same connector that the power pins are located on, on an Arduino MEGA 2560. Reset is active low, which means that a low signal (0V or GND) must be applied to the reset pin to reset the ATmega2560 microcontroller. On the Arduino MEGA 2560, the reset pin is pulled high via a 10k resistor, which means that an external normally open reset switch can be connected to the reset pin and GND as shown in Figure 3.23 if an external reset switch is needed. When the switch is open, the reset pin is pulled to 5V via the 10k resistor on the Arduino, keeping it out of reset. If the switch is momentarily closed, the reset pin is pulled low to GND, resetting the microcontroller. When the switch is released, the 10k resistor keeps the microcontroller out of reset again, allowing it to start running the bootloader and then the currently loaded sketch. The reset pin resets only the main microcontroller on the Arduino MEGA 2560 and not the ATmega16U2. This means that the Arduino will not be taken off the USB bus if it is reset using either the reset pin or the on-board reset button, when it is plugged into a host computer via USB.

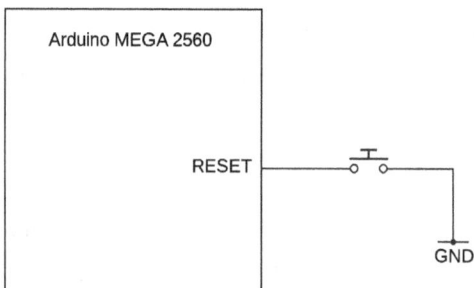

Figure 3.23: Connecting an External Reset Switch to an Arduino MEGA 2560

Active low pin labels normally have a line above them to show that they are active low, which means RESET would be written $\overline{\text{RESET}}$, but this is not done on the Arduino MEGA 2560 reset label.

3.3.9 IOREF Pin

The IOREF pin (input/output reference) is connected directly to the Arduino MEGA 2560 5V pin. IOREF is a standard pin where a shield plugged into an Arduino board can detect

Chapter 3 • Pin Reference and Interfacing

the voltage that the board operates at so that it can switch in the correct voltage level translator circuits for the board. In this way the same shield can be used for 5V and 3.3V Arduino boards. See chapter 9 for more on shield compatibility between Arduino boards.

3.3.10 AREF Pin

The AREF pin allows an alternate reference voltage to be used with the ADC converter for reading analog input voltages on pins A0 to A15. Analog voltages on A0 to A15 are limited to a maximum voltage that is equal to the reference voltage. By default the reference voltage is 5V taken from the 5V supply. If a more stable or different reference voltage is required, it can be applied to the AREF pin.

Figure 3.24 shows an example of a 3V reference applied to the AREF pin of an Arduino MEGA 2560. The 3V reference voltage is derived from a REF3030 voltage reference chip which steps down an input voltage of 3.3V to 3V. This is just one example of a voltage reference chip. There are many other parts available that provide different reference voltages for a range of different input voltages.

The Arduino documentation at www.arduino.cc/reference/en/language/functions/analog-io/analogreference/ gives the input voltage range of the AREF pin as 0V to 5V, however the ATmega2560 datasheet gives the AREF voltage range as 1V to 5V. The datasheet does specify that the minimum value of 1V is given as a guideline only.

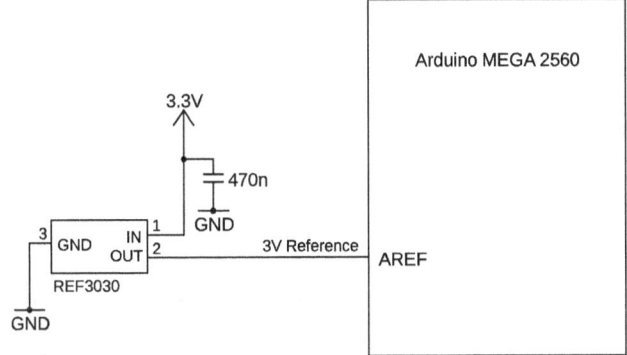

Figure 3.24: Arduino MEGA 2560 with an External ADC Reference Voltage

When using an external reference voltage applied to the AREF pin, analogReference() must be called before reading an analog value on A0 to A15. Call this function as follows.

```
analogReference(EXTERNAL);
```

Cross refer to section 2.7.6 for basic information on the AREF pin.

Arduino MEGA 2560 Hardware Manual

3.4 ICSP Header on Main Microcontroller

Figure 3.25 shows the pinout of the ICSP header for the main microcontroller found near the middle of the Arduino MEGA 2560 board. The ICSP header is used to program the ATmega2560 microcontroller using an external programmer. It is also used by some shields, such as the Ethernet shield to connect to these pins. Programmer documentation and documentation for AVR microcontrollers that use this type of programming header usually refer to it as the ISP (In-System Programming) header. Only on Arduino boards is it referred to as the ICSP header. Notice that the ICSP header pins are basically all of the SPI bus pins, except that the SS pin is not present. In addition to the SPI bus pins, the reset pin is found on the ICSP header.

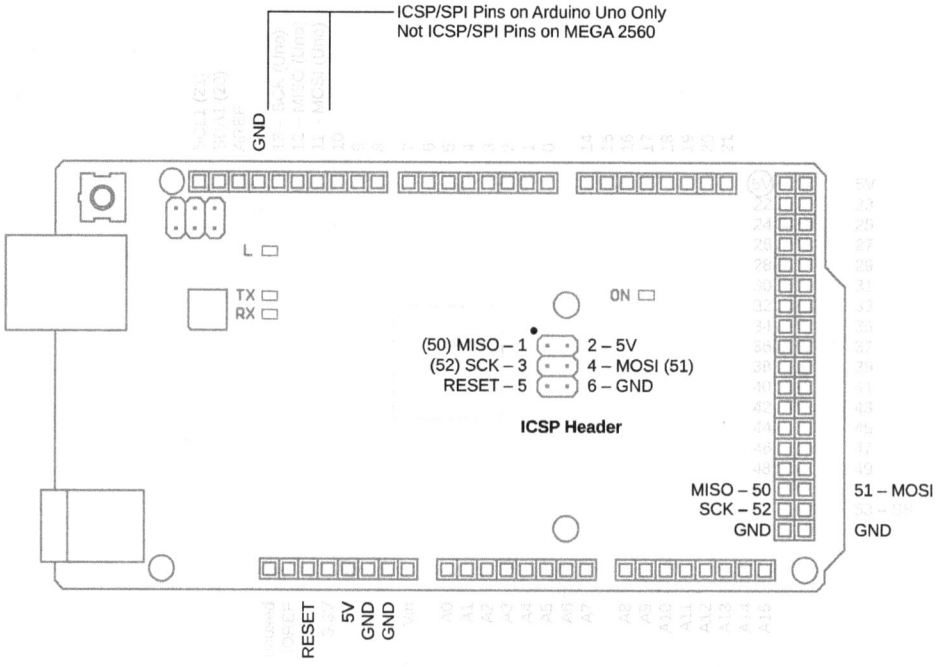

Figure 3.25: ICSP Header Pins and Connections to Arduino MEGA 2560 Pins

All of the ICSP header pins are available on the Arduino MEGA 2560 socket headers at the edges of the board. If an external circuit is connected to these pins and an external programmer is used on the ICSP header, the circuit may interfere with the programmer. One of the differences between the Arduino Uno and the Arduino MEGA 2560 is that the ICSP/SPI pins on the header sockets around the edges of the board do not line up. As

Chapter 3 • Pin Reference and Interfacing

can be seen in Figure 3.25, an Arduino Uno has ICSP/SPI pins on digital pins 11 to 13, while they are found on pins 50 to 52 on the Arduino MEGA 2560.

Cross refer to section 1.1.4.11 – ICSP Header, for basic information on the ICSP header, and section 2.8 – Programming Headers, for an example of connecting an external programmer to the ICSP header. Section 2.9.4 – ICSP SPI Pins and Reset, shows the ICSP header pin names and connections to the Arduino pins at the edge of the Arduino MEGA 2560 board. These same ICSP header pins used to program the ATmega2560 are also the SPI pins – cross refer to 3.1.2 – Shared SPI Pins.

3.5 ICSP Header on USB Microcontroller

Figure 3.26 shows the pinout for the ICSP header that connects to the ATmega16U2 USB microcontroller. Although this header has the same pinout and names as the main ICSP header, it is separate from the main ICSP header. The pins of this header connect to the ATmega16U2 only. In the Arduino MEGA 2560 schematic these pins are labeled MISO2, MOSI2, SCK2 and RESET2 to distinguish them from the same pins on the main ICSP header, and the ICSP header is labeled ICSP1.

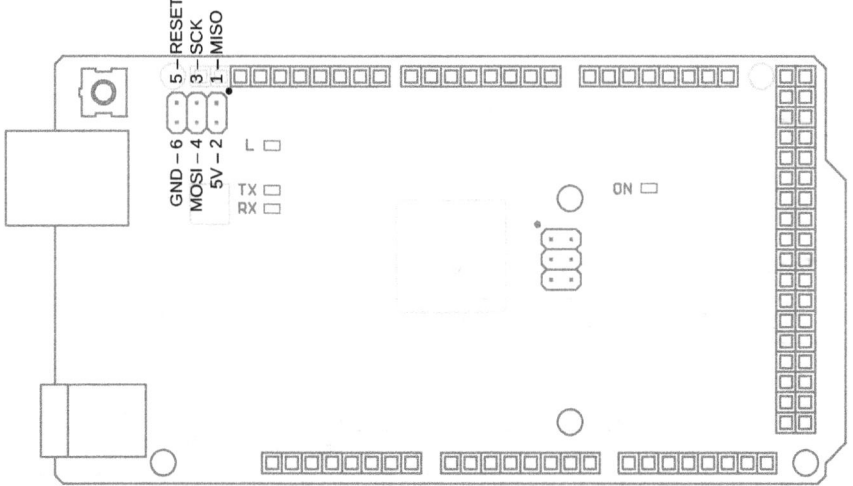

Figure 3.26: ICSP Header Pinout for the ATmega16U2 USB Microcontroller

3.6 JP5 Header on USB Microcontroller

Four pins connect from the ATmega16U2 USB microcontroller to the JP5 header solder pads as shown in Figure 3.27. Arduino have not given any explanation for these pins or solder pads, and it is assumed that they have been taken to the pads so that advanced users who are programming the ATmega16U2 can easily access these pins for convenience for whatever application they want. The equivalent pins are connected to a header named JP2 on Arduino Uno boards, only the header name changes between the Uno and MEGA 2560.

Table 3.4 shows the pin names of the JP5 header and the alternate functions of these pins. Use of these pins is for advanced users who must refer to the ATmega16U2 datasheet for the explanation of these alternate functions.

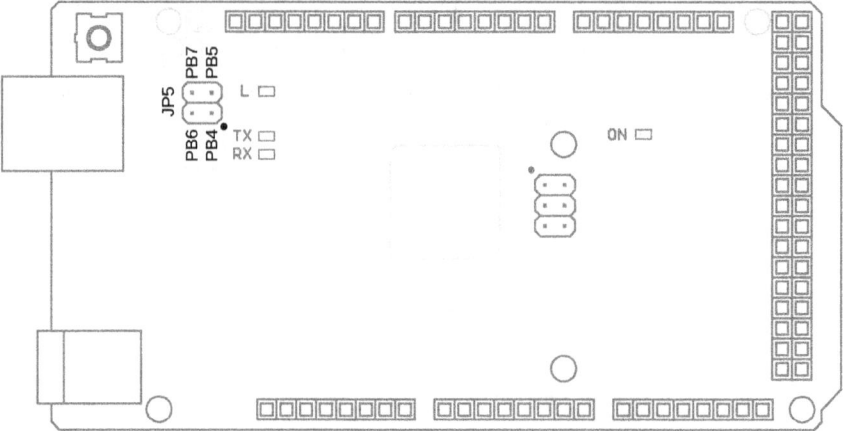

Figure 3.27: JP5 Pinout on the Arduino MEGA 2560

Table 3.4: JP5 Pins and Alternate Functions

JP5 Header Pin	ATmega16U2 Port Pin	Alternate Pin Functions
1	PB4	T1 / PCINT4
2	PB6	PCINT6
3	PB5	PCINT5
4	PB7	PCINT7 / OC0A / OC1C

Chapter 3 • Pin Reference and Interfacing

In the Arduino MEGA 2560 schematic, JP5 is inverted, or flipped over as if it were to be placed on the bottom layer of the board, but on the board itself, JP5 is correctly oriented for the top layer of the board. This may cause some confusion when looking at the schematic and then Figure 3.27, but if the Eagle CAD file for the board is opened, it can be clearly seen that Figure 3.27 has the correct pin names for JP5.

3.7 JTAG Pins

Basics of JTAG pins are covered at the end of the previous chapter, chapter 2, in section 2.9.5. Figure 3.28 below shows the JTAG pins on an Arduino MEGA 2560.

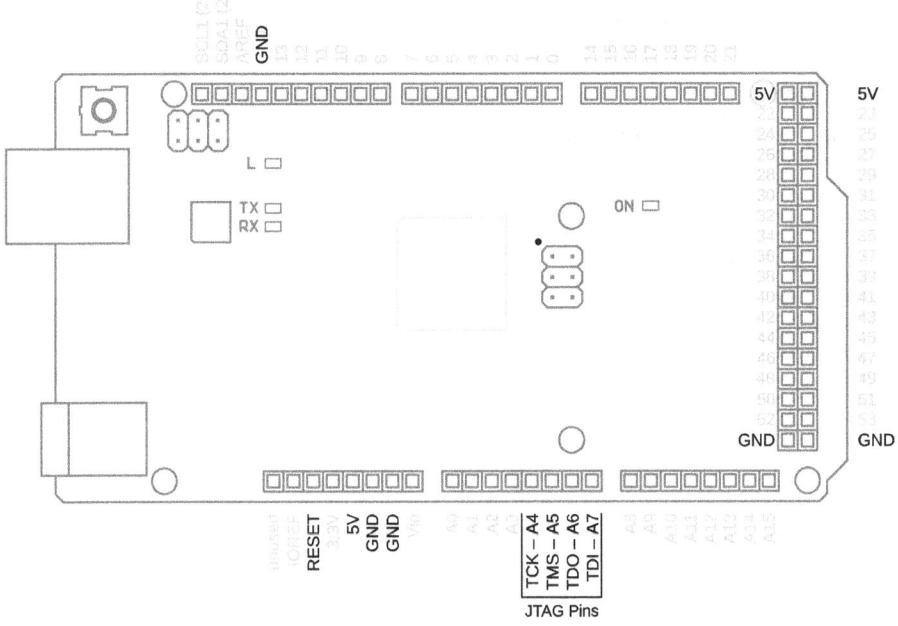

Figure 3.28: JTAG Pins on an Arduino MEGA 2560

3.8 Finding the Datasheets

Anyone wanting to find out more about the microcontrollers on an Arduino MEGA 2560 board can refer to the datasheets for these devices. Datasheets are essential for advanced users who are programming the hardware directly, for example in plain C language, or for developers writing driver libraries for the Arduino.

143

3.8.1 ATmega2560 Datasheet

Find the ATmega2560 datasheet at www.microchip.com/wwwproducts/en/ATmega2560 on the Microchip website. Find the datasheet as well as application notes and other documentation under the Documents tab on the page.

3.8.2 ATmega16U2 Datasheet

Go to www.microchip.com/wwwproducts/en/ATmega16u2 to find the datasheet for the ATmega16U2 microcontroller used as the USB to serial bridge chip on Arduino MEGA 2560 boards.

3.8.3 Datasheets for Other Components

Datasheets for other components used on Arduino MEGA 2560 boards can easily be found by searching the internet. Refer to chapter 6 where the part numbers for components can be found in the circuit diagram and parts list. Simply enter the part number into a search engine to find the datasheet for the part.

Chapter 4 • Power Reference

In this power reference chapter for the Arduino MEGA 2560, the power supply from both USB and external sources are explained. Specifications for external and USB power are included.

Power supply circuits on the Arduino MEGA 2560 board are simplified by breaking them up into sections in the circuit diagram. Each section is then explained.

In this Chapter

- Power sources and specifications
- On-board power supply and regulator circuit diagram
- Differences between the Arduino MEGA 2560 and Uno power circuits
- Power supply protection

Arduino MEGA 2560 Hardware Manual

4.1 Power Supply Specification

This section summarizes the power supply specification of an Arduino MEGA 2560 in the categories that follow.

4.1.1 Operating Voltage

The Arduino MEGA 2560 operates at 5V which is derived either from the USB 5V or from an external power supply that is dropped to 5V by the on-board regulator. An on-board regulator with part number LD1117S50 is specified in the Arduino MEGA 2560 Rev3e circuit diagram. In the Arduino Uno Rev3e circuit diagram, the 5V regulator has a part number of NCP1117ST50, which is essentially the same device, but from a different manufacturer. There are a number of different manufacturers that supply a compatible part for this type of regulator, and it was found that two different Arduino MEGA 2560 boards had different regulator part numbers, namely AZ1117CH-5.0 and NCP1117ST50. It is assumed that a compatible part is selected during manufacture, and the exact part could change, depending on availability. Table 4.1 summarizes three of these devices and some of their specifications.

Table 4.1: Comparison of Compatible 5V LDO Regulators

Part Number	Manufacturer	Output Current	Max. Input Voltage	Tolerance
LD1117S50	STMicroelectronics (www.st.com)	800mA	15V	±1.0%
NCP1117ST50	ON Semiconductor (www.onsemi.com)	1.0A	20V	±1.0%
AZ1117CH-5.0	Diodes Incorporated (www.diodes.com)	1.0A	18V	±1.0%

As can be seen in Table 4.1 the absolute maximum input voltage and output current of the 5V regulator used on Arduino boards can vary, depending on the device part and manufacturer.

In addition to the 5V regulator on the Arduino MEGA 2560, a 3.3V regulator drops the 5V supply to 3.3V which is available on the Arduino 3.3V pin. This regulator has an output voltage tolerance of 1.5%. The 3.3V regulator can deliver a maximum current of 150mA.

Cross refer to section 3.3.7 for information on the Arduino MEGA 2560 power pins.

Chapter 4 • Power Reference

4.1.2 USB Power Input

USB power from a USB 2.0 port is specified as 5V ± 5% and up to 500mA current. The USB 5V is protected by a resettable fuse that will disconnect the USB 5V should more than 500mA be drawn from the USB port. This fuse has a small resistance which means that as more current is drawn from the USB port, the voltage drop across the fuse will increase. The actual voltage supplied to the Arduino will therefore be the USB voltage minus this small volt drop. Cross refer to section 2.4.1 and 2.4.2 for information on USB power and USB cable specification.

4.1.3 External Power Jack Input

An external power input of 7 to 12V DC can be supplied to the power jack input that is found on the same end of the board as the USB connector. Arduino specify the limits of this input as 6 to 20V and warn that a voltage less then 7V may result in the 5V regulator supplying less than 5V which may make the board unstable. A voltage more than 12V can cause the 5V regulator to overheat and damage the board. See the next section for the pinout and polarity of the external power jack.

4.1.4 External Power Jack Pinout

When an external supply of 7 to 12V DC is supplied to the power jack, the center pin of the jack must be connected to positive of the power supply. The external power jack is a 2.1mm barrel connector. Figure 4.1 shows the pinout of the power connector as well as a typical symbol from a power supply that indicates it is wired with the center pin positive. Cross refer to section 2.4.3 for information on external power and section 2.4.4 for information on battery powering the Arduino MEGA 2560.

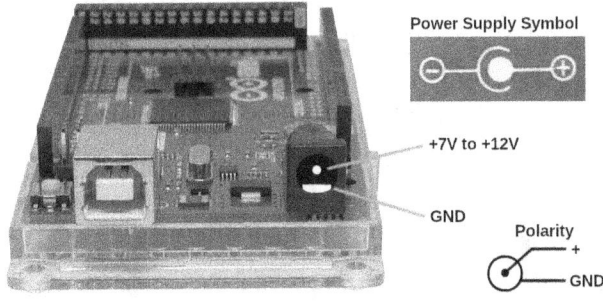

Figure 4.1: External Power Jack Pinout and Polarity

Arduino MEGA 2560 Hardware Manual

4.1.5 Vin Pin as Power Input

Vin, found on the power header socket of the Arduino MEGA 2560, can be supplied with 7 to 12V DC. The Arduino documentation states that a battery can be connected between Vin and GND to power the Arduino MEGA 2560 from a battery. Positive of the battery must connect to the Vin pin. Cross refer to section 2.4.4 for information on battery powering the Arduino MEGA 2560.

4.2 Power Circuit

Figure 4.2 on the next page shows the power supply circuit of the Arduino MEGA 2560 broken up into parts to make it simpler to understand. Each part of the power supply circuit is explained in the sections that follow.

4.2.1 External Power In and 5V Regulator

Connector X1 seen at the top left of Figure 4.2 is the 2.1mm barrel connector jack for the external power supply. The external power is fed to IC1, the 5V regulator, through diode D1. This 5V regulator only functions when external power is supplied to the Arduino MEGA 2560. When powered from USB alone, this regulator is not used.

4.2.2 Power On Indicator LED

The green ON LED seen at the top right of Figure 4.2 switches on when it receives 5V from either the 5V regulator or from USB.

4.2.3 USB Power In

X2, seen at the bottom left of Figure 4.2, is the USB connector on the Arduino MEGA 2560. It is shown here without the USB data lines connected. USB +5V input is connected to resettable fuse F1. USB GND (UGND in the figure) connects to GND via a normally closed link consisting of two solder pads and a connecting track. This allows the track to be broken to separate the USB GND from the main GND on the board. The pads allow it to be soldered closed again. This connector is found under the Arduino MEGA 2560 near the pins of the USB connector. It is more difficult to seen on older Arduino MEGA 2560 REV3 boards because it is covered in solder mask paint. On newer REV3 boards, the pads of this link are exposed and clearly visible as tinned pads.

Chapter 4 • Power Reference

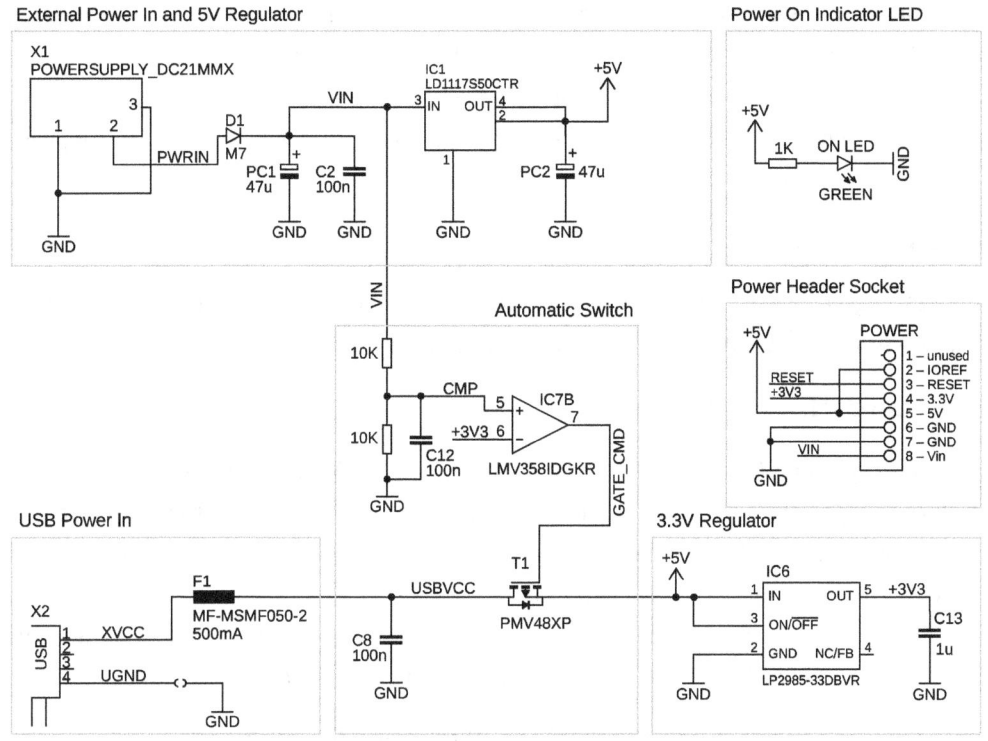

Figure 4.2: Arduino MEGA 2560 Power Supply Circuit

4.2.4 Automatic Switch

An automatic switch detects whether external power is supplied to the Arduino MEGA 2560, and if it is, disconnects the USB 5V supply. If external power is not detected, USB power is switched onto the +5V points shown in Figure 4.2. The automatic switch consists of operational amplifier IC7B working as a comparator. If no external power is connected to the Arduino, and it is powered from USB alone, assume that the output of the op-amp is at GND, switching the P-channel MOSFET T1 on which supplies USB 5V to the circuit. The + pin of the op-amp will then be at a voltage of approximately 2.25V, and the – pin at a voltage of +3.3V. This causes the op-amp to keep transistor T1 on which keeps the USB +5V connected to the Arduino +5V connections. The 2.25V on the + pin of the op-amp comes from 5V from the USB fed back through the internal protection diode of regulator IC1, which loses about 0.5V from the diode forward voltage drop and appears on VIN in the circuit diagram and can be measured on the Vin pin. The two 10k resistors on the + input of the op-amp act as a voltage divider, dividing this 4.5V by two to get about 2.25V.

If external power is supplied to the Arduino MEGA 2560, then the two 10k resistors acting as a voltage divider put half VIN onto the + pin of the op-amp, which is higher than the +3.3V on the − pin. This causes the op-amp to switch transistor T1 off, disconnecting the USB positive voltage from the rest of the circuit. +5V from the 5V regulator then supplies 5V to the Arduino MEGA 2560.

4.2.5 3.3V Regulator

The 3.3V regulator simply produces +3.3V from +5V that is supplied to it. This +5V will either be from the USB or from the 5V regulator if powered externally.

4.2.6 Power Header Socket

+5V, +3.3V, VIN and GND are all connected to pins on the Arduino MEGA 2560 POWER header socket as can be seen in Figure 4.2. At the right of the connector in the figure are the pin names found silkscreened on the Arduino MEGA 2560 board (except for pin 1, unused). +5V in the circuit becomes 5V on the connector, +3.3V becomes 3.3V, VIN becomes Vin and GND remains GND. These are just slightly different names for the same things found in the Arduino MEGA 2560 schematic and on the Arduino MEGA 2560 board.

4.2.7 Differences Between the MEGA 2560 and Uno Power Circuits

Although the Arduino MEGA 2560 power circuit and the Arduino Uno power circuit are essentially identical in functionality, there are some slight differences in the circuits. These differences are discussed in the sections that follow and apply to the Rev3e versions of the circuit diagram or schematic for both boards.

4.2.7.1 External Power In and 5V Regulator

In the Arduino MEGA 2560 external power in and 5V regulator part of the circuit, as shown in Figure 4.2, 100n capacitor C2 is connected to the input pin of the 5V regulator IC1. On the Arduino Uno, it is connected to the output pins of this regulator.

The 5V regulator on the Arduino MEGA 2560 has a reference designator of IC1 and a part number of LD1117S50CTR. On the Arduino Uno, the same 5V regulator has a reference designator of U1 and part number NCP1117ST50T3G.

4.2.7.2 Power On Indicator LED

In the power on indicator LED part of the circuit, the Arduino MEGA 2560 has one 1k resistor in series with the green ON LED. The Arduino Uno has two 1k resistors in parallel

Chapter 4 • Power Reference

with each other, making up the equivalent of a 500Ω series resistor connected to the green ON LED. In other words the Arduino Uno has the same circuit, but with an additional 1k resistor in parallel with the existing 1k resistor shown in Figure 4.2.

4.2.7.3 USB Power In

5V from pin 1 of the USB connector X2 is labelled XVCC on the Arduino MEGA 2560. On the Arduino Uno, the USB 5V from pin 1 of USB connector X2 is labelled XUSB.

4.2.7.4 Automatic Switch

In the automatic switch part of the power supply circuit of Figure 4.2, the Arduino MEGA 2560 uses the second op-amp in the dual op-amp device LMV358IDGKR that connects to pins 5, 6 and 7 of the op-amp package. In the Arduino Uno, the first op-amp in this dual op-amp package is used, connecting to pins 1, 2 and 3 of the package.

Although the dual op-amp is the same part LMV358IDGKR on both the MEGA 2560 and Uno, this part is designated IC7 on the MEGA 2560, and IC7B for the op-amp from this package that is used in the automatic switch part of the circuit. On the Arduino Uno, it is designated U5, and U5A for the op-amp in the package used for the automatic switch.

The Arduino MEGA 2560 adds two 100n capacitors to the automatic switch circuit that the Arduino Uno does not have. C12 on the + input of the op-amp IC7B, and C8 on the junction between fuse F1 and transistor T1.

Transistor T1 on the Arduino MEGA 2560 has a part number of PMV48XP, while on the Arduino Uno, T1 has a part number of FDN340P. Both transistors are P-channel MOSFETs.

4.2.7.5 3.3V Regulator

The only difference between the 3.3V regulator circuit on the Arduino MEGA 2560 and Arduino Uno is that the reference designator for the regulator is IC6 on the Arduino MEGA 2560 and U2 on the Arduino Uno.

4.3 Power Supply Protection

The power supply circuit shown in Figure 4.2 has some protection against reverse polarity connection, current overload and short circuit as described in the sections that follow.

4.3.1 Reverse Polarity Protection

Diode D1, as seen in Figure 4.2, offers some basic reverse polarity protection to power supplied to the external power jack. If external power is supplied to the Arduino MEGA 2560 via the Vin pin, then this diode is bypassed and no reverse polarity protection is available.

4.3.2 5V Regulator Protection Features

5V regulator IC1 offers output current limiting and thermal shutdown. This device has an unlimited output short circuit duration, which means that shorting its output will not destroy the device because internal protection circuits protect it from output short circuits. An internal thermal limiting circuit protects this regulator against excessive temperature. If the device gets too hot, the output will switch off until it cools down to a suitable temperature. All of the 5V regulator devices from Table 4.1 at the beginning of this chapter offer current limiting and thermal shutdown.

4.3.3 3.3V Regulator Protection Features

IC6, the 3.3V regulator, has over-current and thermal protection. This device also has internal short circuit protection that prevents the device from being destroyed by a short circuit on its output.

4.3.4 USB Overload Protection

Resettable fuse F1 is a 500mA fuse that protects the USB 5V from overload and short circuit. The fuse will automatically reset when the overload or short circuit is removed.

Chapter 5 • MEGA 2560 Firmware and Bootloader

Firmware is present on both the main Arduino MEGA 2560 microcontroller and the USB to serial bridge microcontroller. This firmware is factory loaded when the Arduino MEGA 2560 is manufactured.

Firmware on the main microcontroller is known as the bootloader and allows software sketches to be loaded to the Arduino from the Arduino IDE via the USB connection.

The USB to serial bridge microcontroller on the Arduino MEGA 2560 has DFU bootloader firmware and firmware that gives it the USB to serial bridge functionality. The DFU bootloader allows the USB to serial firmware to be updated using the USB connection without the need for an external programmer.

This chapter explains all of the firmware found on the Arduino MEGA 2560.

In this Chapter

- Updating the USB to serial firmware using DFU
- Using Atmel Studio to back up and load new firmware
- How to reload the USB to serial bridge microcontroller firmware using ICSP
- Loading the main microcontroller bootloader to an ATmega2560 chip
- Microcontroller fuse settings
- Purpose of the RESET-EN solder jumper

5.1 Updating the USB to Serial Bridge Firmware using DFU

The most basic task that an Arduino user can do with the ATmega16U2 microcontroller is to update its operational firmware using the DFU (Device Firmware Update) method. This means that the firmware or software that gives this device its USB to serial bridge function can be updated using the USB port on the Arduino MEGA 2560. Most Arduino users should never need to do this, however it is included in this manual to make it complete. Advanced users may also want to use the DFU programming method to put their own custom software into the ATmega16U2. DFU programming requires no external programmer or additional hardware device. Some additional software will need to be downloaded to do the programming.

For Windows computers, download the FLIP (Flexible In-system Programmer) software from Microchip at www.microchip.com/developmenttools/ProductDetails/FLIP
For additional information on Arduino DFU programming and for DFU programming using Linux and Mac, see www.arduino.cc/en/Hacking/DFUProgramming8U2 on the Arduino website. A brief description of DFU programming an Arduino MEGA 2560 using the Microchip FLIP software on a Windows computer follows.

Before updating the ATmega16U2 firmware, download and install the FLIP software, as mentioned in the previous paragraph. Connect the Arduino MEGA 2560 to a USB port of the computer, as would be done to upload a sketch. Connect the RESET pin of the ATmega16U2 ICSP header to GND and then disconnect it in order to reset the ATmega16U2. Make sure to connect to the RESET signal on the ICSP header near the USB connector and not the one near the middle of the board. Refer to Figure 3.26 in section 3.5 of chapter 3 for the pinout of the ICSP header. The RESET pin of the header can be connected to GND on the header or on one of the header sockets at the edge of the board.

After resetting the ATmega16U2, start the FLIP software. Click the chip icon or select Device ▶ Select… from the top menu of the FLIP software. In the dialog box that pops up, scroll down to find ATmega16U2 and click it to select it. Click the OK button in the dialog box to accept. Click the USB icon and then USB on the menu that pops up, or select Settings ▶ Communication ▶ USB from the top menu of the FLIP application. Choose File ▶ Load HEX File from the top menu. Use the dialog box that opens to navigate to the firmware file for the ATmega16U2. This can be found in the Arduino IDE folder in **arduino-1.8.13\hardware\arduino\avr\firmwares\atmegaxxu2\arduino-usbserial** which can easily be found if the zipped Arduino IDE software was downloaded and unzipped to the Windows Desktop as described in section 1.1.5 of chapter 1. The base folder of the above path will be different for different versions of the Arduino IDE software. Find the file **Arduino-usbserial-atmega16u2-Mega2560-Rev3.hex** from the above path and select it in the FLIP dialog box and then click the OK button. Finally click the Run button in the main FLIP application window. Erase, Program and Verify should be selected by default above this button. The Flash memory in the ATmega16U2 will be erased and programmed with the selected HEX file. After the Flash memory has been programmed, unplug the USB cable from the Arduino MEGA 2560 and then plug it back in. If everything went well, the new ATmega16U2 firmware will start running and the Arduino will appear in Windows as a COM port device as would normally be expected. The board can now be loaded with sketches using the Arduino IDE software as usual.

5.2 Atmel Studio

Atmel Studio is a full IDE with C and C++ development tools that can be used to develop software for AVR and other microcontrollers that were originally manufactured by Atmel but now by Microchip. Atmel Studio contains a device programming utility that can be used not only for loading firmware to both the ATmega16U2 and ATmega2560 microcontrollers in the form of HEX or BIN files, but can also be used to set the fuses on these devices. Fuses are used to set the start-up state of some of the microcontroller settings such as the initial clock frequency as well as to provide write protection to some of the Flash memory segments.

Arduino users who want to program the bootloader and set the correct fuse settings on an ATmega2560 microcontroller have the option of using the Arduino IDE, as described in section 2.8.2 of chapter 2, or to use Atmel Studio and its device programming utility. It is less likely that fuse settings will need to be changed on the Atmega2560, as there is less chance that this microcontroller would be replaced. On Arduino Uno boards where the main microcontroller can easily be replaced because of the chip socket, the fuse settings of a new blank microcontroller need to be changed. Fuse settings of an ATmega328P from an Arduino Uno board can be found in the *Arduino Uno Hardware Manual, ISBN 1-54292-181-3*, by the same author. There are other methods of programming both the Flash and fuses of new microcontrollers such as using command line applications in Linux and Windows (usually using the *avrdude* utility), but using Atmel Studio is far easier. To summarize, Atmel Studio is available only for Windows and requires a USB programming device such as the Atmel-ICE to program microcontrollers through the ICSP header. A command line utility is also available for programming AVR microcontrollers and can be used with a variety of USB or other programming devices, including home-made programmers. Alternatively use the Arduino IDE (section 2.8.2).

Those Arduino users who want to load the bootloader to the ATmega2560 microcontroller and set its fuses, program the ATmega2560 directly using C or C++, or even program the ATmega16U2 to load both the DFU firmware and operational firmware, may want to install Atmel Studio. Remember that a USB programming device that connects to the ICSP header is also required when using Atmel Studio. Currently the Atmel-ICE USB programmer is the main programmer available from Microchip for programming AVR devices, as well as SAM ARM devices. Two other programmers that were formerly available from Atmel and then Microchip, and are both USB programmers, are the AVRISP mkII and AVR Dragon, but are no longer available. Users who still have these older devices can use them with Atmel Studio. Find more information about the Atmel-ICE on the Microchip website at:
www.microchip.com/developmenttools/ProductDetails/atatmel-ice

To install Atmel Studio, go to www.microchip.com/mplab/avr-support/atmel-studio-7 on the Microchip website. At the time of writing, Atmel Studio version 7 was the current version. Atmel Studio can be installed by either using the web installer or offline installer. The web installer requires a small file to be downloaded and run, which will then download and install the selected Atmel Studio components. The offline installer is a big file that can be downloaded and run to do the Atmel Studio installation on one or more computers without needing to connect to the internet or download anything else while installing. Go to wspublishing.net/avr-c/installing-atmel-studio-7/ for instructions with screen captures that shows how to install Atmel Studio in detail.

Atmel Studio and a USB programming device are used in the sections that follow for backing up the firmware from the ATmega16U2 and ATmega2560 microcontrollers, programming new firmware to these devices and for setting their fuses. The connector found on Atmel-ICE and other AVR programmers are actually ISP headers or connectors and not ICSP, but connect to the ICSP headers on Arduino MEGA 2560 boards. In the text that follows the name ICSP is used instead of ISP to avoid confusion.

5.3 USB Microcontroller Firmware

There are two firmware applications that are present in the Flash memory of the USB microcontroller (ATmega16U2) on an Arduino MEGA 2560. First, the DFU firmware is a bootloader that allows the operational software of the ATmega16U2 to be updated using the USB connection of the Arduino, as discussed in section 5.1 of this chapter. The operational software that gives the ATmega16U2 its USB to serial bridge functionality is the second firmware program found in the Flash memory of this microcontroller.

Arduino MEGA 2560 boards prior to revision 3 were fitted with an ATmega8U2. Table 5.1 shows the memory sizes of the ATmega8U2 and ATmega16U2. This manual refers to the ATmega16U2 as the USB microcontroller chip that is found on all new Arduino MEGA 2560 boards, rather than the ATmega8U2.

Table 5.1: Memory Sizes for the ATmega16U2 and ATmega8U2

Device	Flash Memory	SRAM	EEPROM
ATmega16U2 (Arduino MEGA 2560 REV3)	16k	512 bytes	512 bytes
ATmega8U2 (Arduino MEGA 2560 REV1 and REV2)	8k	512 bytes	512 bytes

5.3.1 Backing up the ATmega16U2 Firmware with Atmel Studio

As a precaution, the firmware on the ATmega16U2 can be copied from this device on the Arduino MEGA 2560 board and saved to HEX and BIN files using the device programming utility found in Atmel Studio. In this way, if anything goes wrong when loading new firmware to the ATmega16U2, the original firmware can be restored. Atmel Studio must be installed on the computer used to read the firmware from the microcontroller. Additionally, a USB programming device, such as the Atmel-ICE is needed.

When plugging the ICSP connector from the programmer into the ICSP header for the ATmega16U2 on the Arduino MEGA 2560, the key on the connector prevents the connector from being pushed into the header because it bumps up against the header socket at the edge of the board. The key on the connector refers to the small raised plastic key in the middle of the connector which prevents the connector from being inserted into a shrouded header the wrong way around. A shrouded header has a slot that the key fits into. A solution to this problem is to use short wires that have a male pin on one end and female socket on the other end. These are usually referred to as DuPont wires or cables. Plug the male end of 6 of these wires into the connector on the programmer and the female ends into the corresponding pins of the ATmega16U2 ICSP header on the Arduino MEGA 2560. Refer to Figure 3.26 in section 3.5 of chapter 3 which shows the header and which pin is pin 1, for connecting the programming cable. As few users will need to program the ATmega16U2, rather than using up space in this book with an image of the connection, refer to the supporting website wspublishing.net for detailed images of the connection.

Plug the programmer, such as an Atmel-ICE, into the USB port of the computer. Plug the ICSP connector of the programmer into the ICSP header near the USB connector, as described in the previous paragraph, making sure that it is connected the right way around. Now power the Arduino MEGA 2560 board, either via a USB cable, or using an external power supply.

Start Atmel Studio and click the Device Programming icon on the top toolbar, or select Tools ▶ Device Programming from the top menu in Atmel Studio. In the Device Programming dialog box that pops up, select the programmer being used under Tool, e.g. Atmel-ICE if this is the tool being used. Under Device, select ATmega16U2 for an Arduino MEGA 2560 REV3 board, or ATmega8U2 for a REV2 or REV1 board. Make sure that the Interface is set to ISP. Click the Apply button. To check that the programmer and target device have been set up correctly and that Atmel Studio can "see" the target device, click the Read button next to Device signature. If all is set up correctly, the device signature and target voltage will be read from the ATmega16U2.

In the Device Programming dialog box, click Memories in the left column. Click the Read… button in the Flash section of the dialog box. Use the Save As dialog box to navigate to the folder to save the Flash contents to. In the same dialog box, give the target file a name in the File name: field. The file type can be changed from the default Intel Hex (.hex) type to binary (.bin) if desired, but the default is fine. Click the Save button when ready. The device programming utility will read the contents of the ATmega16U2 Flash memory and save it to the selected file. In Windows, use File Explorer to navigate to the destination folder that was chosen. The HEX or BIN file should be found in this folder. The file, whether HEX or BIN format, contains the entire Flash memory contents, and not just the firmware found in the Flash. This means that it also contains the blank bytes from the Flash, which make the file bigger than the original HEX file that was used to factory load the DFU and operational firmware. The HEX or BIN file can now be used to restore the entire Flash memory contents of the ATmega16U2 if ever needed. Programming this file to memory can also be done using the device programming utility from Atmel Studio as described in section 5.3.4 that follows in this chapter.

5.3.2 DFU Bootloader Firmware

C source code for the DFU bootloader firmware can be found in the Arduino IDE folder **arduino-1.8.13\hardware\arduino\avr\firmwares\atmegaxxu2\arduino-usbdfu** where the base folder of this path will be different for different versions of the Arduino IDE. At GitHub github.com/arduino/ArduinoCore-avr/tree/master/firmwares/atmegaxxu2/arduino-usbdfu is the link to the same source code.

To actually restore the DFU firmware, together with the USB to serial bridge firmware, **arduino-1.8.13\hardware\arduino\avr\firmwares\atmegaxxu2** in the Arduino IDE folder contains the combined HEX file that has both of these firmware programs in one file. The file **Arduino-COMBINED-dfu-usbserial-atmega16u2-Mega2560-Rev3.hex** in this folder can be loaded to an Arduino MEGA 2560 to restore both the DFU firmware and USB to serial bridge firmware at the same time. Refer to section 5.3.4 that follows for information on using Atmel Studio to program a HEX file to the ATmega16U2.

The DFU bootloader firmware gives the ATmega16U2 its ability to load new operational software to its Flash memory using the DFU method described in section 5.1 of this chapter.

5.3.3 USB to Serial Bridge Firmware

C source code and the HEX file for the USB to serial bridge firmware can be found in the Arduino IDE folder **arduino-1.8.13\hardware\arduino\avr\firmwares\atmegaxxu2\ arduino-usbserial** which contains the HEX file for the USB to serial bridge on its own. This is the file used in section 5.1 of this chapter that explains how to load this file to the Arduino MEGA 2560 using the DFU method. It is available here uncombined with the DFU firmware so that the DFU method can be used to update the USB to serial bridge firmware using a USB connection. The same source code and HEX files can be found on GitHub at github.com/arduino/ArduinoCore-avr/tree/master/firmwares/atmegaxxu2/arduino-usbserial which contains the latest version of this code and HEX files.

Arduino MEGA 2560 Hardware Manual

The USB to serial bridge firmware sets up the ATmega16U2 as a USB device that relays serial data between the main Arduino MEGA 2560 microcontroller (ATmega2560) and the computer connected to the Arduino MEGA 2560 USB port.

5.3.4 Programming the USB Microcontroller using ICSP

Connect a USB programmer to the ICSP header for the ATmega16U2 found near the USB connector as described in section 5.3.1 of this chapter. In fact connect to the Arduino MEGA 2560 using a USB programmer and Atmel Studio exactly as described in section 5.3.1 – the only difference is that the ATmega16U2 will be programmed instead of reading the contents of its Flash memory.

In Atmel Studio, open the Device Programming utility by clicking the Device Programming icon, or clicking Tools ▶ Device Programming from the top menu. In the dialog box that pops up, select the correct USB programmer under Tools, select ATmega16U2 under Device, select ISP under Interface and then click the Apply button. Click the Read button under Device signature to make sure that the settings are correct and that the Device Programming utility can connect to the target microcontroller. If all of the settings are correct, the device signature will be retrieved and target voltage read and displayed in the dialog box (only after clicking the Read button).

To load a HEX file to the ATmega16U2, click Memories in the left column of the Device Programming dialog box. Click the browse for file button [...] in the Flash section of the dialog box to open a dialog box that will be used to navigate to the desired HEX file. The HEX file can be any HEX file that is made to run on the ATmega16U2 microcontroller of the Arduino MEGA 2560. This could be the HEX file from section 5.3.1 of this chapter that was retrieved from the ATmega16U2, or combined DFU firmware file described in section 5.3.2. Navigate to the desired HEX file using the dialog box and then click the Open button. Click the Program button in the Flash section of the Device Programming dialog box to load the selected HEX file to the ATmega16U2.

After loading the new firmware to the ATmega16U2, power down the Arduino MEGA 2560 and then unplug the USB programmer from it. Power the Arduino again and it should work as expected – verify by loading a sketch to the Arduino from the Arduino IDE.

5.3.5. ATmega16U2 Fuse Settings

In order to see the fuse settings of the ATmega16U2 or to change them, connect to the ATmega16U2 using a USB programmer exactly as described in the previous section, section 5.3.4. Open the Device Programmer as described, but instead of Flash in the left column of this dialog box, click Fuses. Most Arduino users should never need to change the fuse settings for the ATmega16U2. The default Arduino MEGA 2560 settings for the ATmega16U2 fuses are include in Table 5.2 below in case they ever need to be set back to their correct settings.

Table 5.2: Fuse Settings for the ATmega16U2 on the Arduino MEGA 2560

Fuse Name	Value
EXTENDED.BODLEVEL	Brown-out detection level at VCC=3.0V
EXTENDED.HWBE	☑ checked
HIGH.DWEN	☐ unchecked
HIGH.RSTDISBL	☐ unchecked
HIGH.SPIEN	☑ checked
HIGH.WDTON	☐ unchecked
HIGH.EESAVE	☐ unchecked
HIGH.BOOTSZ	Boot Flash size=2048 words start address=$1800
HIGH.BOOTRST	☐ unchecked
LOW.CKDIV8	☐ unchecked
LOW.CKOUT	☐ unchecked
LOW.SUT_CKSEL	Ext.Crystal Osc. 8.0- MHz; Start-up time: 16K CK + 4.1ms

When the fuses are set as shown in Table 5.2, the fuse registers will have the following values, as seen at the bottom of the Fuses section in the Device Programming dialog box.

EXTENDED	0xF4
HIGH	0xD9
LOW	0xEF

More information on each fuse and what the fuse settings do can be found in the ATmega16U2 datasheet.

5.4 Main Microcontroller Bootloader

If the main microcontroller (the ATmega2560) is ever replaced on an Arduino MEGA 2560 and does not have a bootloader already programmed into it, or if the bootloader is erased, the bootloader will need to be loaded to this device. This can be done using Atmel Studio and an external USB programmer that connects to the ICSP header. Programming is done in the same way as has already been described for the ATmega16U2, but the ICSP header near the middle of the board, must be used. In the same way, the bootloader can be backed up from an ATmega2560 that already contains a bootloader. These actions are explained further in the sections that follow and include the fuse settings for the ATmega2560, when used on an Arduino MEGA 2560. The bootloader can also be quickly restored from within the Arduino IDE as has already been described in section 2.8.2, but with Atmel Studio installed, this will not work because of a driver clash.

5.4.1 Backing up the ATmega2560 Firmware with Atmel Studio

As a precaution, the firmware on the ATmega2560 can be copied from this device on the Arduino MEGA 2560 board and saved to HEX and BIN files using the device programming utility found in Atmel Studio. This is especially appropriate when using a clone board that may have a different bootloader than the one used on genuine Arduino MEGA 2560 boards.

Plug a USB programmer, such as an Atmel-ICE, into the computer USB port, and then plug the cable with the 6 pin socket connector from the programmer into the ICSP header near the middle of the Arduino MEGA 2560 board. Refer to Figure 3.25 in section 3.4 – ICSP Header on Main Microcontroller, for the pinout of the ICSP header for the ATmega2560 which shows where pin 1 is. The raised key on the 6-pin connector must point to the USB connector on the MEGA 2560. Figure 2.9 in section 2.8.1 of chapter 2 shows the correct orientation of an Atmel-ICE programmer plugged into the ICSP header of an Arduino MEGA 2560. Power up the Arduino MEGA 2560 using either USB or an external power supply.

Start Atmel Studio and open the Device Programming utility by either clicking the Device Programming icon on the top toolbar, or by selecting Tools ▶ Device Programming from the top Atmel Studio menu. In the Device Programming dialog box, select the correct USB programmer under Tool, select ATmega2560 under Device, make sure that ISP is selected under Interface, finally click the Apply button. To check that everything is set up correctly and that Atmel Studio can connect to the target device, click the Read button under Device signature. If all is well, the device signature and target voltage will be read and displayed in the Device Programming dialog box.

In the left column of the Device Programming dialog box, click Memories. In the Flash section of Memories in the dialog box, click the Read... button to navigate to a folder to save the HEX file to that will be retrieved from the Flash memory of the ATmega2560. At the bottom of the Save As dialog box enter the name of the HEX file that will be saved – this can be any valid name of your choice. Click the Save button when done. The Device Programming utility will read the contents of the ATmega2560 Flash memory and save it to a HEX file of the chosen name. This HEX file can be used to restore the original firmware to the ATmega2560 at any time. The HEX file includes the entire contents of the Flash memory including whatever user sketch was programmed in the Flash at the time of creating the HEX file.

5.4.2 Bootloader Firmware – stk500v2

Arduino MEGA 2560 boards use the stk500v2 bootloader in the ATmega2560. Source code and HEX files for the stk500v2 bootloader can be found in the Arduino IDE folder in the path **arduino-1.8.13\hardware\arduino\avr\bootloaders\stk500v2** where the base folder will have a different name for different versions of the Arduino IDE. The same files can be found at github.com/arduino/ArduinoCore-avr/tree/master/bootloaders/stk500v2 on GitHub.

5.4.3 Restoring the Bootloader

The stk500v2 bootloader can be restored to the ATmega2560, or loaded to a new blank ATmega2560 microcontroller using Atmel Studio and an external USB programmer, as has already been described in this chapter for the ATmega16U2. Use the same method for connecting to the ATmega2560 from Atmel Studio that was used for backing up the bootloader from section 5.4.1. See section 7.2 in chapter 7 for information on replacing the ATmega2560 microcontroller on an Arduino MEGA 2560 board.

To load the stk500v2 bootloader to the ATmega2560 on the Arduino MEGA 2560, connect the USB programmer to the ICSP header near the middle of the board as is described in section 5.4.1 earlier in this chapter. Open the Device Programming utility in Atmel Studio, and connect to the programmer and ATmega2560 in the same way. Click the Memories item in the left column of the Device Programming dialog box. Click the [...] button in the Flash section of the dialog box to open a dialog box that is used to navigate to the HEX file to load to the ATmega2560. The HEX file for restoring the bootloader can either be the HEX file created when backing up the bootloader, as described in section 5.4.1, or the correct HEX file from **arduino-1.8.13\hardware\arduino\avr\bootloaders\stk500v2** which for the Arduino MEGA 2560 is **stk500boot_v2_mega2560.hex**. Select the correct HEX file in the dialog box and then click the Open button. Back in the Device Programming dialog box, click the Program button in the Flash section of the dialog box. If everything is set up correctly, the Flash will be programmed with the selected HEX file.

If the bootloader was loaded to a new blank ATmega2560, the fuses must be set correctly in this device before continuing, as described in the next section. If the fuses are already set correctly, close the Device Programming dialog box in Atmel Studio and unplug the power from the Arduino MEGA 2560. Disconnect the USB programmer from the Arduino and then power up the Arduino again. If the fuses are already set correctly, then test the newly loaded bootloader by opening the Arduino IDE and loading a test sketch to the Arduino using the normal USB cable method.

5.4.4 ATmega2560 Fuse Settings

A new blank ATmega2560 must first have the stk500v2 bootloader loaded to it as described in the previous section. ATmega2560 fuses must then be set correctly for use in the Arduino MEGA 2560. Fuse values can be read and set using the Device Programming utility in Atmel Studio. To read and set the fuses, first connect an external USB programmer to the ICSP header near the middle of the Arduino MEGA 2560 as is described in section 5.4.1 earlier in this chapter. In Atmel Studio, open the Device Programming utility, choose the correct settings for the tool, device and interface as already described in section 5.4.1 and then click the Apply button to connect. In the left column of the Device Programming dialog box, click the Fuses item. The fuses must be programmed to the values shown in Figure 5.1 and Table 5.3. When these settings have been made, the fuse register values at the bottom of the dialog box will be:

EXTENDED	0xFD
HIGH	0xD8 (EESAVE unchecked) or 0xD0 (EESAVE checked)
LOW	0xFF

Checking the EESAVE box (HIGH.EESAVE) is optional and not set on new Arduino MEGA 2560 boards. This fuse, if checked in the dialog box, will protect the EEPROM memory contents when the chip is erased. It was found that the EESAVE fuse was checked on older Arduino MEGA 2560 boards, but not on new boards.

Chapter 5 • MEGA 2560 Firmware and Bootloader

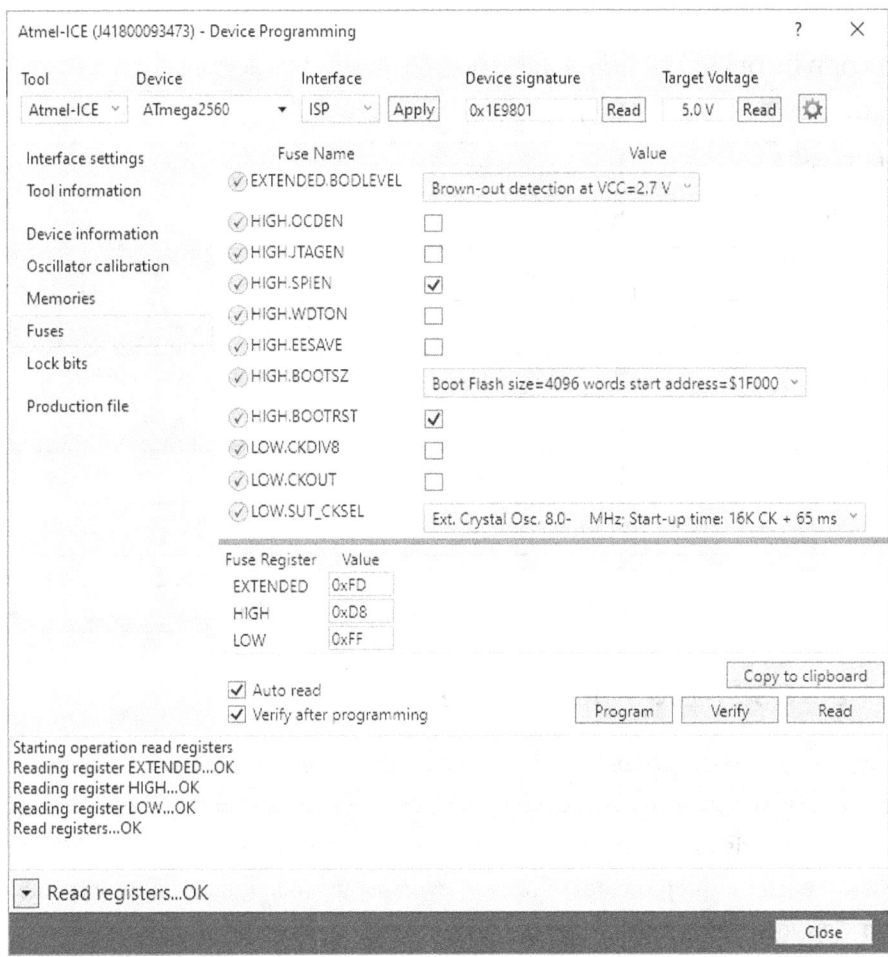

Figure 5.1: ATmega2560 Fuse Settings for the Arduino MEGA 2560

After making changes to the fuse settings, click the Program button near the bottom of the dialog box. This will program the new fuse values to the ATmega2560. Click OK in the warning dialog box to continue. Close the Device Programming dialog box, unplug the power from the Arduino MEGA 2560 and then unplug the USB programmer. Plug the Arduino MEGA 2560 into the computer USB port and then load a sketch to it from the Arduino IDE to make sure that the bootloader is working and that the fuse settings are correct.

Table 5.3: Fuse Settings for the ATmega2560 on an Arduino MEGA 2560

Fuse Name	Value
EXTENDED.BODLEVEL	Brown-out detection level at VCC=2.7V
HIGH.OCDEN	☐ unchecked
HIGH.JTAGEN	☐ unchecked
HIGH.SPIEN	☑ checked
HIGH.WDTON	☐ unchecked
HIGH.EESAVE	☐ unchecked, or ☑ checked, see text
HIGH.BOOTSZ	Boot Flash size=4096 words start address=$1F000
HIGH.BOOTRST	☑ checked
LOW.CKDIV8	☐ unchecked
LOW.CKOUT	☐ unchecked
LOW.SUT_CKSEL	Ext.Crystal Osc. 8.0- MHz; Start-up time: 16K CK + 65 ms EXTXOSC_8MHZ_XX_16KCK_65MS

5.5 The RESET-EN Solder Jumper

Some of the AVR USB programmers have debugging capability, such as the Atmel-ICE and the older now obsolete AVR Dragon. Debugging capabilities refers to the ability of the USB programmer/debugger to work in conjunction with software such as Atmel Studio, and allow the user or programmer to access the main microcontroller on the Arduino in order to view the contents of its memory and internal registers, as well as to single-step through source code. At present this capability is not available in the Arduino IDE.

Arduino MEGA 2560 boards with the ATmega2560 microcontroller have two different programming/debugging interfaces called debugWIRE and JTAG. By comparison, Arduino Uno boards only have a debugWIRE interface and do not have JTAG. In order to use the debugWIRE debugging capabilities of a USB programmer/debugger, it is plugged into the ICSP header as it normally would be done for programming the Flash memory of the target AVR device, or for reading fuse values. A C or C++ program can be loaded to the AVR via the USB programmer/debugger using Atmel Studio. Atmel Studio can then be used to debug the target AVR through the debugWIRE connection. In order for debugWIRE to work on the ATmega2560 on Arduino MEGA 2560 boards, reset circuitry must be disconnected from the reset pin. Arduino MEGA 2560 boards have a solder link labeled RESET-EN that consists of two solder pads connected by a circuit board track. The track between the solder pads must be cut through in order to disconnect part of the reset circuitry from the reset pin when using debugWIRE. The connection can be remade by soldering the two solder pads together. Figure 5.2 shows the location of the RESET-EN solder pads on the Arduino MEGA 2560.

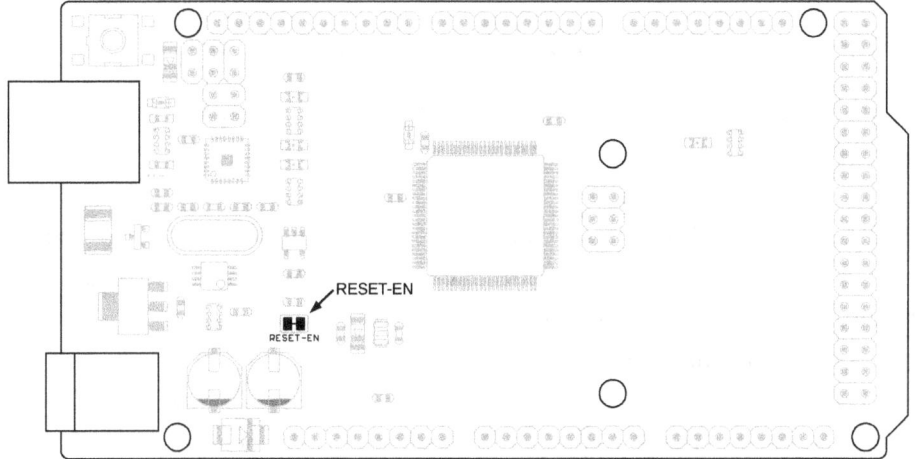

Figure 5.2: Location of the RESET-EN Solder Jumper on an Arduino MEGA 2560

An alternative to using debugWIRE on an Arduino MEGA 2560 and having to cut the RESET-EN link is to use the JTAG interface for programming and debugging. Before using the JTAG interface, the JTAGEN (HIGH.JTAGEN) fuse must be set using the USB programmer/debugger connected to the ICSP header, as was done when reading fuses in this chapter. This enables the JTAG interface and the programmer/debugger can then be disconnected from the ICSP header and connected to the JTAG pins. The JTAG interface does not use the RESET pin as the debugging interface like debugWIRE does, but uses RESET only to reset the microcontroller, so there is no need to open RESET-EN when using JTAG. Refer back to Figure 3.28 in section 3.7 of chapter 3 for the Arduino MEGA 2560 JTAG pinout.

Refer to the documentation of the JTAG programmer/debugger that you are using to see how to connect the device to the Arduino JTAG pins. For the Atmel-ICE, this information can be found in the Atmel-ICE User Guide that is available for download from the Microchip website at www.microchip.com/DevelopmentTools/ProductDetails/atatmel-ice

Advanced features such as debugging via either debugWIRE or JTAG will only be used by advanced Arduino users who are typically programming the board using plain C and Atmel Studio. Those readers interested in learning the C language to program Arduino boards may be interested in the book *C Programming with Arduino, ISBN 978-1-907920-46-2* by the same author and published by Elektor. This book contains a chapter on debugging Arduino MEGA 2560 and Arduino Uno boards using Atmel Studio.

5.6 Alternative Firmware Programming Methods

Using an Arduino as an ISP (In-system programmer) is described on the Arduino website at www.arduino.cc/en/Tutorial/ArduinoISP

See chapter 2, section 2.8 for more information on loading sketches to the Arduino MEGA 2560 using an external programmer and the Arduino IDE. Refer to the same section for information on restoring the bootloader to the main microcontroller, also using an external programmer and the Arduino IDE.

Refer to www.arduino.cc/en/Hacking/DFUProgramming8U2 for additional information on DFU programming the ATmega16U2.

Chapter 6 • Circuit Diagram and Components

Although the circuit diagram for the Arduino MEGA 2560 is available online in both PDF and Eagle EDA formats, this chapter enhances the circuit diagram and breaks the circuit diagram up into easier to reference and understand sections.

This chapter also includes the component list of all of the parts found on the Arduino MEGA 2560 board and in the schematic, as well as the location of parts on the board itself.

Parts are usually difficult to locate on the board, especially the smaller parts such as resistor packs and capacitors, because the board is compact and there is no space to silkscreen reference designators for the parts. The diagram in this chapter that shows the location of all components on the board is a great reference that can be used to easily locate any component.

In this Chapter

- Arduino MEGA 2560 block diagram
- Arduino MEGA 2560 circuit diagram enhanced, and split into three easy to reference figures
- Component list for the Arduino MEGA 2560
- Location of parts on the board
- Component quick reference table

6.1 Circuit Diagram

The circuit diagram for REV 3 (Rev3e) Arduino MEGA 2560 boards follows in this chapter and is shown as a block diagram that consists of three main parts, namely, the power supply circuit, the USB microcontroller circuit and the main microcontroller circuit with header sockets. Each of these three parts are then presented as separate circuits in the sections that follow. The block diagrams for the Uno and MEGA 2560 are basically the same, with the differences being the details in each block.

6.1.1 Block Diagram

The block diagram, seen in Figure 6.1, is a top level view of the Arduino MEGA 2560 circuit diagram that shows how the different parts of the circuit interconnect. The power supply circuit is supplied with power from the 2.1mm jack and from the USB 5V. This circuit then supplies 5V to the rest of the Arduino and 3.3V to the 3.3V pin. The USB microcontroller circuit connects to the main microcontroller circuit via the TX0 and RX0 serial port lines and reset line via C7. This allows the Arduino IDE to reset the main microcontroller in order to start its bootloader which then allows a new sketch to be loaded to the main microcontroller using the TX0 and RX0 lines. GND is not shown in the block diagram, but is common throughout. Vin is also omitted from the figure, but connects from the 2.1mm jack through a diode to a pin on the header sockets.

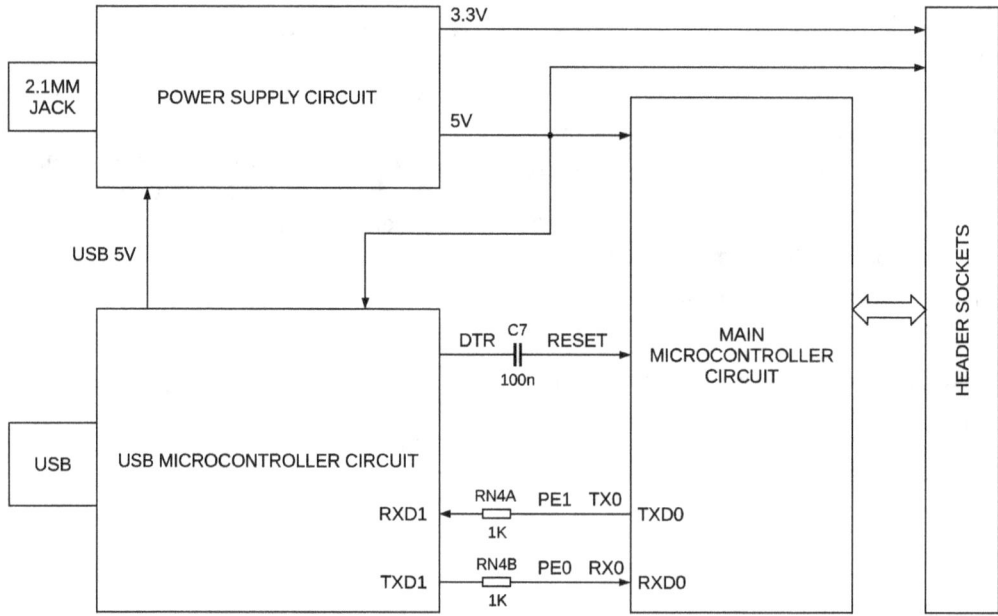

Figure 6.1: Block Diagram of Arduino MEGA 2560 Schematic or Circuit Diagram

6.1.2 Main Microcontroller Circuit

Figure 6.2 shows the main microcontroller circuit containing the ATmega2560 device. Something to note in the circuit diagram is the unusual names for reference designators, such as RESET for the reset switch, where one would expect a reference designator such as SW1, or similar, for a switch. The same for the L LED – L is the actual reference designator rather than LED1, D1, or similar.

Header socket connectors have reference designators of ADCH and ADCL for the analog pins headers, COMMUNICATION for the communication header, POWER for the power header, PWML for PWM pins 2 to 7, and XIO for the double-row header at the end of the boards containing pins 22 to 53. The exception to these designator names is JP6 which contains digital/PWM pins 8 to 13. The circuit diagram in Figure 6.2 is enhanced to include all of the header names, and the pin names as they appear silkscreened on an Arduino MEGA 2560 board. The reference designator names, as mentioned above, are found in the component list of Table 6.1 in section 6.2 of this chapter.

In the circuit diagram of Figure 6.2, double arrows for the RESET signal, PE0 (RX0) and PE1 (TX0) show connections to the USB microcontroller part of the circuit in Figure 6.3. These connections are as we have already seen in the block diagram of Figure 6.1.

Two errors have been corrected that were found in the original Arduino MEGA 2560 Rev3e circuit diagram. In the original circuit diagram, the main microcontroller, IC3, has a part number of ATMEGA2560-15AU, but this is incorrect. The part number has been corrected in Figure 6.2 to ATMEGA2560-16AU. 16 in the part number is the speed grade indicator that denotes 16MHz, there is no 15MHz part. The second error is also to do with IC3 and is found on pin 2 of this microcontroller. In the original circuit diagram, the pin is labeled as (RXD0/PCIN8) PE0 inside the body of the symbol. This is incorrect, it should be (RXD0/PCINT8) PE0, the mistake is that PCIN8 should be PCINT8. It has been updated in the circuit of Figure 6.2.

6.1.3 USB Microcontroller Circuit

The USB microcontroller circuit containing the ATmega16U2 device can be seen in Figure 6.3. Double arrows that connect the RESET, PE0 and PE1 lines to the main ATmega2560 microcontroller circuit have been added to the circuit in the figure. The circuit in Figure 6.3 has been cleaned up to make it easier to read, especially where text was overlapping in the original circuit diagram.

Arduino MEGA 2560 Hardware Manual

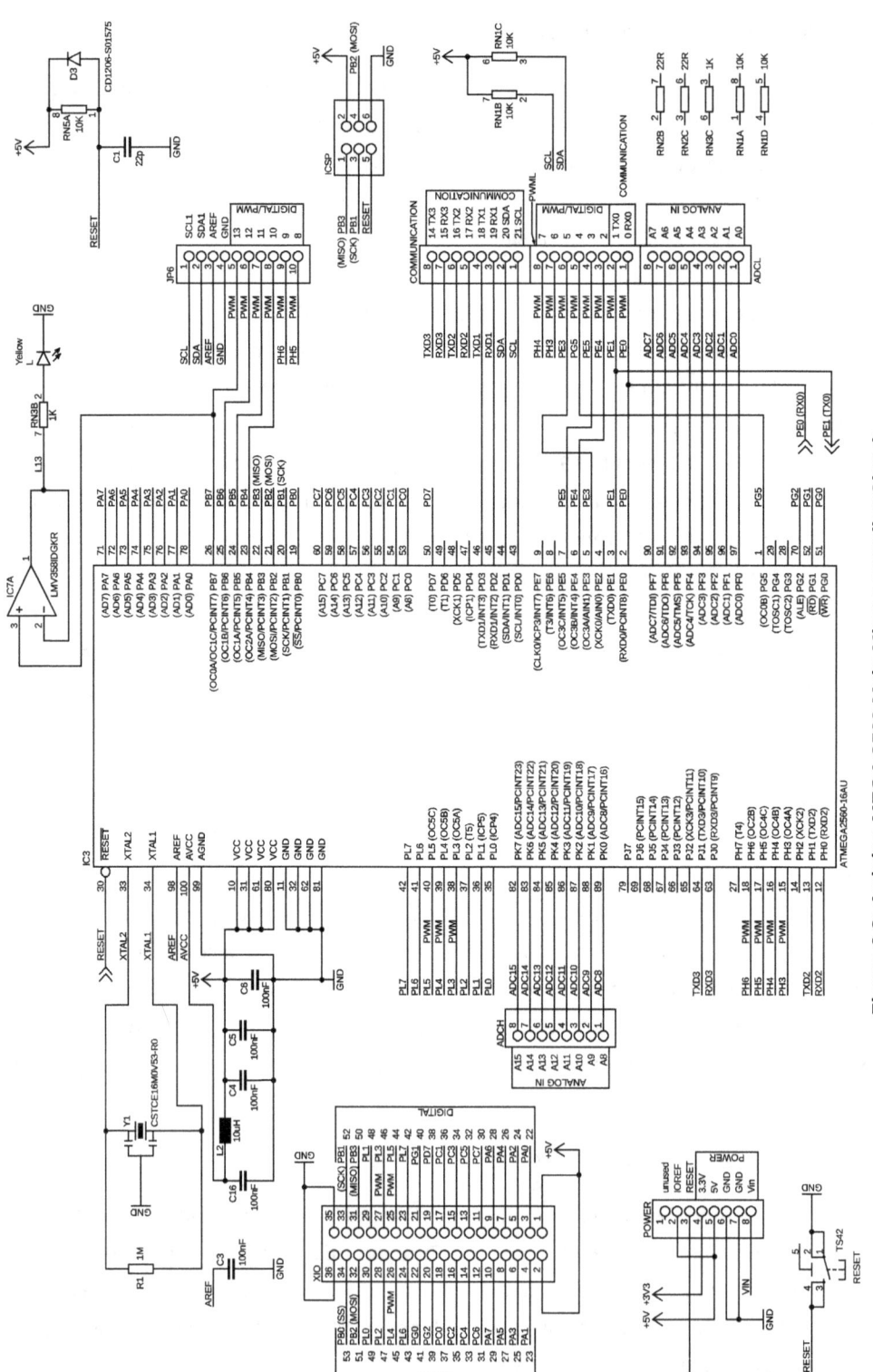

Figure 6.2: Arduino MEGA 2560 Main Microcontroller Circuit

Chapter 6 • Circuit Diagram and Components

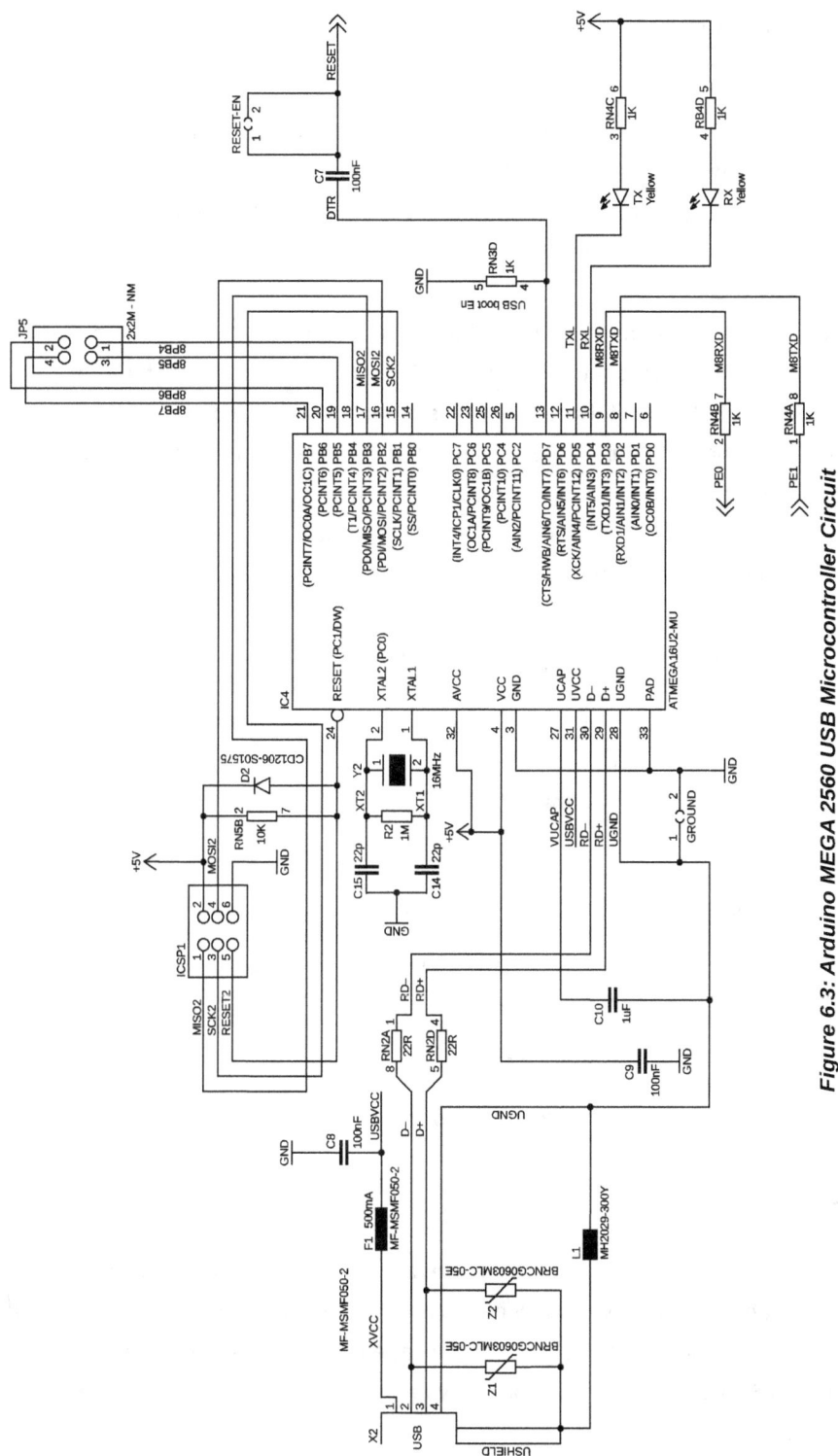

Figure 6.3: Arduino MEGA 2560 USB Microcontroller Circuit

173

Arduino MEGA 2560 Hardware Manual

6.1.4 Power Supply Circuit

Figure 6.4 shows the power supply circuit of the Arduino MEGA 2560. Cross refer to Figure 4.2 in section 4.2 of chapter 4 which shows the same circuit but includes both the USB connector and power header socket. The USB connector is missing from Figure 6.4 because it is part of the USB microcontroller circuit of Figure 6.3. The power header socket is found in the main microcontroller circuit of Figure 6.2.

USBVCC, seen connected to transistor T1 in Figure 6.4, connects to fuse F1 from the Arduino MEGA 2560 USB microcontroller circuit in Figure 6.3. Refer to chapter 4 for details of the power supply circuit. Note that IC7 is a dual op-amp chip that contains two op-amps. IC7B is one op-amp from IC7 and is used as the comparator in the power supply circuit. IC7A is the other op-amp from IC7 that is found in the main microcontroller circuit of Figure 6.2, and is used as a unity gain buffer for the L LED. IC7 is powered by its pins 8 and 4 as can be seen in Figure 6.4

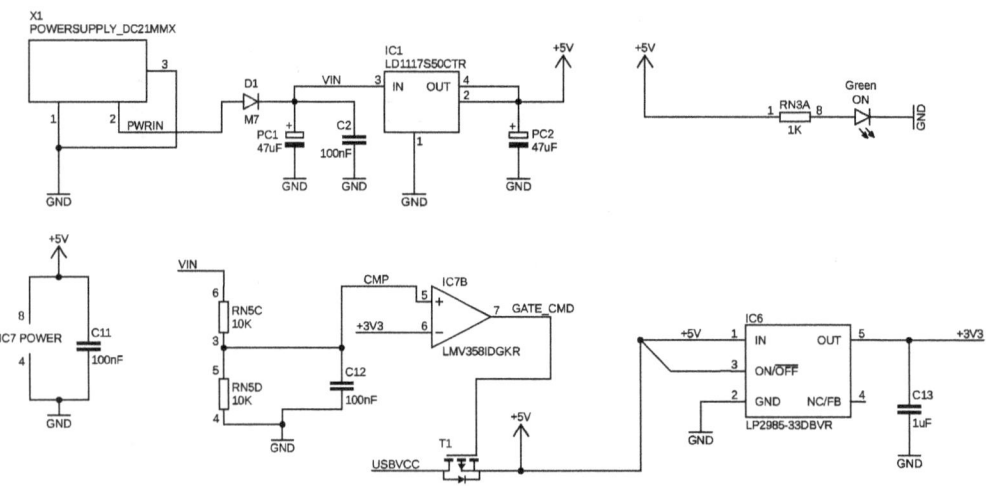

Figure 6.4: Arduino MEGA 2560 Power Supply Circuit

6.2 Component List

Table 6.1 contains the component list for all of the components found on the Arduino MEGA 2560. The table extends over a few pages and lists the components in alphabetical order by reference designator. The device and package columns use the names provided from the circuit via Eagle EDA and may not always make sense. Read the comments column for a better description of the part.

Table 6.1: Arduino MEGA 2560 Component List

Reference Designator	Value	Device	Package	Comments
ADCH	FH254-108DF08500V	0058_FH254-108DF08500V	1X08	Analog Pins High (A8 - A15)
ADCL	FH254-108DF08500V	0058_FH254-108DF08500V	1X08	Analog Pins Low (A0 - A7)
C1	22p	0014_22PF_0603	C0603-ROUND	Capacitor
C2	100nF	0015_100NF_0603	C0603-ROUND	Capacitor
C3	100nF	0015_100NF_0603	C0603-ROUND	Capacitor
C4	100nF	0015_100NF_0603	C0603-ROUND	Capacitor
C5	100nF	0015_100NF_0603	C0603-ROUND	Capacitor
C6	100nF	0015_100NF_0603	C0603-ROUND	Capacitor
C7	100nF	0015_100NF_0603	C0603-ROUND	Capacitor
C8	100nF	0015_100NF_0603	C0603-ROUND	Capacitor
C9	100nF	0015_100NF_0603	C0603-ROUND	Capacitor
C10	1uF	0006_1UF_0603/ GRM188R61E105KA12D	C0603-ROUND	Capacitor
C11	100nF	0015_100NF_0603	C0603-ROUND	Capacitor
C12	100nF	0015_100NF_0603	C0603-ROUND	Capacitor
C13	1uF	0006_1UF_0603/ GRM188R61E105KA12D	C0603-ROUND	Capacitor
C14	22p	0014_22PF_0603	C0603-ROUND	Capacitor
C15	22p	0014_22PF_0603	C0603-ROUND	Capacitor
C16	100nF	0015_100NF_0603	C0603-ROUND	Capacitor
COMMUNICATION	FH254-108DF08500V	0058_FH254-108DF08500V	1X08	Communication Pins
D1	M7	0020_M7	SMB	Diode
D2	CD1206-S01575	0012_CD1206-S01575	MINIMELF	Diode
D3	CD1206-S01575	0012_CD1206-S01575	MINIMELF	Diode
F1	MF-MSMF050-2 500mA	0002_MF-MSMF050-2	L1812	500mA resettable fuse
GROUND	-	SJ	SJ	Etched jumper
IC1	1870_LD1117S50CTR	1870_LD1117S50CTR	LINEAR_SOT223	5V regulator
IC3	ATMEGA2560-16AU	0023_ATMEGA2560-16AU	TQFP100	Main microcontroller
IC4	ATMEGA16U2-MU	0007_ATMEGA16U2-MUR	MLF32	USB microcontroller

Table 6.1: Arduino MEGA 2560 Component List continued...

Reference Designator	Value	Device	Package	Comments
IC6	LP2985-33DBVR	0008_TEXLP2985-33DBVR	SOT23-DBV	3.3V regulator
IC7	LMV358IDGKR	0021_LMV358IDGKR	MSOP08	Dual op-amp
ICSP	ICSP	0114_PH254-203DF118A00V	2X03	Main ICSP header
ICSP1	ICSP	0114_PH254-203DF118A00V	2X03	ICSP header for USB microcontroller
JP5	2x2M - NM	PINHD-2X2	2X02	4 pads at ICSP1
JP6	FH254-110DF08500V	1216_FH254-110DF08500T30	1X10	Arduino pins 8 to 13 header socket
L	Yellow	0044_KPT-2012YC	CHIPLED_0805	L LED on pin 13
L1	MH2029-300Y	0001_BLM21PG300SN1D_/_MH2029-300Y 0805		Inductor at USB connector
L2	10uH	0715_CV201210-100K	0805	Inductor for analog supply
ON	Green	0043_KPT-2012SGC	CHIPLED_0805	Power ON LED
PC1	47uF	0113_47UF	PANASONIC_D	Capacitor
PC2	47uF	0113_47UF	PANASONIC_D	Capacitor
POWER	FH254-108DF08500V	1217_FH254-108DF08500T21	1X08	POWER pins header socket
PWML	FH254-108DF08500V	1218_FH254-108DF08500T20	1X08	PWM low connector for pins 0 to 7
R1	1M	0004_0603_1M	R0603-ROUND	Resistor
R2	1M	0004_0603_1M	R0603-ROUND	Resistor
RESET	TS42	0946_TS42031-160W-TR-7260	TS42	Reset push-button switch
RESET-EN	-	SJ	SJ	Etched jumper
RN1	10k	0016_064R_10K_/_CAY16-103J4LF	CAY16	Resistor network
RN2	22R	0003_064R_22R_/_CAY16-220J4LF	CAY16	Resistor network
RN3	1K	0005_064R_1K_/_CAY16-102J4LF	CAY16	Resistor network
RN4	1K	0005_064R_1K_/_CAY16-102J4LF	CAY16	Resistor network
RN5	10k	0016_064R_10K_/_CAY16-103J4LF	CAY16	Resistor network

Table 6.1: Arduino MEGA 2560 Component List continued...

Reference Designator	Value	Device	Package	Comments
RX	Yellow	0044_KPT-2012YC	CHIPLED_0805	RX LED for USB
T1	PMV48XP	0297_PMV48XP	SOT-23	P-channel MOSFET
TX	Yellow	0044_KPT-2012YC	CHIPLED_0805	TX LED for USB
X1	POWERSUPPLY_DC21MMX	POWERSUPPLY_DC21MMX	POWERSUPPLY_DC-21MM	2.1mm power in jack
X2	USB-B_TH	0056_USB-B-S-RA-WT-SPCC	PN61729	USB B-type connector
XIO	18x2F-H8.5	0060_FH254-218DF08500V	2X18	Double row header socket for pins 22 to 53
Y1	CSTCE16M0V53-R0	0011_CSTCE16M0V53-R0	RESONATOR	16MHz ceramic resonator for main microcontroller clock
Y2	16MHz	0019_P011052006_16M	QS	16MHz crystal for USB microcontroller
Z1	BRNCG0603MLC-05E	0010_BRNCG0603MLC-05E	CT/CN0603	Protection varistor for USB data line
Z2	BRNCG0603MLC-05E	0010_BRNCG0603MLC-05E	CT/CN0603	Protection varistor for USB data line

C16 and L2 were added to newer Arduino MEGA 2560 REV3 boards which are referred to as Rev3e boards in the schematic and build files. On older REV3 boards these two components are not present. They form a power supply filter for the analog power pin AVCC of the ATmega2560 microcontroller. This pin supplies power to the ADC in the ATmega2560.

GROUND and RESET-EN are both normally closed solder pad jumpers that are made out of copper PCB track on the board. The connecting track between the pads on these components can be cut with a sharp blade to open circuit these components. Solder can be used to join the pads back together again if they are ever cut.

6.3 Component Positions on the Board

Figure 6.5 on the next page shows the position of each of the components on the Arduino MEGA 2560 board. The corresponding components can be found in the circuit diagram of Figures 6.2, Figure 6.3 and Figure 6.4, as well as in the component list of Table 6.1. Table 6.2 below Figure 6.5 is a convenient simple component list for quick part lookup.

Arduino MEGA 2560 Hardware Manual

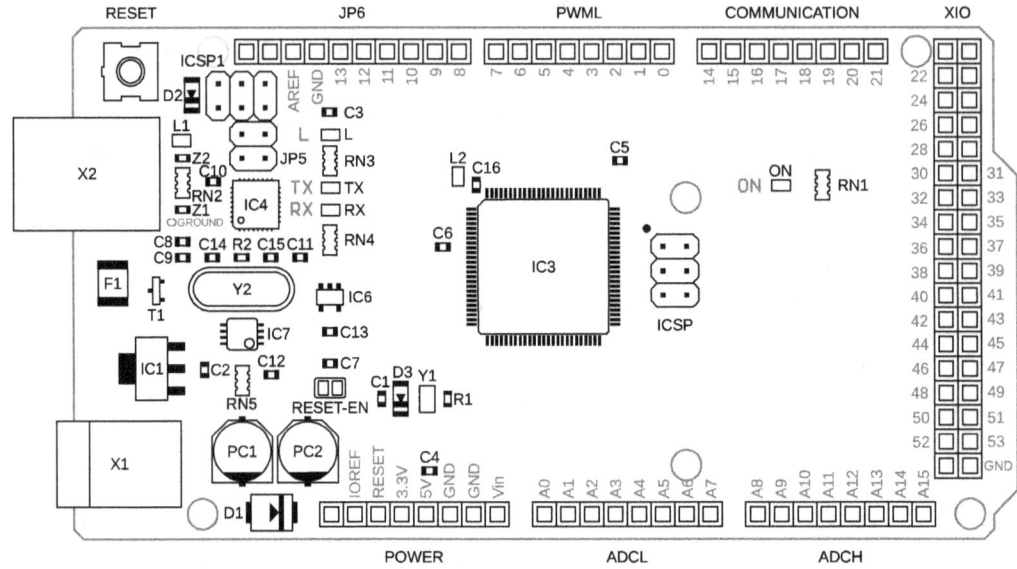

Figure 6.5: Component Positions on the Arduino MEGA 2560 Board

Table 6.2: Component Quick Reference

ADCH	1 × 8	D2	CD1206-S01575	PWML	1 × 8
ADCL	1 × 8	D3	CD1206-S01575	R1	1M
C1	22p	F1	MF-MSMF050-2	R2	1M
C2	100nF	GROUND	Etched jumper	RESET	TS42
C3	100nF	IC1	LD1117S50CTR	RESET-EN	Etched jumper
C4	100nF	IC3	ATMEGA2560-16AU	RN1	10k
C5	100nF	IC4	ATMEGA16U2-MU	RN2	22R
C6	100nF	IC6	LP2985-33DBVR	RN3	1K
C7	100nF	IC7	LMV358IDGKR	RN4	1K
C8	100nF	ICSP	2 × 6	RN5	10k
C9	100nF	ICSP1	2 × 6	RX	Yellow LED
C10	1uF	JP5	2 × 2	T1	PMV48XP
C11	100nF	JP6	1 × 10	TX	Yellow LED
C12	100nF	L	Yellow LED	X1	2.1mm Jack
C13	1uF	L1	MH2029-300Y	X2	USB-B_TH
C14	22p	L2	10uH	XIO	2 × 18
C15	22p	ON	Green LED	Y1	CSTCE16M0V53-R0
C16	100nF	PC1	47uF	Y2	16MHz Crystal
COMMUNICATION	1 × 8	PC2	47uF	Z1	CG0603MLC-05E
D1	M7	POWER	1 × 8	Z2	CG0603MLC-05E

Note that the GROUND solder jumper is on the bottom layer of the board and can be seen between Z1 and C8 in Figure 6.5. Connector names for the header sockets of the Arduino pins around the edges of the board are placed outside the board area in Figure 6.5, as well as the RESET label for the reset push-button switch. On new Arduino MEGA 2560 revision 3 boards, connectors at the edges of the board down the length consist of single molded pieces with silkscreen labels for each pin. Connectors JP6, PWML and COMMUNICATION are all joined into one molded connector. On the opposite side of the board, POWER, ADCL and ADCH are joined into one molded connector. On older revision 3 boards, and earlier revision boards, these are separate connectors, 3 on each side of the board. There is no IC2 or IC5 in the circuit. IC numbering goes IC1, IC3, IC4, IC6 and IC7.

6.4 Getting an Electronic Copy of the Circuit Diagram

Arduino hardware is open-source and the circuit diagram and source files for the circuit diagram and board design are freely available to examine and modify within the terms of the Creative Commons license. Find the circuit diagram in PDF format, and the circuit diagram and PCB design file in Eagle format at store.arduino.cc/arduino-mega-2560-rev3 for the Arduino MEGA 2560. Look under the DOCUMENTATION tab for these files.

To view the files in Eagle format, the Eagle EDA software package will need to be downloaded from www.autodesk.com/products/eagle/free-download and installed. Eagle EDA software is available for Windows, Mac and Linux. Although Eagle is a commercial product, it can run as a limited version for hobbyists that has certain restrictions, but is fine for examining the Arduino MEGA 2560 schematic and board files. Eagle has been moved to a subscription service for the paid version. Registration is needed for both free and paid models, meaning that you will need to supply an email address to register.

Chapter 7 • Fault Finding and Measurement

This chapter is dedicated to fault finding on the Arduino MEGA 2560. Basic fault finding techniques are covered. An explanation of how to remove a faulty microcontroller from an Arduino MEGA 2560 and replace it with a new one is included for advanced users.

In order to test an Arduino MEGA 2560 board, various measurements need to be made. Test points on the board are shown in order to make voltage measurements to compare to when testing a faulty board. Both DC voltage measurements that can be tested with a multimeter and various AC waveform measurements are covered that can be measured using an oscilloscope.

Examples that capture PWM, UART, TWI and SPI signals on an oscilloscope in this chapter can be used as a reference when setting up an oscilloscope to test these signals in a project.

In this Chapter

- Basic fault finding on the Arduino MEGA 2560
- Replacing the Arduino MEGA 2560 main microcontroller and bootloader firmware
- Making voltage measurements using a multimeter
- Making waveform measurements using an oscilloscope
- PWM, UART, TWI and SPI signal oscilloscope examples

7.1 Basic Fault Finding and Repair

Some basic fault finding on the Arduino MEGA 2560 has already been covered in chapter 1. Refer to section 1.5.3 – Basic Testing, for the first things to look for on a faulty Arduino MEGA 2560 board. Knowing the history of the board can be a big help when fault finding. What happened to cause it to fail? Did it fail while in use, and if so, what was connected to it? If a heavy load was connected to it, a pin on the ATmega2560 microcontroller could be burned out, or even the microcontroller itself. If the board was known to be working and then failed the next time it was used, this could point to possible mechanical damage if it was packed away in an unsuitable place, or perhaps damage from static electricity.

Except for the 16MHz crystal for the ATmega16U2 and connectors on an Arduino MEGA 2560 board, all electronic components are surface mount devices soldered to the top of the board. This makes repair more difficult for the average hobbyist or maker. Some of the bigger devices, such as the 5V regulator, are easier to replace than small devices with fine pitch pin spacing. It is up to each individual to decide whether replacing a part is too difficult or not. Inexperienced users could end up damaging the board more when attempting to do a repair, so discretion is advised.

Replacing the main microcontroller on an Arduino MEGA 2560 should only be attempted by users experienced in surface mount soldering and repair. Unlike the Arduino Uno that has a 28-pin socketed through-hole mounting microcontroller, the Arduino MEGA 2560 has a 100-pin surface mount microcontroller. Replacing this device on an Arduino MEGA 2560 makes for a challenging repair job. Although this job is fairly difficult, the next section provides information on replacing the main microcontroller for those users who are willing to attempt this repair.

In the sections that follow, test points for measuring voltages on an Arduino MEGA 2560 are shown, which can be used when fault finding in order to determine if voltages at the various points are at the correct levels, or if they indicate a fault.

7.2 Replacing the Main Arduino MEGA 2560 Microcontroller

If the Arduino MEGA 2560 main microcontroller is damaged or faulty, replace it with a new device. Replacement of the main ATmega2560 microcontroller on an Arduino MEGA 2560 board, as described in this section, requires some equipment. Firstly, a rework station that

Chapter 7 • Fault Finding and Measurement

has a hot air gun, or stand-alone hot air soldering station is needed. A hot air gun sold at hardware stores that is usually used for paint stripping and similar work is not suitable. These types of hot air guns do not have fine temperature control, and have big nozzles that make them unsuitable for heating a small area on a circuit board. Secondly, a soldering iron with a hoof soldering iron tip used for drag soldering is needed to do drag soldering when replacing the microcontroller. Liquid flux or flux paste is needed in addition to solder when doing drag soldering. Finally, a programmer is needed for loading the bootloader to the new microcontroller, and setting its fuses through the ICSP header.

7.2.1 Replacement Part

Replace the 100-pin TQFP packaged microcontroller on the Arduino MEGA 2560 with a new 16MHz device that has the part number **ATMEGA2560-16AU**. The suffix AU in the part number denotes the packaging of this device as a 100-lead TQFP package type. This microcontroller is available from a number of different online stores. Be sure _not_ to get an ATmega2560V-8AU, which has a maximum speed of only 8MHz.

7.2.2 Removing the Old Microcontroller

As can be seen in the rectangular area marked near the middle of the board in Figure 7.1, there are a number of components that are close to the ATmega2560 microcontroller IC3. It is very difficult to replace IC3 without first removing the components in the marked area.

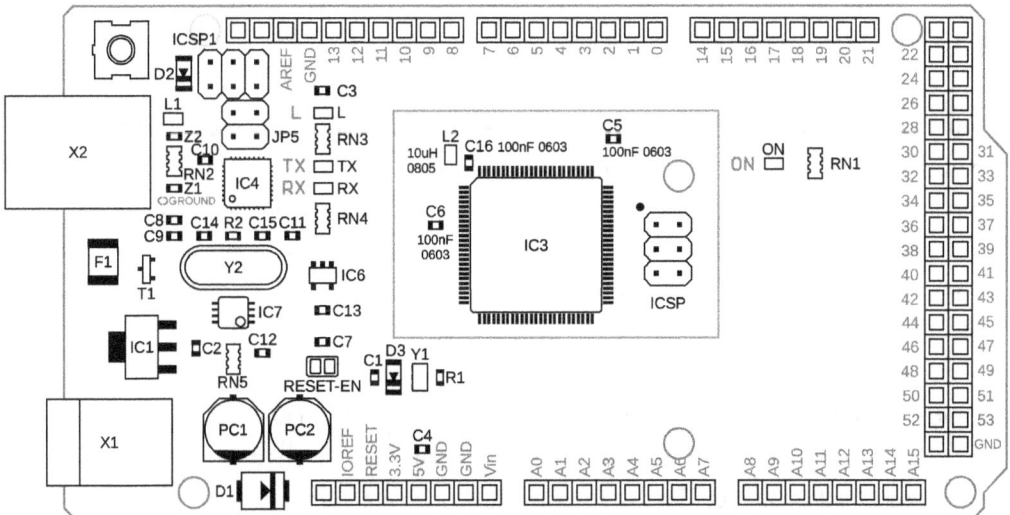

Figure 7.1. Removing the ATmega2560 Microcontroller

It is suggested to first remove the 6-pin header ICSP by heating it with a hot air gun from underneath the board, and then pulling it out from the top using tweezers or pliers. 10µH inductor L2 should be removed, followed by the 100nF capacitors C5, C6 and C16. It may be prudent to have spare 0603 footprint 100nF capacitors, as well as a spare 0805 footprint 10µH inductor, should these parts need to be replaced – it may not be possible to recycle them after removal. Replacing these capacitors and inductor with new parts will be a lot easier than trying to reuse the old parts. It will also be easier to replace the ICSP header with a new one, although cleaning the solder off this header and reusing it will be easier than trying to recycle the surface mount inductor and capacitors.

After removing the components immediately surrounding IC3, use a hot air gun to heat the pins around IC3. Be careful not to heat and melt the plastic Arduino pin header sockets at the edges of the board. When the solder that is holding IC3 to the board melts, lift IC3 off the board.

7.2.3 Soldering the New Microcontroller

After removing IC3 and the surrounding components, clean up the remaining solder from the pads of these components by using solder wick. Use either solder wick or a solder sucker to clean solder out of the holes on the board for the ICSP header.

When the excess solder has been removed from the pads of the components that were removed, clean up any flux from the board using a flux remover solvent. After this step, the board is ready to replace the components.

Place the new ATmega2560 microcontroller in position on the board, making sure to orient it correctly by finding pin 1 on the microcontroller, and pin 1 on the microcontroller footprint on the board. Pin 1 is marked on the body of the ATmega2560 microcontroller at one of the corners that has a 45° bevel and a dot on the top of the body near the beveled corner. Pin 1 can be seen at the top left of IC3 in Figure 7.1 on the previous page, at C16. It is at the top of the left row of pins of IC3 in the figure.

Position the ATmega2560 microcontroller so that all of the pins line up with the pads on the board. Use a magnifying glass to check alignment. Once aligned, tack one or two pins with a blob of solder at a corner, and again at the opposite corner.

Chapter 7 • Fault Finding and Measurement

With the microcontroller tacked in place by solder, it is suggested to use the drag soldering method to solder IC3 to the board. Start with all of the pins on one of the sides of the microcontroller that has not been tacked. Drag soldering is usually done by first applying flux to the pins down one side of the microcontroller. Use a soldering iron with a hoof type soldering iron tip. Add a ball of solder to the soldering iron tip and then drag it down the row of pins that has flux applied to it. If there is enough flux on the pins then only enough solder will be left on each pin as the ball of solder is dragged down the pins.

After soldering one side of the microcontroller to the board, do the opposite side. Finally solder the remaining two sides, always applying enough flux to the pins and using the drag soldering method.

Replace the 100nF capacitors C5, C6 and C16, and then inductor L2. Use either a fine tipped soldering iron to replace these chip capacitors and inductor, or solder paste from a syringe and a hot air station. Use flux remover solvent to clean up the board after finishing the surface mount soldering. Replace the 6-pin header ICSP to finish the repair job.

7.2.4 Loading the Bootloader

Use a USB programmer to load the bootloader to the new ATmega2560 microcontroller, refer to section 2.8.2 of chapter 2 for information on how to restore the bootloader using the Arduino IDE. Refer to section 5.4 of chapter 5 for more information on loading the bootloader to the microcontroller using Atmel Studio. If using Atmel Studio, be sure to also program the microcontroller fuses as described in section 5.4.4.

7.3 Voltage Measurements

One of the simpler tests to perform on an Arduino is to measure its voltages at various points on the board in order to determine if faulty power components or power supply are the cause of problems on the board. In the two sections that follow, voltages at certain test points on an Arduino MEGA 2560 board are shown, so they can be compared to measurements made on a board under test. The first section shows measurements on a board powered from USB, and the second section, a board powered from an external power supply.

Use a multimeter set to voltage when making voltage measurements on an Arduino MEGA 2560. If the multimeter is not an autoranging type, be sure to set it on a suitable voltage scale for the voltage being measured. When making measurements, especially on small electronic components, be careful not to short out any pins with the probe tip on the multimeter lead. A lead with a very sharp tip is less likely to slip and short pins together. All voltage measurements are made relative to GND. Insert a jumper wire into one of the GND pins of the socketed headers and then use the alligator clip attachment on the black COM lead of the multimeter to clip onto the other end of the jumper wire. This frees up a hand that would otherwise have to hold the COM lead to a GND point, making it slightly easier to take measurements.

To prevent voltage fluctuations when making DC voltage measurements on the Arduino MEGA 2560, it is suggested to load a blank sketch to the Arduino. A blank sketch can be found in the Arduino IDE under File ▶ Examples ▶ 01.Basics ▶ BareMinimum from the top menu. This leaves all hardware in its default state and causes program execution to enter an endless loop so that no hardware is being used, switched or operated. With the blank sketch loaded, the L LED stays on.

7.3.1 Powered from USB

Figure 7.2 shows various test points to take DC voltage measurements at in order to check that power is reaching these areas on the board. The sections that follow describe how to perform measurements at the points marked in the figure.

7.3.1.1 5V Test Points

First, and most obvious, is to check that 5V is present on the 5V pin of the POWER header socket, as shown in Figure 7.2. 5V should also be present at the top of the double-row header at the end of the board, as marked in the figure. Pin 2 of the ICSP header is an easy to reach 5V measurement point. 5V that is close to the ATmega2560, IC3, can be measured across capacitor C5 at the top right of IC3 as shown in the figure.

7.3.1.2 USB Power and 3.3V Circuit Test Points

The actual USB input voltage can be measured on resettable fuse F1 at the XVCC point that can be seen in Figure 7.2. Be very careful not to short out the probe point of the multimeter lead to the USB connector casing, which is connected to GND, when measuring the XVCC voltage. On the other end of fuse F1 is USBVCC that will be at a slightly lower voltage than XVCC because of the voltage drop across fuse F1. With the blank sketch loaded to the Arduino MEGA 2560 and both the L and ON LEDs on, the

Chapter 7 • Fault Finding and Measurement

voltage drop across the fuse will be around 0.05V to 0.06V. As more current is drawn from the Arduino, so will the voltage drop across F1 increase.

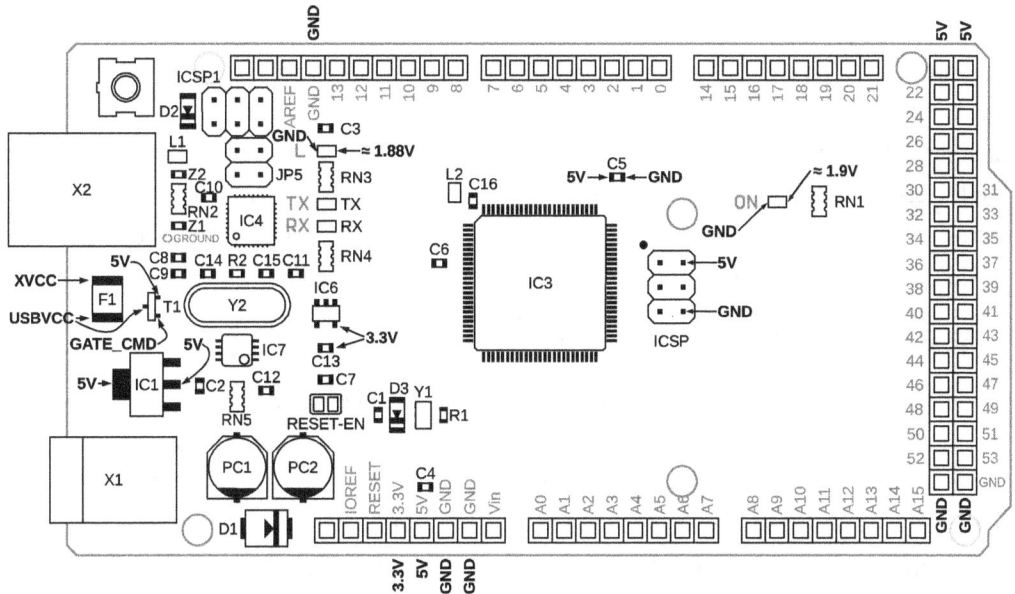

Figure 7.2: Voltage Test Points on an Arduino MEGA 2560 when USB Powered

USBVCC is fed into transistor T1, which switches it onto the 5V pins of the Arduino MEGA 2560 if no external power supply is present, and the Arduino is powered from USB alone. The voltage drop across the transistor, when it is on, between USBVCC and 5V is so small that it is insignificant. This 5V is then fed onto the output of the 5V regulator IC1, as can be seen in Figure 7.2, where 5V appears on the tab and middle pin of this regulator. Because of the internal protection diode in voltage regulator IC1, the 5V voltage appears on the input pin of this regulator where it drops to about 4.5V. Of course the 5V regulator is not used at all when the Arduino MEGA 2560 is powered from USB alone, but the 5V being fed back into IC1 is simply an effect of this regulator being in the circuit. This feedback voltage of around 4.5V can be measured on the Vin pin of the Arduino.

If 5V reaches the 3.3V regulator IC6, then 3.3V should be present on the Arduino MEGA 2560 3.3V pin. This voltage can also be measured directly on IC6, and on C13, as indicated in Figure 7.2. The output pin of the 3.3V regulator IC6 connects directly to C13.

7.3.1.3 Measuring Voltage on the L and ON LEDs

A voltage of around 1.9V will be measured on the ON LED at the end indicated in Figure 7.2. 5V is supplied to this LED from a resistor in resistor network pack RN3, and not RN1 that is close by it. RN1 provides pull-up resistors for the TWI bus SCL and SDA lines. Around 1.8V to 1.9V will be measured on the L LED as indicated in Figure 7.2. Both of these measurements are for a working board when both of these LEDs are on. Here is another subtle difference between the Arduino MEGA 2560 and the Arduino Uno – both the L LED and ON LED are rotated 180° around on the Arduino MEGA 2560. In other words GND is at the right of each LED and positive voltage at the left on an Arduino Uno board that is oriented in the same direction, with the USB connector at the left.

7.3.2 Powered from External Power Supply

When an Arduino MEGA 2560 is powered from external power alone, the input voltage can be measured on diode D1 at the PWRIN point as shown in Figure 7.3 on the next page. VIN is the input voltage on the other side of D1, which is the same as PWRIN minus the voltage drop across D1. The voltage drop across D1 is around 0.7V to 0.8V, which means that if the input voltage PWRIN is 12V, VIN will be around 11.3V. Note that the 0.7 to 0.8V drop across D1 is measured at low load. When current at the maximum rated value of 1.0A for this device is pulled through it, this voltage drop can be up to 1.1V.

When testing the voltages on an externally powered Arduino MEGA 2560, first make sure that PWRIN and VIN are present. VIN can be measured on the diode as indicated in Figure 7.3, and also on the Vin pin of the POWER header socket. If PWRIN and VIN are present on the board, make sure that it reaches the 5V regulator IC1. If IC1 is working properly, the regulated 5V will appear on the output pin of this device, as can be seen in Figure 7.3. If 5V is present on the output pin of the regulator, then it should be present at all of the other 5V measurement points indicated in the figure, including on the POWER header socket, and at the top of the double row socket at the end of the board. To make sure that 5V is reaching the main microcontroller, IC3, test for 5V across capacitor C5, and test for 5V on pin 2 of the 6-pin ICSP header.

After making sure that 5V is present on the board, check that 3.3V is present on the 3.3V pin of the POWER header socket. 3.3V should be present on IC6, which can also be measured on C13, as indicated in Figure 7.3. 3.3V is used as the reference voltage in the automatic switch circuit that switches USB 5V on if there is no external power, or powers

Chapter 7 • Fault Finding and Measurement

the circuit from 5V that is derived from external power if external power is connected. Refer back to Figure 4.2 in section 4.2 of chapter 4 for details of this circuit.

LED voltages of the L and ON LEDs can also be measured as shown in the Figure 7.3 for these devices when they are both on. Voltage values for the LEDs are approximate values and measured values should be close to these values, but don't have to match them exactly.

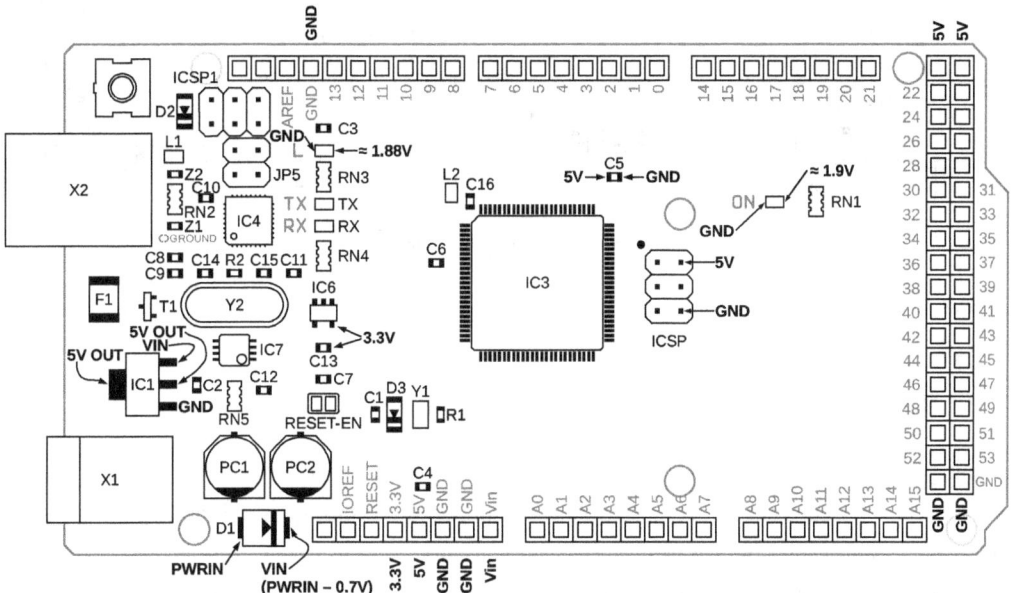

Figure 7.3: Measuring Voltage on an Externally Powered Arduino MEGA 2560

7.4 Waveform Patterns and Measurement

Although some multimeters can measure frequency, which can be useful to indicate the presence of an AC signal, one really needs an oscilloscope to properly measure and test an AC waveform pattern or signal. All oscilloscope measurements in this section were made with a PicoScope 2000 series digital PC oscilloscope, model number 2205A. This is a 25MHz bandwidth oscilloscope that is more likely to be used by hobbyists and makers on a budget. If using a different oscilloscope, make adjustments as necessary to the oscilloscope setups described in the text of this section. Figure 7.4 shows the test points that are used in the sections that follow to test for various AC waveforms.

Arduino MEGA 2560 Hardware Manual

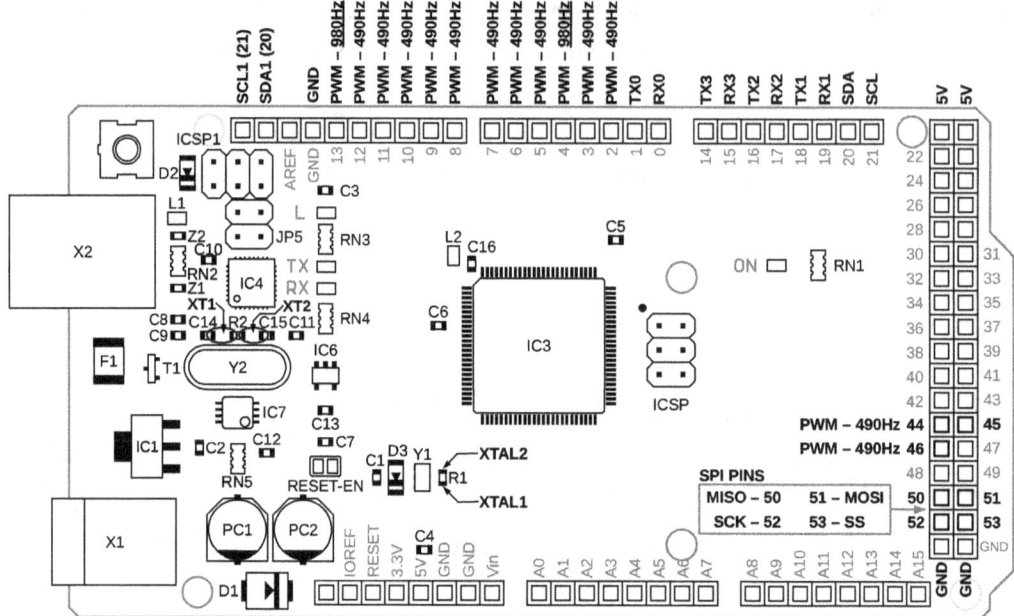

Figure 7.4: Test Points for Making Oscilloscope Measurements on an Arduino MEGA 2560

7.4.1 Testing for Presence of Microcontroller Clocks

Testing for the presence of the main clock frequency on a microcontroller can help to determine if the microcontroller is working or not. Both the main microcontroller and USB microcontroller each operate from a 16MHz clock that can be measured on the pins of these microcontrollers, or components attached to these pins. Test for the clock on IC3, the ATmega2560, at the points XTAL1 and XTAL2 marked in Figure 7.4.

Figure 7.5 shows the clock frequency measured on test point XTAL1 at R1 using a 25MHz bandwidth oscilloscope set to 50 ns/div and the probe set to 10X. As can be seen in the figure, the clock signal is distorted, attenuated and offset from 0V. The reason for the distortion is because the capacitance of the oscilloscope probe interferes with the oscillator circuit. Input capacitance of the probes supplied with the PicoScope 2205A is 14pF to 18pF when set to 10X, and even higher when set to 1X (70pF to 120pF). Some oscillator circuits will actually stop working when an oscilloscope probe is attached to them. Besides the probe capacitance problem, to capture a proper 16MHz signal, a much higher bandwidth oscilloscope is needed. In this basic test with a lower bandwidth oscilloscope, even though the signal appears distorted, it is still useful to indicate if the clock signal is present. Absence of a clock signal can also indicate that the fuse settings

Chapter 7 • Fault Finding and Measurement

of the ATmega2560 are incorrect, see section 5.4.4 for more details. The following was set on the oscilloscope to capture the clock frequency seen in Figure 7.5:

- A channel Probe set to ×10 by clicking A on the top toolbar
- Collection Time set to 50ms/div using the top toolbar
- Trigger Mode set to Auto, or Single for a single capture on the bottom toolbar
- Input Range left on Auto next to A on the top toolbar

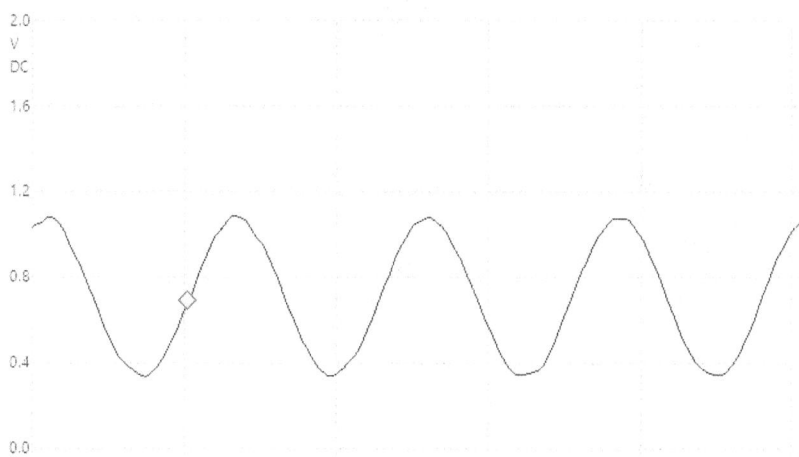

Figure 7.5: 16MHz Clock Frequency as it Appears on a 25MHz Bandwidth Oscilloscope

Measure the clock frequency of the USB microcontroller, the ATmega16U2 IC4, at the XT1 or XT2 test points as shown in Figure 7.4. This clock signal can be measured on C14 or C15, which also connect to either end of R2, as shown in the figure. Measuring at the XT1 point with the previous oscilloscope settings will produce a waveform identical to that of Figure 7.5. Again, the presence of this signal can help identify if the microcontroller is at least being clocked.

7.4.2 Testing for PWM Waveforms

Figure 7.6 shows a PWM signal or waveform from pin 2 of an Arduino MEGA 2560 running the sketch that follows on the next page. The sketch generates a 10% duty cycle square wave on pin 2. Use the sketch to generate PWM (Pulse Width Modulation) waveforms on each of the 15 PWM pins of the Arduino MEGA 2560. As can be seen in the comments of the sketch, each PWM pin is set to generate a square wave signal with a different duty cycle. Use the sketch as a reference when testing the PWM signals on an Arduino MEGA

2560 project. Each PWM pin can be tested in turn using the same oscilloscope channel for each pin. Refer back to Figure 7.4 for the PWM pins and frequencies. The two PWM pins that have 980Hz PWM frequencies are underlined in the figure. Refer to section 2.7.4.4 of chapter 2 for more information on PWM pins.

```
void setup() {
  analogWrite(2, 26);    // PWM 10% 490Hz
  analogWrite(3, 38);    // PWM 15% 490Hz
  analogWrite(4, 51);    // PWM 20% 980Hz
  analogWrite(5, 64);    // PWM 25% 490Hz
  analogWrite(6, 77);    // PWM 30% 490Hz
  analogWrite(7, 89);    // PWM 35% 490Hz
  analogWrite(8, 102);   // PWM 40% 490Hz
  analogWrite(9, 115);   // PWM 45% 490Hz
  analogWrite(10, 128);  // PWM 50% 490Hz
  analogWrite(11, 140);  // PWM 55% 490Hz
  analogWrite(12, 153);  // PWM 60% 490Hz
  analogWrite(13, 166);  // PWM 65% 980Hz
  analogWrite(44, 179);  // PWM 70% 490Hz
  analogWrite(45, 191);  // PWM 75% 490Hz
  analogWrite(46, 204);  // PWM 80% 490Hz
}

void loop() {
}
```

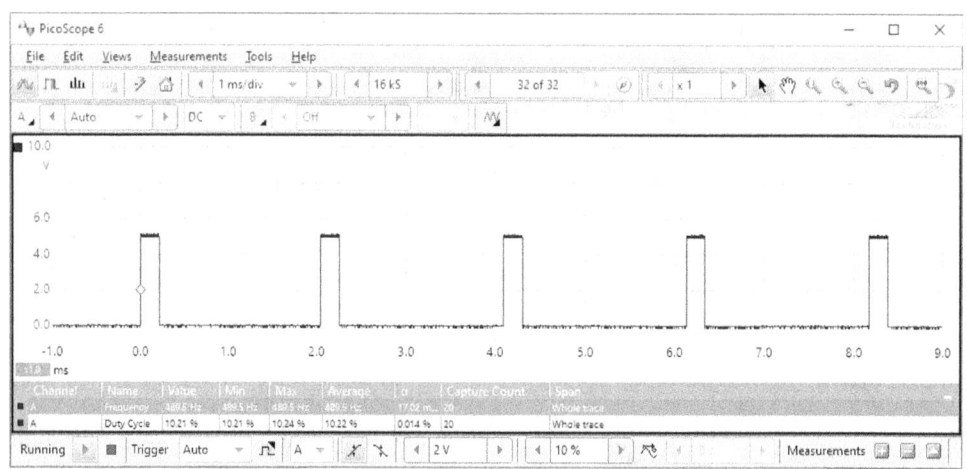

Figure 7.6: PWM Waveform with 10% Duty Cycle and Oscilloscope Settings

Oscilloscope settings for measuring PWM waveforms can be seen in Figure 7.6. Frequency and duty cycle of the measured waveform can be displayed, as seen near the

Chapter 7 • Fault Finding and Measurement

bottom of Figure 7.6, by clicking the + sign next to the Measurements label at the bottom right of the PicoScope window. After clicking the + sign, an Add Measurement dialog box pops up. In the dialog box, use the Select the type of measurement drop-down list to add Frequency. Click the + sign again to add Duty Cycle in the same way.

Figure 7.7 shows a sample of PWM waveforms from three different PWM pins of an Arduino MEGA 2560 running the sketch from the previous page. The top waveform has a 25% duty cycle and frequency of 490Hz measured on pin 5. Pin 13 generates a 65% duty cycle waveform at a frequency of 975Hz, and can be seen in the middle of the figure. The stated 980Hz PWM frequency for pin 13 and pin 4 in the Arduino documentation is rounded up from 975Hz. At the bottom of Figure 7.7 is an 80% duty cycle 490Hz PWM waveform measured on pin 46 of the Arduino.

Note that the duty cycle and frequency measurements will in most cases never be exact round numbers. This is partly because of component tolerances that do not produce exact frequencies. Duty cycles will seldom be exact because the calculated values will often have to be rounded up or down to produce an approximate value.

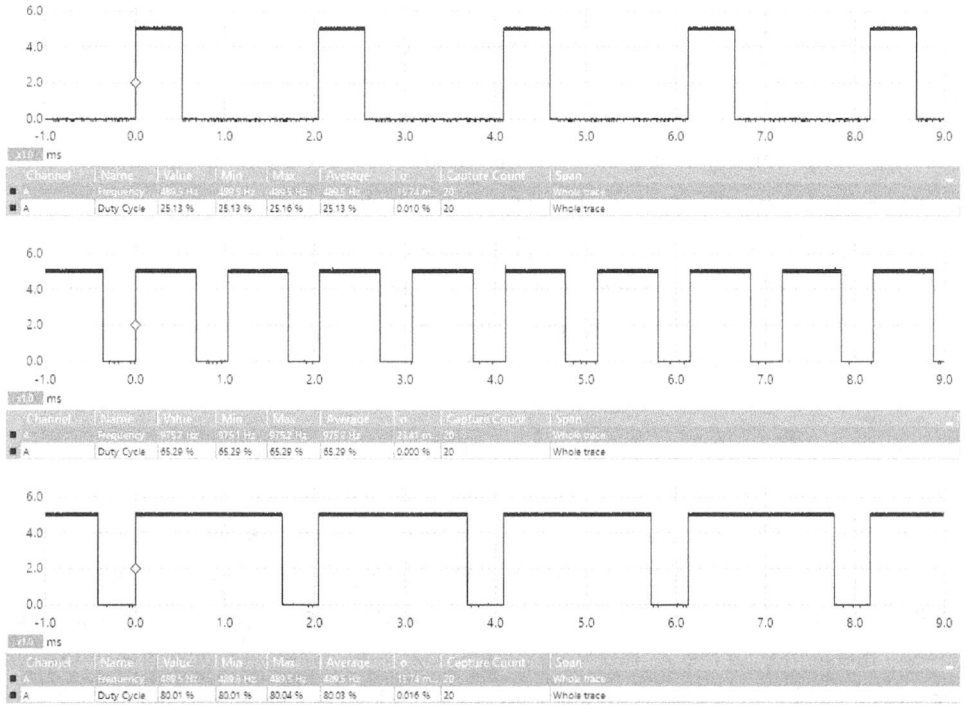

Figure 7.7: Sample PWM Waveforms from an Arduino MEGA 2560

7.4.3 Testing UART Outputs

A square wave can be generated on any of the UART transmit pins by sending an uppercase U character out of the serial port. The square wave signals can then be measured using an oscilloscope to see if the UART serial ports are working. Use the UART test sketch that follows to generate the square wave on pin 1 (TX0), pin 18 (TX1), pin 16 (TX2) and pin 14 (TX3) of an Arduino MEGA 2560. Modify the sketch as needed for your own tests, for example, initialize each UART with a different baud rate such as 1200, 2400, 4800 and 9600. This improves the test, as it can be used to verify that each UART is indeed generating its own output waveform.

```
void setup() {
  Serial.begin(9600);
  Serial1.begin(9600);
  Serial2.begin(9600);
  Serial3.begin(9600);
}

void loop() {
  Serial.print('U');    // Pin 1,  TX0
  Serial1.print('U');   // Pin 18, TX1
  Serial2.print('U');   // Pin 16, TX2
  Serial3.print('U');   // Pin 14, TX3
}
```

If the UARTs are working, a square wave with a 50% duty cycle and frequency of approximately 4.8kHz will be seen on the oscilloscope when measuring on each of the UART TX pins. The frequency will be 4.8kHz for a baud rate setting of 9600, as set in the above sketch. When the Serial Monitor window is opened from the Arduino IDE, the top line of the window will fill up with the letter 'U', which comes from pin 1 (TX0). This is the letter sent by Serial.print() in the sketch.

Some oscilloscopes such as the PicoScope can decode serial data, such as UART data. This can be useful when debugging a project that is sending and receiving serial port data using the UART. In the PicoScope software, the UART data can be decoded by selecting Tools ▶ Serial Decoding from the top menu. In the dialog box that pops up, click Create and then select UART (RS-232, RS-422, RS-485) near the bottom of the list that pops up. Although this item from the list has RS-232, RS-422 and RS-485 in brackets, it works with plain UART TTL level signals as well. A new UART dialog box opens which allows the oscilloscope channel to be selected as well as the UART settings for the UART under test.

Chapter 7 • Fault Finding and Measurement

Select the appropriate settings in the dialog box and then click the OK button. For example, if using oscilloscope channel A, and a baud rate of 9600 with the UART set up by the previous sketch, use the following settings:

- Data: A
- Threshold: 2 V
- Hysteresis: 500mV
- Baud Rate: 9.6 kbaud
- Data Bits: 8
- Parity: None
- Stop Bits: 1
- Bit Order: LSB

The oscilloscope software now decodes the UART signal and displays the data. For a baud rate of 9600, set the Collection Time to 200µs/div on the top toolbar to fit a complete data byte in the oscilloscope window with start and stop bits. Figure 7.8 shows the UART data from an Arduino MEGA 2560 running the sketch from the listing on the previous page.

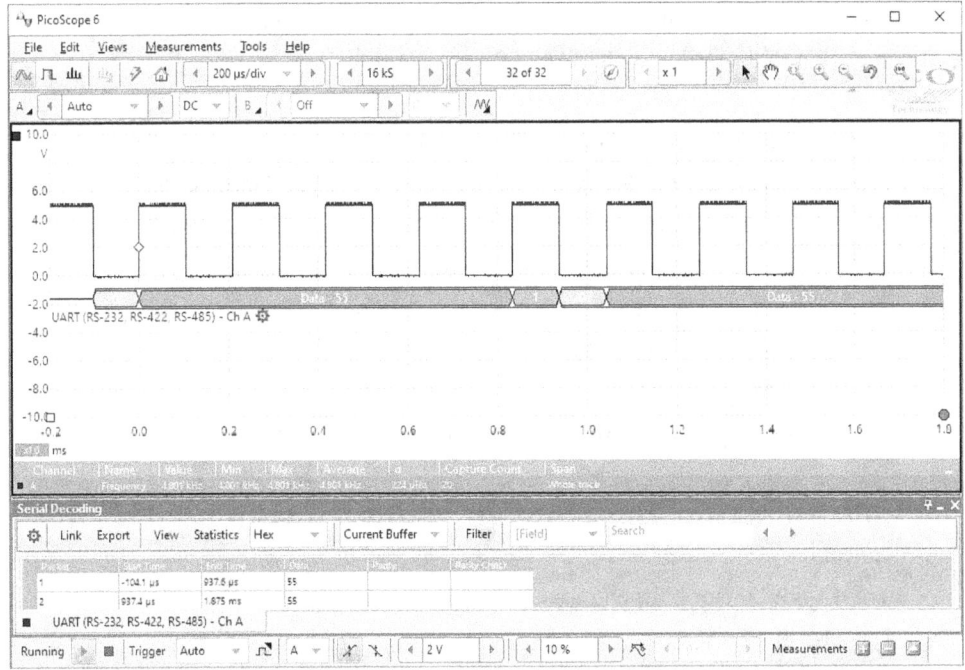

Figure 7.8: Arduino MEGA 2560 UART TX Signal and Data on a PicoScope

7.4.4 TWI Signals

A PicoScope 2205A can be set up to capture I²C or TWI signals which can aid in fault finding on projects that use TWI devices. The simple sketch below can be used to test the TWI bus signals without the need to attach a TWI device to this bus.

```
#include <Wire.h>

void setup() {
  Wire.begin();
  Wire.beginTransmission((0xA0 >> 1));
  Wire.write(0x00);
  Wire.endTransmission();
}

void loop() {
}
```

To capture TWI signals on an Arduino MEGA 2560 using a PicoScope oscilloscope, start by connecting oscilloscope channel A to Arduino pin 21 – the TWI SCL, or clock signal. Connect channel B of the oscilloscope to Arduino pin 20 – the TWI SDA, or data signal. Refer back to Figure 7.4, or Figure 3.16 from section 3.3.4 in chapter 3 for the TWI pinout on an Arduino MEGA 2560. TWI pins near the USB connector (SDA1 and SCL1) could be used instead, as these pins are directly connected to pin 20 and pin 21. Be sure to load the above sketch to the Arduino MEGA 2560 under test.

With the oscilloscope attached to the Arduino TWI pins as described, and the sketch loaded to the Arduino, start the PicoScope software. On the top PicoScope tool menu, enable channel B by changing it from the default Off to ±10V, also change channel A from the default Auto to ±10V, so that both channel A and B are now set to ±10V and DC. If the scope probes are set to 10X, use the drop down menu for channel A and then B on the top toolbar to select x10 for the Probe setting on each channel. Select Tools ▶ Serial Decoding from the top menu and then click Create in the dialog box that pops up. On the menu that pops out, click I2C. Change settings in the I2C dialog box as follows:

- Data: B
- Clock: A
- Threshold: 1V (for both channels)
- Hysteresis: 20mV
- Bus Speed: Standard-mode (100 kbits/s)

Chapter 7 • Fault Finding and Measurement

Click OK in the dialog box after making the changes. Click OK in the Serial Decoding dialog box to close it. Set the Collection Time setting on the top toolbar to 50 µs/div.

By default the oscilloscope should be stopped, if not, click the stop button on the bottom toolbar at the left. On the same toolbar, change the Trigger setting to Single. Now click the green start button on the bottom toolbar at the left. Move the yellow trigger level symbol on the oscilloscope area of the screen up above 0V, and to the left of the screen so that the Threshold is around 2V and Pre-trigger about 10%, as can be seen on the bottom toolbar – hover the mouse cursor over the boxes on the toolbar so that the tool tip pops up to help identify each field. Finally press the RESET button on the Arduino to start the TWI sketch running. If all is set up correctly, the TWI communications will be displayed in the oscilloscope display area of the screen. Click B on the top menu to pop the B channel menu out and then use the Offset field to move the B channel below the A channel signal for easier viewing, by setting it to a negative value. About -30% should be fine.

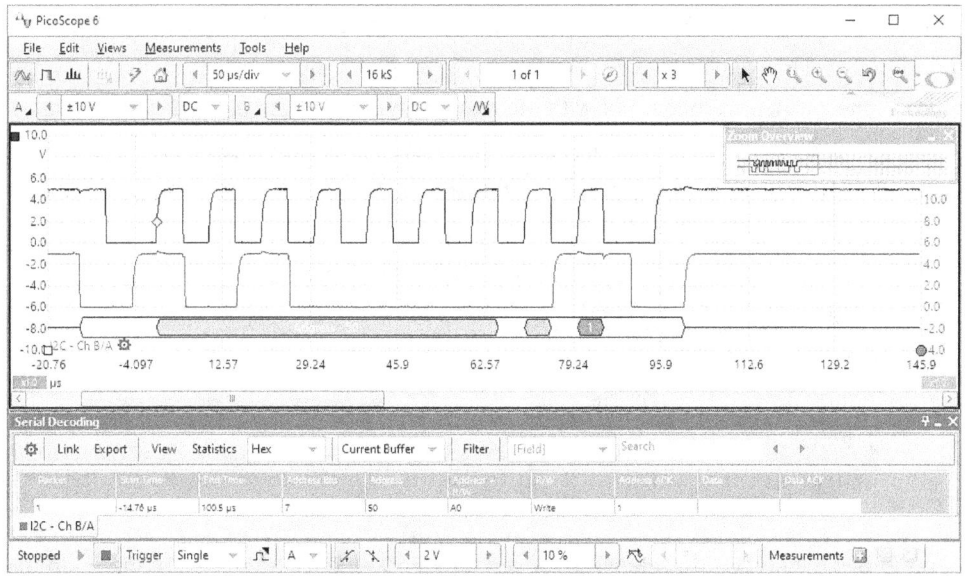

Figure 7.9: Arduino TWI Signals Captured on an Oscilloscope

Figure 7.9 shows the TWI signals captured while running the sketch from the previous page. The TWI clock or SCL is at the top of the figure and the data, or SDA signal, is below it. A zoom of × 3 was applied to the signals using the Horizontal Zoom field on the top toolbar of the PicoScope window.

Arduino MEGA 2560 Hardware Manual

7.4.5 SPI Signals

To capture SPI signals on a PicoScope, load the following sketch to the Arduino MEGA 2560. The sketch simply sends a character out on the MOSI pin continually (digital pin 51). Refer back to Figure 7.4, or to Figure 3.18 in section 3.3.5 of chapter 3 for the location of the SPI pins.

```
#include <SPI.h>

void setup() {
  SPI.begin();
  SPI.beginTransaction(SPISettings(10000, MSBFIRST, SPI_MODE1));
}

void loop() {
  SPI.transfer('U');
  delay(1);
}
```

Connect channel A of the PicoScope to Arduino pin 52 (SCK) and channel B to Arduino pin 51 (MOSI). The oscilloscope must now be set up much the same as it was for TWI signals in the previous section, but with the exception that SPI is selected in the Serial Decoding dialog box, and a higher collection time and higher number of samples is selected in order to get a decent signal on the scope. The PicoScope is set up as follows:

- Channel A and B: ±10V, DC, Probe x10 (if probes set to 10X)
- Collection Time: 200 ms/div
- Number of Samples: 2 MS
- Trigger: Single
- Threshold: 2V
- Pre-trigger: 0%

Open the SPI dialog box by selecting Tools ▶ Serial Decoding from the top menu. In the Serial Decoding dialog box, click the Create button and then select SPI from the menu that pops up. Choose the following settings in the SPI dialog box.

Channels:
- Data: B
- Clock: A

Chapter 7 • Fault Finding and Measurement

- Threshold (both):   1V
- Hysteresis (both):   20mV
- Clock Edge: Rising
- Chip Select: Leave blank

Configuration:

- Clock Edge: Rising
- Chip Select State: Low (does not matter because this signal is not connected)
- Bit Order: MSB

Display:

- Display packets in: ASCII (for Graph and Table)

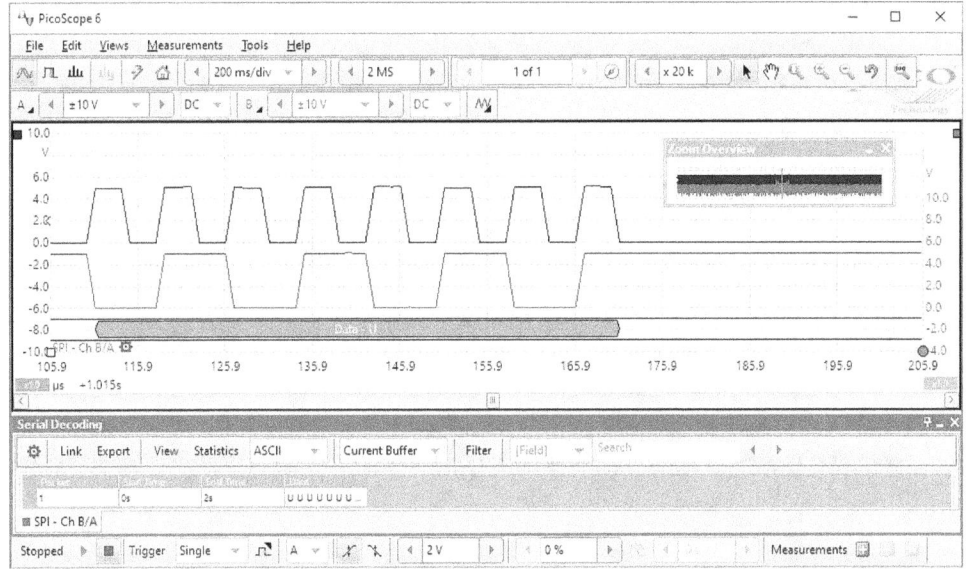

Figure 7.10: Arduino MEGA 2560 SPI Signals Captured on a PicoScope

Click OK in the SPI dialog box after changing the settings. Click OK in the Serial Decoding dialog box to close it. Click the green button on the bottom toolbar at the left to start capturing the SPI signals.

When the oscilloscope stops capturing, zoom in using the Horizontal Zoom control on the top toolbar. Offset the data signal from the clock signal by clicking B on the top toolbar and then using the Offset control to change the offset to -30%. To get a decent view of a data

199

character, it is necessary to zoom in to about x5k to x20k. The captured data should then look something like Figure 7.10. Because ASCII was selected in the PicoScope software SPI settings, the data is displayed as an ASCII character – the uppercase 'U' that is sent by the Arduino sketch can be seen in the Data field on the oscilloscope display.

Chapter 8 • Mechanical Dimensions and Templates

Dimensions of the Arduino MEGA 2560 as well as positioning and size of its mounting holes are presented in this chapter.

Dimensions are useful when making an Arduino MEGA 2560 clone board, making a shield to fit an Arduino MEGA 2560, when measuring for placing an Arduino project in an enclosure or when drilling a base plate for mounting.

Rather than including all of the dimensions and sizes on a single drawing, they have been spread over several drawings to prevent clutter and for easier reference.

In this Chapter

- Measurements, tolerance and scale
- Arduino MEGA 2560 length, width and mass
- Arduino MEGA 2560 and shield dimensions and spacing

8.1 Measurements, Tolerance and Scale

The Arduino MEGA 2560 board was designed with the Eagle EDA CAD software package using thousands of an inch as the unit of measurement (a thousandth of an inch is also referred to as a mil). Inches are therefore the "official" measurement system of the board. Dimensions in this chapter are given in inches as well as millimeters. All dimensions are subject to manufacturing tolerances so the actual board size may vary slightly from the measurements given.

Images in this chapter are not to scale. Refer to wspublishing.net for an image of the Arduino MEGA 2560 that can be printed to scale and used as a template for drilling a base plate when mounting an Arduino. Also find Arduino MEGA 2560 drill templates at the very back of this book after the index.

8.2 Length, Width and Mass

Table 8.1 and Figure 8.1 show the length and width of the Arduino MEGA 2560 board as well as the overall length when including the USB connector. As the board was designed using inches, millimeter values have been converted from inches.

Table 8.1: Arduino MEGA 2560 Dimensions

Measurement	Inches	Millimeters	Arduino
Board Length	4 in	101.6 mm	101.52 mm
Board Width	2.1 in	53.34 mm	53.3 mm
Length with USB Connector	4.25 in	107.95 mm	–

The size of the Arduino MEGA 2560 PCB, or printed circuit board, is given as 4 inches long by 2.1 inches wide. This works out to 101.6mm long by 53.34mm wide. As can be seen in the right column of Table 8.1, dimensions given by Arduino on the Arduino MEGA 2560 REV3 page are 101.52mm long by 53.3mm wide. These values were taken from the page at the time of writing.

Weight of the board is given as 37g (thirty seven grams) on the Arduino MEGA 2560 REV3 web page which works out to 1.31oz (one point three one ounces). Measurements taken on two Arduino MEGA 2560 boards gave a mass of 34g or 1.2oz for one, and 36g or

1.27oz for the other. The clear plastic base that is packaged with new Arduino MEGA 2560 REV3 boards has a mass of 15g or 0.53oz. These measurements are of course dependent on the tolerance of the weighing scale used.

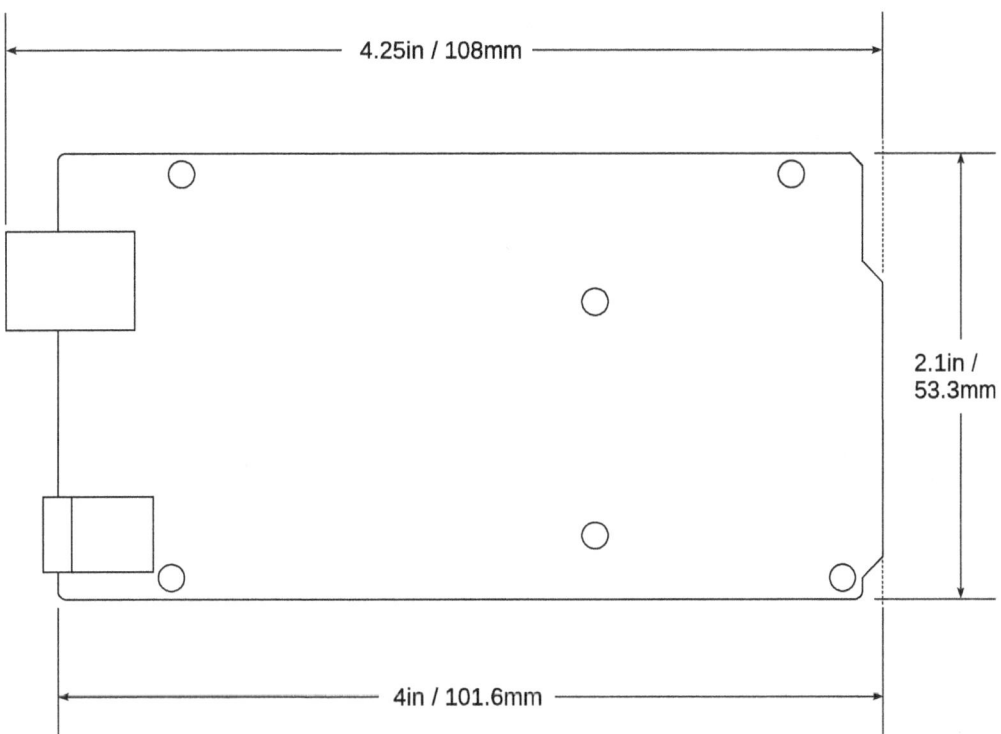

Figure 8.1: Arduino MEGA 2560 Length and Width

8.3 Mounting Hole Spacing and Size

Arduino MEGA 2560 boards have six mounting holes, four near to the corners of the board, but all offset from the corners, one near the main ICSP header, and one near the edge of the board at the A6 analog pin. Hole size diameter of all mounting holes is 3.2mm or 0.126 inch. Figure 8.2 shows the distances between the mounting holes and edges of the board. Although the hole diameters are in metric, or millimeters, the position of the holes are in imperial or inches – these measurements are displayed in inches and converted to millimeters in the figure.

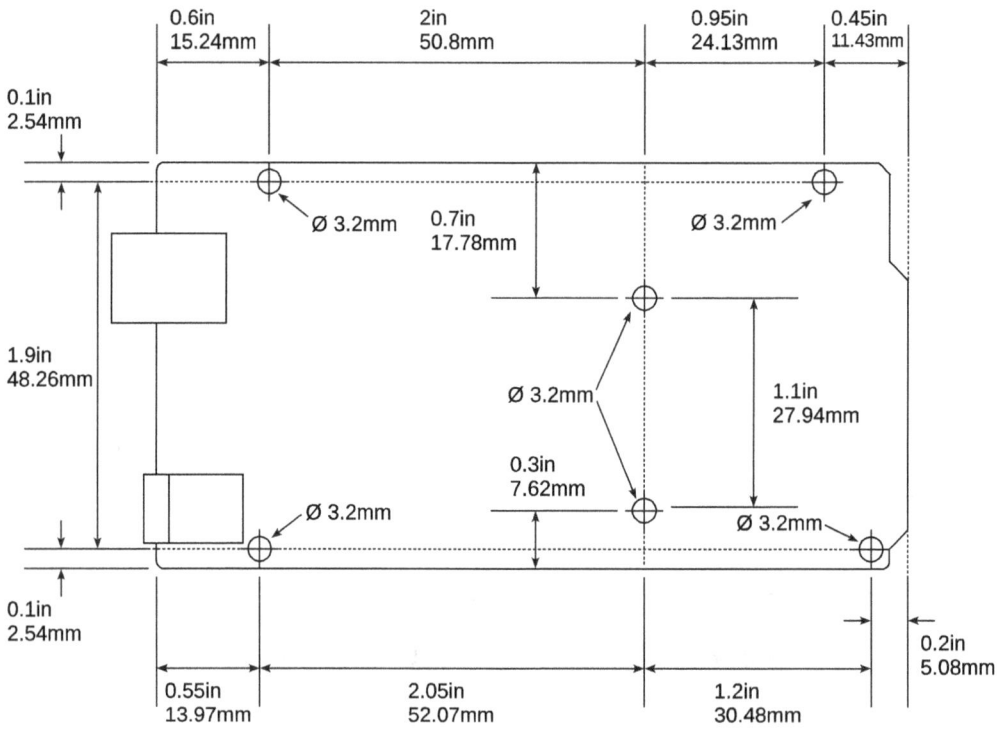

Figure 8.2: Arduino MEGA 2560 Hole Spacing and Dimensions

Mounting holes were placed on the board in Eagle EDA using a grid of 100mills except for the bottom left hole (near the external power input in Figure 8.2), and the top right hole, which were both placed using a 50mil grid. These two mounting holes are both on a horizontal 100mil grid line, but on a vertical 50mil grid line.

Chapter 8 • Mechanical Dimensions and Templates

8.4 Shape Dimensions

Shape dimensions refers to the irregular cutout of Arduino MEGA 2560 boards which have a particular shape cut out at the end of the board. Figure 8.3 shows the dimensions for the cutout shape.

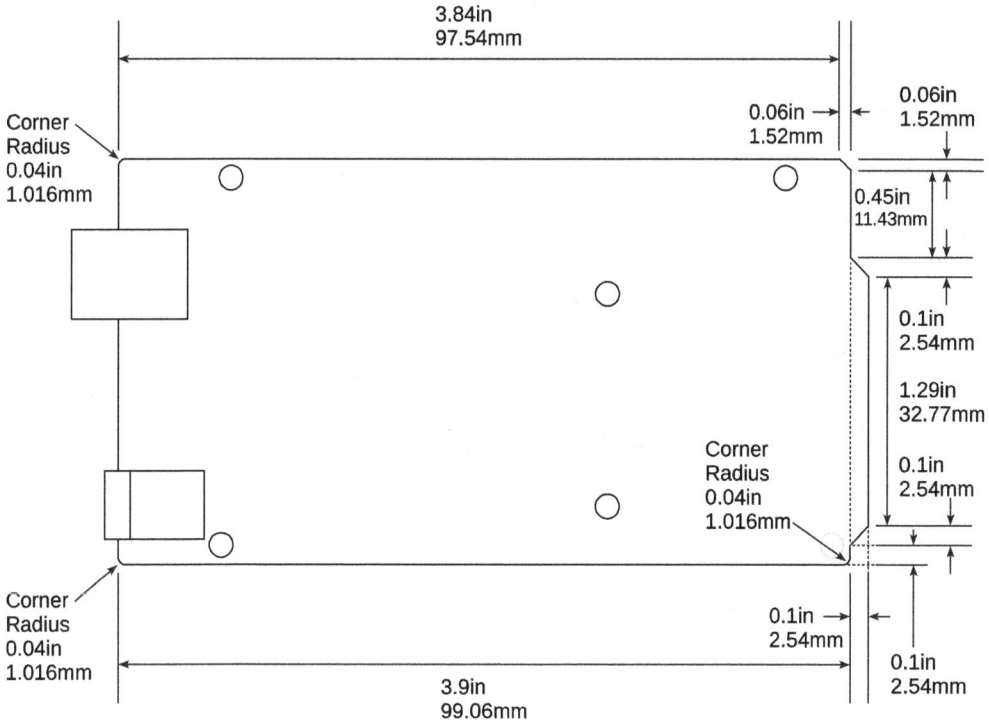

Figure 8.3: Arduino MEGA 2560 Shape Dimensions

8.5 Header Positions

Figure 8.4 shows the positions for the header sockets at the edges of an Arduino MEGA 2560 and the ICSP header near the middle of the board. These header socket positions are needed when making a shield that fits on top of the Arduino MEGA 2560 and plugs into the header sockets. Some shields also plug into the ICSP header in addition to plugging into the header sockets, for example the Ethernet shield.

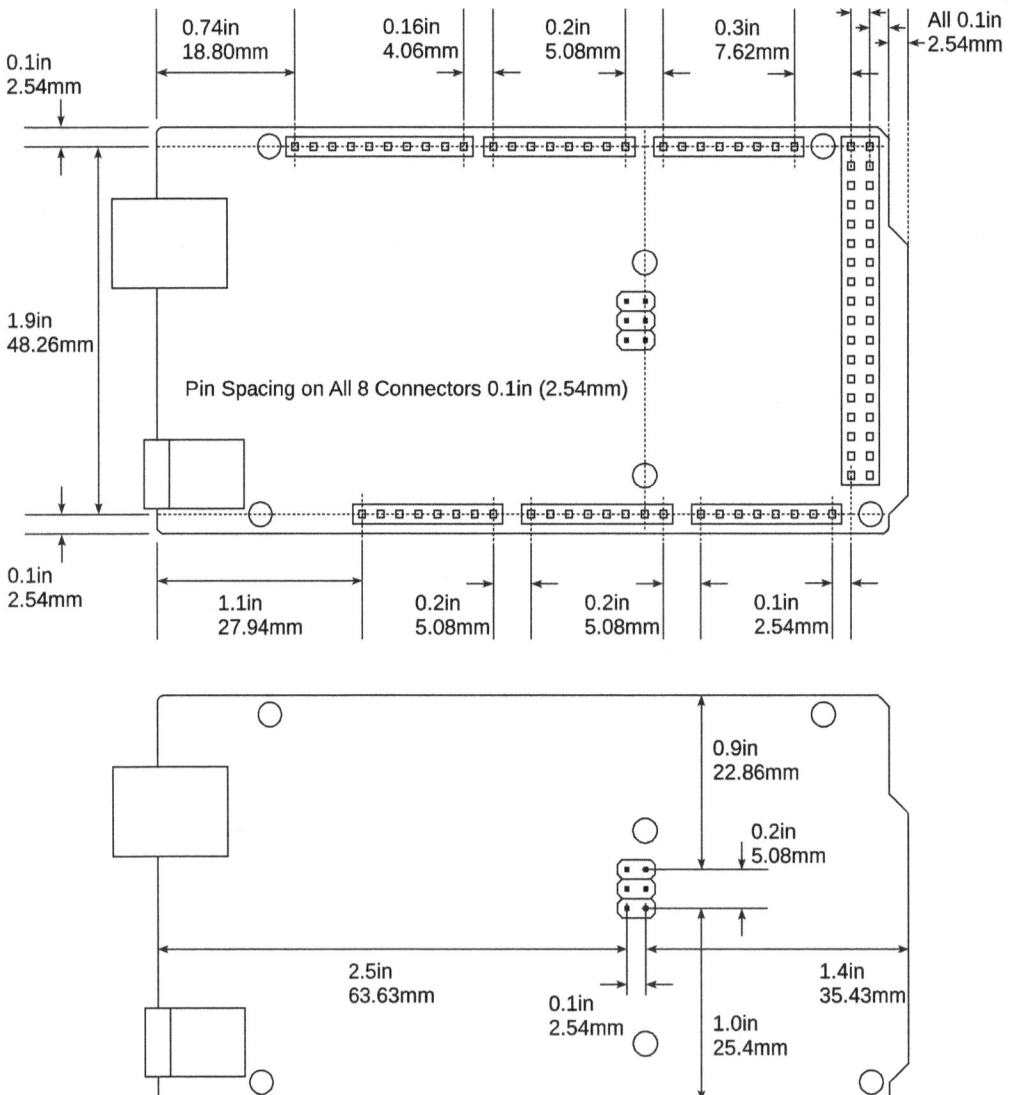

Figure 8.4: Arduino MEGA 2560 Header Positions

Chapter 8 • Mechanical Dimensions and Templates

8.6 Shield Reverse Connection Protection

Figure 8.5 shows that all of the header sockets on the Arduino MEGA 2560 are aligned to a 0.1in or 100mil vertical grid lines, except for the top left header in the figure that is offset from this grid. A shield that has pins underneath it with the same spacing can not be plugged in the wrong way around because of the offset header that provides reverse connection protection. This protects the Arduino MEGA 2560 from having both the small Arduino Uno sized form factor shield, or full sized Arduino MEGA 2560 sized shield, being plugged in the wrong way around.

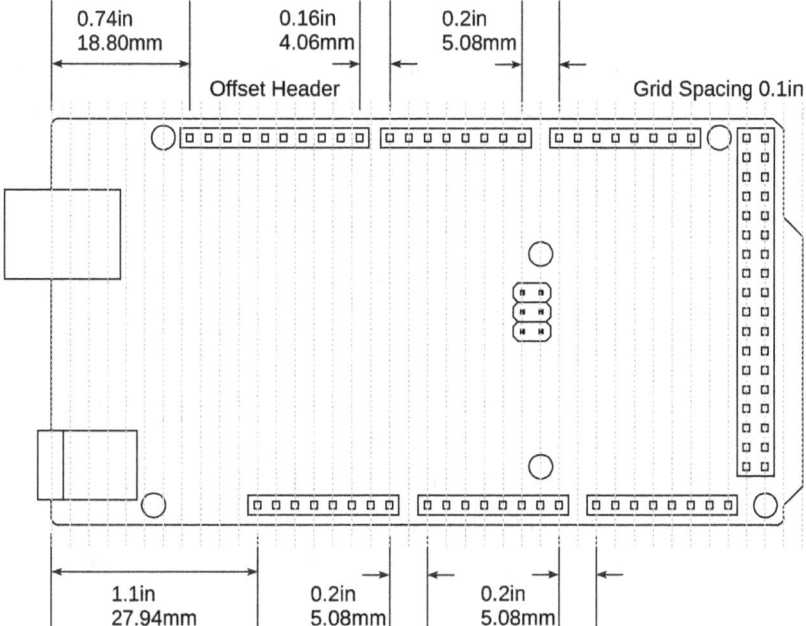

Figure 8.5: Shield Reverse Connection Protection with Offset Header

8.7 Using Strip-board as a Shield

Strip-board, also known by the brand name Veroboard, can be used to make a shield, one problem being that the offset header that is shown in the previous section does not line up with the holes in the strip-board. If the pins on the offset header are not needed, they can be left unconnected. An alternative is to solder header pins into the strip-board that have long pins, which can then be bent to fit into the offset header. Another problem with strip-board on an Arduino MEGA 2560 is with the double row connector at the end of the board. Connecting strips on the strip-board short out all of the pins down a row. Either each strip must be cut between every pin on these two rows, which is difficult and tedious, or the strip-board must not be attached to the double row connector at the end of the board. Using a prototype shield is another method that can be used to make a shield, as was discussed in section 1.1.6.2 of chapter 1.

8.8 Drill Template and KiCad Template

A drill template, in PDF format, for the mounting holes on an Arduino MEGA 2560 that can be used when drilling a base plate for mounting an Arduino MEGA 2560 is available for readers of this book. Be sure to print the file using a 1 to 1 scale so that the printed template is correctly sized. Go to the supporting website at wspublishing.net to find the drill template file. Also find Arduino MEGA 2560 drill templates at the very back of this book after the index. Measure the 1 inch or 1cm marking on these templates before using them to make sure that the printing process did not resize these templates in any way.

Find a KiCad template of an Arduino MEGA 2560 board at wspublishing.net which can be used to create both a custom Arduino MEGA 2560 board or shield that fits the Arduino MEGA 2560 shape and size. KiCad is an open-source EDA CAD package that can be used to draw circuit diagrams and design printed circuit boards. The KiCad software package can be found at kicad-pcb.org where it can be downloaded free of charge and unrestricted.

Chapter 9 • Arduino Shield Compatibility

This chapter looks at what makes Arduino shields either compatible or incompatible with different Arduino models.

Four different Arduino models are used as examples to show shield compatibility problems and solutions.

Examples of commercially available shields are used to show why some shields are compatible with different Arduino models, while others only work on certain models.

In this Chapter

- Issues to consider that make shields compatible between different Arduino models

- Four different Arduino models used to show the compatibilities and the incompatibilities between them

- Practical examples of shields that have incompatibilities and others that are compatible across different Arduino boards

9.1 Shield Compatibility Considerations

The aim of this chapter is to explain Arduino shield compatibility issues for the purpose of understanding why some shields only work with some Arduino boards or models, while not with others. This chapter is also for those Arduino users who want to design shields or build prototype shields that are compatible between various Arduino models.

Although it is not mandatory to design shields that are compatible across a range of Arduino models, compatibility makes a shield more useful.

9.2 Shield Compatibility Between Arduino Models

There are five main issues when it comes to compatibility of shields between different Arduino models. This section looks at the issues that must be considered, namely shield size, shield voltage, SPI pin compatibility, TWI pin compatibility and shield stacking.

9.2.1 Shield Size

As we have already seen in this manual, an Arduino Uno sized shield can fit both an Arduino Uno sized Arduino board and an Arduino MEGA 2560 sized board. In this chapter, an Arduino Uno size shield is referred to as a half-size shield, and an Arduino MEGA 2560 size shield is referred to as a full-size shield. "Arduino board" or "Arduino boards" refer to any Arduino model or models.

Although a full-size shield will plug into a half-size Arduino, such as an Arduino Uno, the extra pins at the edges of the full-size shield will obviously not plug into anything on the Arduino and will overhang. It is therefore much more likely that a half-size shield will be made to be compatible between both Arduino sizes, while a full-size shield will be made to be compatible with full-size Arduino boards only.

9.2.2 Shield Voltage

Arduino boards operate at one of two voltages, either 5V or 3.3V. This voltage difference causes shield compatibility problems. The IOREF pin was added to newer Arduino board models to allow a shield to detect at which voltage an Arduino board is operating. The shield can then switch voltage level converters in, or simply power the shield from the Arduino board operating voltage. Current rating of the 5V and 3.3V pins must also be taken into consideration, as they vary greatly between models.

Chapter 9 • Arduino Shield Compatibility

9.2.3 SPI Pin Compatibility

The position of the SPI pins on different Arduino models can vary, as was already pointed out in this manual. Shields will only be compatible between many different Arduino models if SPI pins from the ICSP header are used.

9.2.4 TWI Pin Compatibility

TWI pin compatibility has been resolved on new Arduino board models by duplicating the TWI pins at the end of the header socket near the USB connector. It is important to use these duplicated pins in order to make compatible shields. For example, on older Arduino Uno models, TWI pins were only available on analog pins A4 and A5. On Arduino MEGA boards, TWI pins were only available on pins 20 and 21. By duplicating the TWI pins in a common place on new Arduino boards, compatible shields can now be made.

9.2.5 Shield Stacking

When designing a shield it is important to think about compatibility between different shields. While buses such as SPI and TWI buses can be shared between many shields stacked on an Arduino, other pins can not be shared. As an example, the SPI bus needs to individually address each device on the bus. Although the SPI bus shares data and clock lines, each SPI device needs its own address or chip select line, which is simply a spare Arduino digital pin. Other shields must be looked at to see which pins are used for this SPI chip select line, so that the same pin is not used on a shield that is to be compatible.

Some shields can not be stacked because of their mechanical layout. An example is a joystick shield, and LCD shield. If the LCD shield is stacked on the joystick shield, then it blocks access to the joystick. On the other hand, if the joystick shield is stacked on the LCD shield, the LCD screen can not be seen, as the joystick shield blocks it.

9.3 Compatibility Between Four Arduino Models

Four Arduino models have been chosen for comparison to show compatibility and incompatibility issues in this section. Two full-size Arduino boards, the Arduino MEGA 2560 and Arduino Due operate at 5V and 3.3V respectively. Two half-size Arduino boards, the Arduino Uno and Arduino Zero operate at 5V and 3.3V respectively. These four boards were chosen as they include a full-size 5V board, full size 3.3V board, half-size 5V board and half-size 3.3V board, covering all possibilities of size and voltage. These four boards can be seen in Figure 9.1 to Figure 9.4, placed on facing pages for easier comparison.

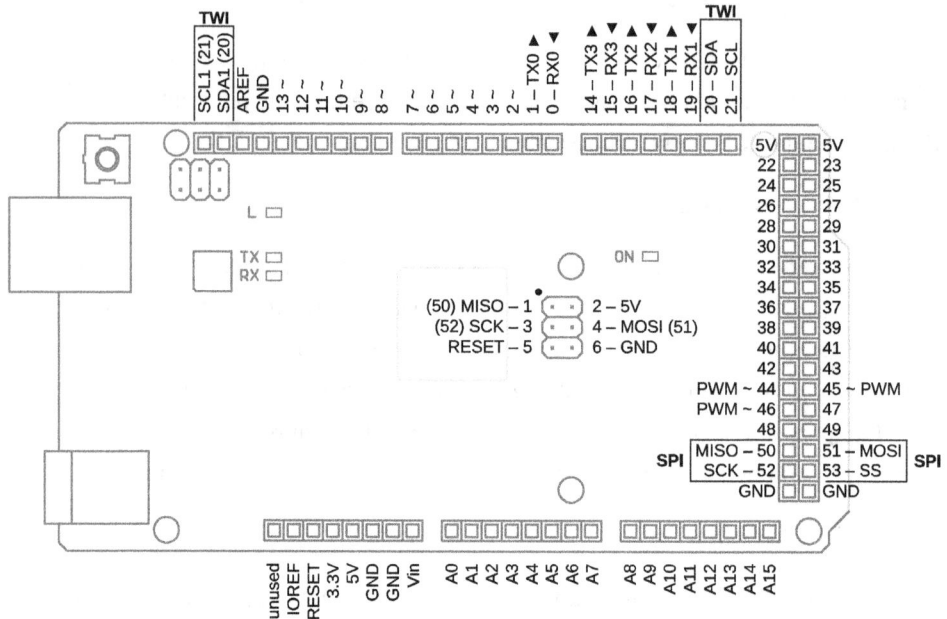

Figure 9.1: Arduino MEGA 2560 Pinout with TWI and SPI Pins Highlighted

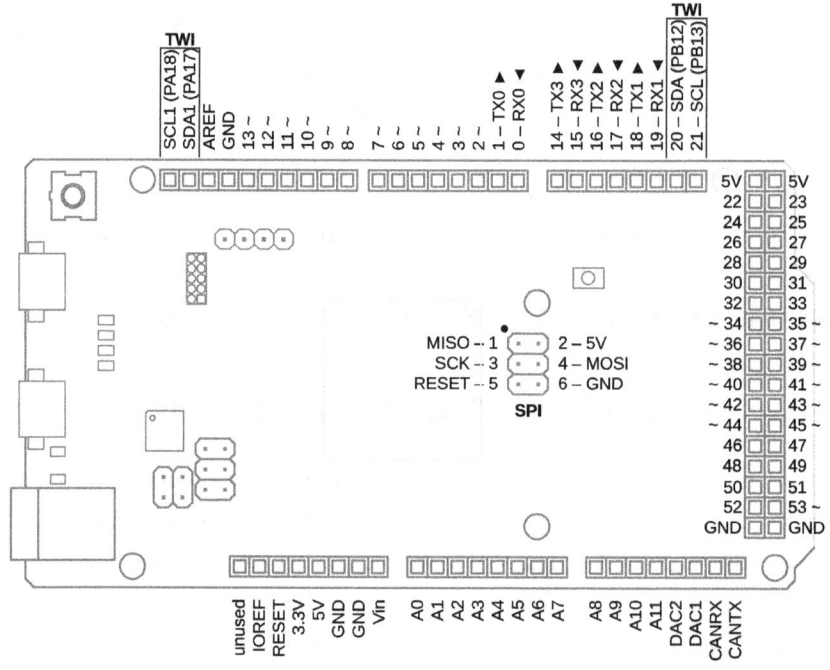

Figure 9.2: Arduino Due Pinout with TWI and SPI Pins Highlighted

Chapter 9 • Arduino Shield Compatibility

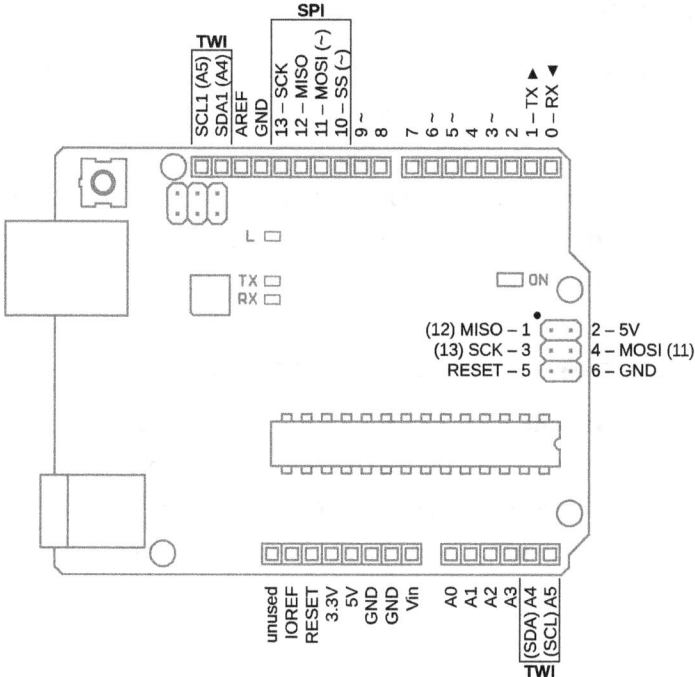

Figure 9.3: Arduino Uno Pinout with TWI and SPI Pins Highlighted

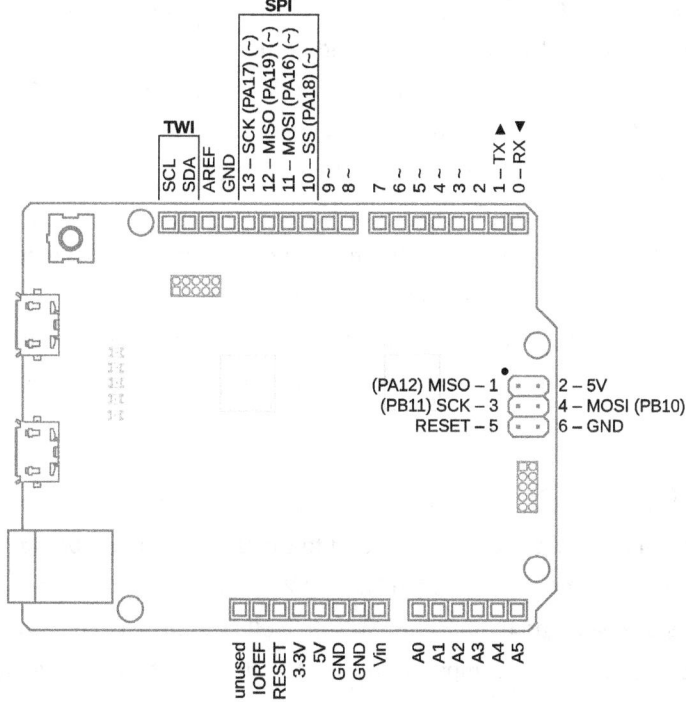

Figure 9.4: Arduino Zero Pinout with TWI and SPI Pins Highlighted

9.3.1 Arduino MEGA 2560

Figure 9.1 shows the **5V** Arduino MEGA 2560 pinout with TWI and SPI pins highlighted. This should be very familiar by now, as this book specifically targets the Arduino MEGA 2560, and all of these pins have been covered in the preceding chapters. Table 9.1 summarizes the maximum current available from the 5V and 3.3V pins. It is important to consider how much current can be drawn from the power pins, especially when aiming to make shields compatible.

Table 9.1: Arduino MEGA 2560 Current

Voltage	Current
5V pin when externally powered	800mA
5V pin when USB powered	500mA
3.3V pin	150mA

9.3.2 Arduino Due

Figure 9.2 shows the **3.3V** Arduino Due pinout with TWI and SPI pins highlighted. The Due has two separate sets of TWI pins, unlike the Arduino MEGA 2560 that joins pin 20 and 21 to SDA1 and SCL1 at the opposite end of the board. As can be seen in Figure 9.2, the Due has Arduino pin 20 and 21 connecting to microcontroller pins PB12 and PB13. The second set of TWI pins is found at the opposite end of the board with SCL1 and SDA1 connecting to microcontroller pins PA18 and PA17.

SPI pins are only found on the SPI/ICSP header near the middle of the board. Although the Arduino Due pinout diagram from the Arduino website shows that pins 10 to 13 are also SPI pins, there is no indication from the microcontroller datasheet that these pins have SPI capability. In any case, they are separate pins from the ones on the SPI/ICSP header.

Because the Arduino Due is a 3.3V board, it has a 3.3V regulator that can supply much more current to the main microcontroller, and to the 3.3V pin of the board, than the Arduino MEGA 2560. As can be seen in Table 9.2, the current rating for the 5V pins of the Arduino Due is the same as the Arduino MEGA 2560. The difference is with the 3.3V pin that can supply up to 800mA compared to only 150mA from the 3.3V pin on the Arduino MEGA 2560. Current on the Due 3.3V pin is limited to below 500mA when USB powered.

Table 9.2: Arduino Due Current

Voltage	Current
5V pin when externally powered	800mA
5V pin when USB powered	500mA
3.3V pin	800mA

9.3.3 Arduino Uno

Figure 9.3 shows the **5V** Arduino Uno pinout with TWI and SPI pins highlighted. On the Uno, both the TWI pins and SPI pins are duplicated. The TWI pins connect A4 and A5 from one side of the board to SDA1 and SCL1 on the other side of the board. SPI pins connect Arduino pins 11 to 13 to the ICSP header. Table 9.3 shows the Uno power pin current rating.

Table 9.3: Arduino Uno Current

Voltage	Current
5V pin when externally powered	1A
5V pin when USB powered	500mA
3.3V pin	150mA

9.3.4 Arduino Zero

Figure 9.4 shows the **3.3V** Arduino Zero pinout with TWI and SPI pins highlighted. The Zero has one set of TWI pins next to the AREF pin. It has two separate SPI channels, one on the ICSP header and one on pins 10 to 13. Table 9.4 shows the Arduino Zero power pin current rating. Current on the Zero 3.3V pin is limited to below 500mA when USB powered.

Table 9.4: Arduino Zero Current

Voltage	Current
5V pin when externally powered	800mA
5V pin when USB powered	500mA
3.3V pin	800mA

9.4 Arduino Shield Pin Compatibility

The four Arduino shields shown in the previous section have what is known as the *Arduino 1.0 pinout*. Arduino 1.0 pinout is an upgrade to older Arduino boards and adds TWI pins next to the AREF pin, as well as the IOREF pin on the power pin header socket. As can be seen from Figures 9.1 to 9.4, Arduino pins are only compatible if the TWI pins next to the AREF pin are used, and SPI pins are taken off the ICSP header. Only new boards with the 1.0 pinout are considered in this chapter. Figure 9.5 shows pins that are common and therefore compatible between the four Arduino models previously discussed. A discussion of the pins seen in Figure 9.5 is found in the sub-sections that follow.

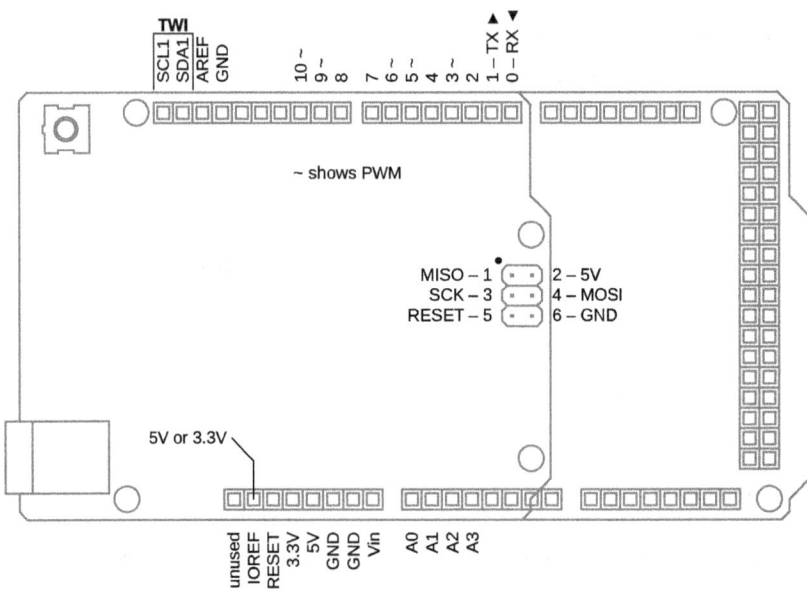

Figure 9.5: Compatible Pins Across Four Arduino Models

9.4.1 TWI Pins

As has already been discussed, the TWI pins next to the AREF pins are the only TWI pins that can be used for proper compatibility. Be aware that on the Arduino MEGA 2560, anything that is connected to these TWI pins also ends up being connected to pins 20 and 21 via the tracks on the Arduino MEGA 2560 board. On the Arduino Uno, anything that is connected to these TWI pins also connects to analog pins A4 and A5. This is not the case with the Arduino Due and the Arduino Zero that both have separate TWI pins that do not connect to anything else on their boards.

9.4.2 SPI Pins

For proper SPI compatibility between different Arduino boards, only the SPI pins from the ICSP header must be used. Because SPI also needs a separate address line or chip select line for each SPI device, a digital pin must be selected for each SPI device that does not conflict with any other SPI device on the bus.

On an Arduino MEGA 2560, whatever connects to the SPI pins on the ICSP header also connects to the SPI pins on digital pins 50, 51 and 52. On the Arduino MEGA 2560, the SS pin, digital pin 53, must always be set up as an output when using the SPI bus. On an Arduino Uno, whatever connects to the SPI pins on the ICSP header also connects to digital pins 11, 12 and 13. In both cases of SPI on the Arduino MEGA 2560 and Arduino Uno, be sure not to use the duplicate SPI pins for anything else. It can be easy to forget that they are duplicated pins and try to used them as digital I/O pins.

9.4.3 Digital Pins

Only digital pins 0 to 10 are common between all four Arduino models discussed. These pins are not duplicated anywhere, so are safe to use as normal digital I/O pins. Remember that digital pins 0 and 1 also connect to the USB bridge chip and will receive data whenever serial data is sent and received from this chip.

9.4.4 Analog Pins

Analog pins A0 to A3 are the only analog pins that are available on all four Arduino models shown in this chapter. A4 and A5 have been left off Figure 9.5 because they are used for TWI on the Arduino Uno. If A0 to A3 are not needed as analog inputs, they can be used as digital I/O pins instead, as already described in this manual.

9.4.5 Power Pins

Power pins on the power header socket connector are identical on all Arduino models discussed in this chapter. Remember that the IOREF pin will be at 5V for 5V Arduino boards, and at 3.3V for 3.3V Arduino boards. Use this pin to detect which voltage to use for a shield.

When deciding whether or not to use the 3.3V pin to power a shield, or a particular chip on a shield, remember that this is limited to 150mA by the Arduino MEGA 2560 and Arduino Uno models. In many cases, if 3.3V is needed, it will be better to use the 5V and step it down to 3.3V using a 3.3V regulator on the shield.

9.5 Example of Shield Compatibility Problems

In this section, we look at some problems and issues on two different shields. We also look at the design of these shields to see how certain problems were overcome by the designers of the shields. The two example shields are a data logger shield and Arduino Ethernet shield.

9.5.1 Data Logger Shield Example

The design of the data logger shield shown in Figure 9.6 is discussed in the sub-sections that follow. There are several design flaws in this shield and it does not work with an Arduino MEGA 2560 without modification. Besides the bad design, the circuit diagram supplied by the manufacturer does not exactly match the actual circuit – the Arduino 1.0 pinout at the AREF pin appears as an extra connector for the TWI pins, the solder jumpers under the board are missing, and there are no symbols representing the extra pads.

Under the board there is text that says "cut off if use in Arduino Mega" with an arrow pointing to two sets of solder pads. With this mention of the Arduino MEGA, one would expect the shield to work with the Arduino MEGA 2560, but it does not. Although this shield is not recommended because of all of these problems, it is used here as a practical example of design problems, and helps with understanding of the Arduino MEGA 2560 and shield compatibility with other Arduino models.

Figure 9.6: Data Logger Shield used as an Example

9.5.1.1 Shield Power

The data logger shield shown in Figure 9.6 powers the SD card directly from the Arduino 3.3V pin. On the Arduino MEGA 2560 and Arduino Uno, we know that this pin can deliver a maximum of 150mA. Many micro SD cards specify current consumption of 100mA when operating in standard mode, but some specify a higher current. This means that if anything else is connected to 3.3V in combination with this shield, there may be power problems when operating the micro SD card. To solve this 3.3V power problem, it would be better to have a 3.3V regulator on the shield that drops 5V from the Arduino 5V pin to 3.3V. A regulator that can deliver about 500mA to 800mA will ensure that there is enough current for the SD card without straining the 3.3V pin on Arduino MEGA 2560 and Uno boards.

A DS1307 RTC (Real-Time Clock) chip is present on the shield, giving it the ability to keep track of the current time and date. This chip is a 5V device, powered from the Arduino 5V pin, which immediately makes it incompatible with 3.3V Arduino models. A solution for the 5V RTC chip is to use a RTC chip that operates over a wide range of voltages. For example the M41T00 from ST Microelectronics operates between 2V to 5.5V. This is just one example of a RTC chip that operates over a wide range of voltages, there are others. If this RTC is powered from the Arduino IOREF pin, then it will be supplied with 5V from 5V Arduino models and 3.3V from 3.3V Arduino models, making the shield compatible with many different Arduino boards.

Another mistake made with the data logger shield design is that the IOREF pin is joined to 5V on the shield. This means that if plugged into a 3.3V Arduino, <u>5V is shorted to 3.3V</u>.

9.5.1.2 ICSP Connector

Figure 9.7 shows why the micro SD card on the data logger shield does not work with an Arduino MEGA 2560. Although the circuit board tracks on the shield connect to the ICSP header, the actual ICSP header placed on the data logger shield, seen at the right of the figure, does not have a socket underneath it to connect to the Arduino ICSP header pins. The Ethernet shield at the left of the figure does have a socket underneath it to connect to the Arduino ICSP pins. This means that when the data logger shield is plugged into an Arduino Uno, it will work because it is picking up the SPI pins from digital I/O pins 11, 12 and 13 on the connector at the edge of the board. On an Arduino MEGA 2560, pins 11, 12 and 13 are not SPI pins. MEGA 2560 SPI pins are only found on the ICSP header and on the double-row connector at the end of the board, which the half-size shield does not connect to.

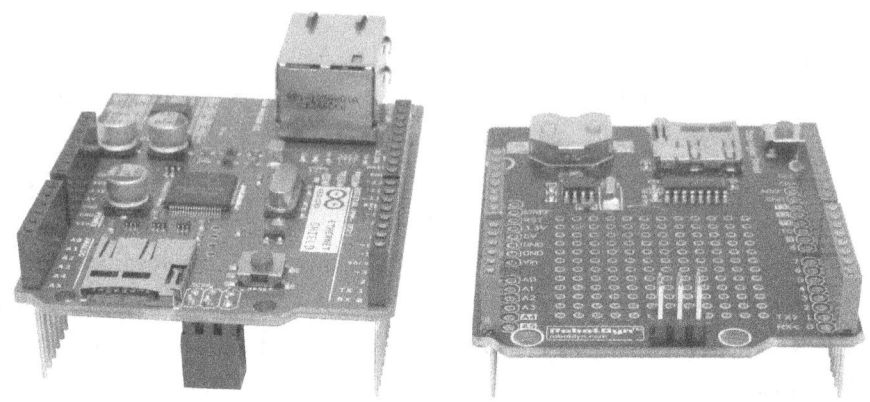

Figure 9.7: ICSP Connectors on the Ethernet Shield (left) and Data Logger Shield (right)

9.5.1.3 TWI Pins

TWI pins on the data logger shield allow the I²C compatible RTC chip on the shield to be accessed by an Arduino. A track on the shield joins the A4 pin, or SDA to the SDA pin on the other side of the board near the AREF pin. A track also joins A5, or SCL to the SCL pin near the AREF pin. This was done to make the board compatible with old Arduino boards that do not have the extra TWI pins near the AREF pins. There are no problems with this arrangement when the shield is plugged into an Arduino Uno because these pins are also joined on the Arduino Uno board.

A problem comes when the shield is plugged into an Arduino MEGA 2560. On an Arduino MEGA 2560, A4 and A5 are separate pins from the SDA and SCL pins near the AREF pin. This means that A4 is shorted to the SDA pin, and A5 is shorted to the SCL pin when this shield is plugged into an Arduino MEGA 2560. To fix this problem, the manufacturer put two sets of solder pads under the board that has a track joining each set. The track between each set of solder pads can be cut to disconnect A5 from SCL on the other side of the board, and A4 from SDA on the other side of the board. This is specifically meant to be done when using the shield with an Arduino MEGA 2560. Of course the micro SD card on the shield does not work with an Arduino MEGA 2560, only the RTC works. If the ICSP header were replaced with a socket, such as the Ethernet shield has, then the shield should work properly. The only issue would be possible power problems with the micro SD card because of power being taken from the 3.3V pin. Also on an Arduino MEGA 2560, the SPI pins from the ICSP header would then connect to pins 11, 12 and 13 via the shield.

9.5.2 Ethernet Shield Example

The official Arduino Ethernet shield is a good example to study when learning about shield compatibility. It is an open-source design and the circuit diagram is freely available. Information on this shield can be found at: store.arduino.cc/arduino-ethernet-shield-2

9.5.2.1 Shield Power

The Ethernet shield is basically a 3.3V shield, but the main Ethernet chip, the W5500 on version 2 shields, is a 3.3V device with 5V tolerant pins. A 3.3V regulator on the shield steps 5V from the Arduino 5V pin down to 3.3V to supply the circuit of the shield, including the W5500 chip. This 3.3V also supplies the micro SD card socket on the shield, ensuring that there is enough current for all devices on the shield. Voltage level translator chips for the SD card SPI lines are powered from 3.3V. The only chip on the shield that is supplied directly by 5V is a CAT811 voltage supervisor chip that takes care of resetting the W5500 chip. Because the only output pin from the CAT811 connects to the 5V tolerant W5500, there is no problem. The manual reset pin of the CAT811 connects to the Arduino RESET pin, but this is also not a problem as it is an input, which means that this shield is compatible with both 3.3V and 5V Arduino models.

To summarize, the Ethernet shield version 2 is a 3.3V shield, but is compatible with both 3.3V and 5V Arduino boards because the W5500 chip has 5V tolerant pins, and also because it derives its 3.3V power from the Arduino 5V pin using a higher current regulator, allowing it to deliver more current than Arduino MEGA 2560 and Arduino Uno 3.3V pins can.

9.5.2.2 ICSP Connector and Stacking

Figure 9.7 on the previous page shows the ICSP connector on the Ethernet shield at the left of the figure. It is a female socket connector that does not have any pins that extend out of the top of the board. This means that although it connects to the SPI pins on the ICSP header below it, a shield that uses SPI pins from the ICSP header can not be stacked on top of it. Had the pins of the ICSP socket under the board been long pins, they would extend through the board allowing a shield to be stacked on top of the Ethernet shield. This means that the Ethernet shield always has to be the top shield on a stack of shields, should any of the other shields need to use the SPI pins from the ICSP header. Remember to consider this when designing a shield. Another problem with the Ethernet shield is that the RJ45 Ethernet connector is higher than the connectors at the edges. If any shield is plugged into the Ethernet shield, it will make contact with the RJ45 connector.

Appendix A • Specifications Quick Reference

The table that follows contains a summary of the Arduino MEGA 2560 technical specifications with references to the appropriate sections in this book where more information can be found on each parameter.

Parameter	Specification	Notes	Reference
Microcontrollers			
Main Microcontroller	ATmega2560-16AU	100 pin TQFP package	1.1.4.1, 2.1, 3.8.1, 5.4, 6.1.2, 7.2
USB Microcontroller	ATmega16U2-MU	ATmega8U2 on boards before rev3	1.1.4.10, 2.8.3, 3.8.2, 5.3.1, 6.1.3
Memory			
Flash Memory	248K bytes	256K bytes minus 8K bytes for bootloader	2.3, 2.3.1
SRAM	8K bytes	Volatile, data memory	2.3, 2.3.2
EEPROM	4K bytes	Non-volatile, data	2.3, 2.3.3
Communications			
UART	4 UARTs (USARTs)	4 serial ports, TX and RX pin pairs	2.7.4.5, 2.9.1, 3.3.6, 7.4.3
TWI	1 TWI port	Two Wire Interface, I²C compatible serial bus	2.3.4, 2.7.4.5, 2.9.3, 3.1.1, 3.3.4, 7.4.4
SPI	1 SPI port	Serial Peripheral Interface serial bus	2.3.4, 2.7.4.5, 2.9.4, 3.1.2, 3.3.5, 7.4.5
Operating Frequencies			
ATmega2560-16AU	16MHz	Generated from external ceramic resonator	2.5, 7.4.1
ATmega16U2-MU	16MHz	Generated from external quartz Crystal	2.5, 7.4.1

Parameter	Specification	Notes	Reference
Voltage Specifications			
Operating Voltage	5V DC	Derived from either USB or external voltage through 5V regulator	1.3.4, 1.5.3.2, 2.4.5, 4.1.1, 6.1.4, 7.3
Input Voltage, USB	5V DC ± 5%	As per USB 2.0 specification	2.4.1, 4.1.2, 4.2.3, 4.3.4, 6.1.3, 7.3.1
Input Voltage, 2.1mm Jack	7 to 12V DC	Center of jack is positive	1.3.4, 2.4.3, 4.1.3, 4.1.4, 4.2.1, 4.3.1, 6.1.4, 7.3.2
Current Specifications			
5V Regulator DC Current	800mA or 1A, see 2.7.1.2 and 4.1.1	Current limited by thermal considerations which depend on input voltage and limited heat sinking on board	2.7.1.2, 4.1.1, 4.3.2
5V USB DC Current	500mA	As per USB 2.0 specification	2.4.1, 4.1.2, 4.3.4
3.3V Pin DC Current	150mA	50mA on pre-MEGA 2560 boards	2.7.1.3, 3.3.7.3, 4.1.1, 4.3.3
I/O Pin DC Current	20mA	Subject to group limit and maximum limit, see reference	2.7.4.2, 3.3.1.1
LEDs			
On LED	Green	Power On Indicator	1.1.4.6, 1.5.3.2, 2.6.1, 4.2.2, 7.3.1.3
L LED	Yellow	User LED	1.1.4.7, 2.6.2, 2.9.2, 7.3.1.3
TX LED	Yellow	Serial TX Indicator	1.1.4.8, 2.6.3
RX LED	Yellow	Serial RX Indicator	1.1.4.9, 2.6.4
Button			
RESET Button	Momentary reset push button	Resets main micro-controller	1.1.4.4, 2.6.5, 2.7.3, 3.3.8
Programming Headers			
ICSP	6-pin (3 × 2) pin header	Programming header for main microcontroller	1.1.4.11, 2.8, 2.9.4, 3.4
ICSP1	6-pin (3 × 2) pin header	ICSP header for USB bridge microcontroller	1.1.4.12, 2.8, 2.8.3, 3.5

Appendix A • Specifications Quick Reference

Parameter	Specification	Notes	Reference
Pins			
Power Pins	GND, 5V, 3.3V, Vin		2.7.1, 3.3.7, 4.1.5, 4.2.6, 4.3
IOREF Pin	I/O voltage reference	Shield voltage reference	2.7.2, 3.3.9, 9.2.2, 9.4
RESET Pin	Active low reset input	Resets main microcontroller	2.7.3, 3.3.8
Digital Pins	54 digital I/O pins, 15 of the digital I/O pins are PWM pins	15 pins have PWM capabilities, some pins multiplexed with TWI, SPI and UARTs	2.7.4, 3.3.1, 3.3.2, 7.4.2
Analog Pins	16 analog input pins connected to internal ADC	Can be configured as digital I/O pins, JTAG on some analog pins	2.7.5, 3.3.3, 2.9.5, 3.7
AREF Pin	Analog reference input, 1V to 5V	Optional external analog input voltage used as ADC reference	2.7.6, 3.3.10
Power and USB Connectors			
USB	USB Type B	USB 2.0 port	1.1.4.2, 2.4.1, 2.4.2, 4.1.2, 4.2.3
Power Jack	2.1mm Barrel	7V to 12V DC input, center positive	1.1.4.3, 2.4.3, 2.4.4, 4.1.3, 4.1.4
Board Dimensions			
Length	101.6mm	4 inches	8.2
Width	53.4mm	2.1 inches	8.2
Mounting Holes			
6 Mounting Holes	3.2mm diameter		1.1.4.13, 8.3
Mass			
Board mass	37g	Measured: 34g, 36g	8.2
Firmware			
Main bootloader on ATmega2560	stk500v2 bootloader	Factory loaded to main microcontroller Flash memory	1.2.2, 5.4
DFU Firmware	Device firmware update	Factory loaded to USB bridge microcontroller	5.1, 5.3, 5.3.2
USB Serial Firmware	USB bridge firmware	Factory loaded to USB bridge microcontroller	1.2.1, 5.1, 5.3, 5.3.3

Index

0
0V 76

1
1.0 pinout 216
16MHz 73
16MHz clock 190

2
2.1mm barrel connector 70, 147
2N7000 117

3
3.3V 44, 73, 77
3.3V pin 77, 137
3.3V regulator 150

5
5V 44, 55, 73, 77
5V pin 76
5V pins 136
5V regulator 137, 147, 148

A
A0 to A15 87
AC load 117
AC waveforms 189
active low 138
ADC 87, 90
alternative pin function 102
ANALOG IN 103
analog input pins 87, 124
Android 60
anti-static 42
anti-static mat 43
anti-static wrist strap 43
Arduino 1.0 pinout 216

Arduino as an ISP 168
Arduino as ISP 93
Arduino Due 214
Arduino DUE 59
Arduino IDE 24, 31, 56
Arduino logos 38
Arduino MEGA 2560 ....24, 214
Arduino MEGA ADK 60
Arduino Uno 24, 215
Arduino Uno SMD 24
Arduino Zero 215
arduino.cc 40
arduino.org 40
Arduino/Genuino 40
AREF 89
AREF pin 139
AT24C16C 125
ATmega16U2 ....29, 31, 41, 47, 77, 157
ATmega16U2 firmware 154
ATmega16U2 fuses 161
ATmega2 63
ATmega2560 ....62, 63, 99
ATmega2560 datasheet 102
ATmega2560 fuses 164
ATmega2560-16AU 62
ATMEGA2560-16AU 183
ATmega8U2 ....41, 47, 157
Atmel 63
Atmel Studio 30, 155
Atmel-ICE 30, 90, 156, 166
automatic switch 137, 149
AVR 62, 63
AVR Dragon 166

B

bandwidth..189
battery..71, 137
baud rate..53
blank sketch..186
block diagram..170
bootloader......................................41, 91, 162
bootloader size..64
breadboard..36, 57
Burn Bootloader.......................................91
buzzer..115

C
C language..31, 168
ceramic resonator....................................73
circuit diagram.......................................170
clock frequency......................................190
clone boards...38
COM port..48
compatible boards...................................38
component list.......................................174
component positions............................177
const..80
Creative Commons...................................38
crystal..74
CS..128
current limiting resistor..........................106
current per pin.......................................111
current sink limits..................................111
current sinking......................................110
current source limits.............................111
current sourcing....................................109

D
data logger shield..................................218
data retention...64
datasheets..143
DC...27
DC voltage measurements....................186
debugging..166

debugWIRE..166
Device Manager......................................48
DFU...31, 154
DFU bootloader firmware.......................159
DFU firmware..157
DFU programming.................................154
digital pins...78
dimensions..202
documentation..57
drill template..208
drivers...47
Due...211
DUE...59
DuPont...158
duty cycle...82

E
Eagle EDA..179
EDA..38, 57
EEPROM...65, 125
EEPROM chips......................................127
EEPROM memory..................................164
ESD...42
Ethernet shield..............................129, 221
external memory......................................65
external power..............27, 44, 70, 147, 148
external power supply.............................77

F
FAQ...57
fault finding.............................47, 54, 182
firmware..29, 40
Flash memory..64
Flash memory size..................................64
Flash wear..64
FLIP..154
floating pin...88
forum...57
frequency..73

Fritzing..57
FT232RL.............................41, 77, 133
FTDI...41
fuse settings.......................................30
fuses..155, 164

G

Genuino..40
GND..76
GND pins..136
GPL..38

H

handling precaution..........................45
hardware revision..............................46
header socket positions..................206
header sockets..................................76
Header sockets..................................29
heap..64
History..46

I

I/O..68
I/O pins..103
I2C..68
I²C..68, 125
ICSP...90
ICSP header..............30, 31, 94, 98, 140
ICSP header pins............................141
ICSP SPI pins...................................94
ICSP1..141
IIC..68
input pins..81
Input/Output...................................103
interfacing.....................45, 68, 103, 118
internal pull-up.................................81
internal pull-up resistors................122
internal reference..............................90
IOREF..47, 77

IOREF pin..138
ISP..140, 156

J

JP5 header.......................................142
JTAG..166

K

KiCad...38
KiCad template...............................208

L

L LED..............................29, 75, 79, 93
LED..74, 104
LED forward voltage......................104
LED_BUILTIN....................75, 79, 103
length...202
level shifters.....................................66
LGPL...38
library reference...............................57
license..38
Linux...49
loading a sketch................................49
logo..38

M

main microcontroller........................62
main microcontroller circuit..........171
maximum current per pin................80
MEGA ADK.......................................59
memory...63
Microchip....................................62, 63
mil..202
MISO..128
MOSFET..117
MOSI..128
mounting holes........................31, 204
multimeter......................................185
multiplexed.....................................102
multiplexed pins...............................88

229

N

N-Channel MOSFET..................117
non-volatile memory...................64

O

official Arduino board..................39
offset header............................207
ON LED..................29, 49, 54, 74, 148
op-amp.................................75, 149
open-source................................38
open-source projects....................57
operating frequency.....................73
operating voltage.................73, 146
order codes................................62
oscilloscope..............................189
output pin..................................78
output pins...............................103
overload...................................152
overrating..................................81

P

PCB..37
PicoScope................................189
pin..29
pin current rating.........................80
pin functions..............................98
pin headers................................76
pin mapping...............................99
pin numbers.............................102
pins..76
PN2222....................................116
ports.......................................101
potentiometer.............................87
power..................................44, 69
POWER.....................................72
POWER header socket................150
power jack................................147
power pins.........................76, 136
power supply..............................70

power supply circuit.............148, 174
precautions..........................42, 45
Processing.................................58
programming..............................31
programming headers..................90
projects.....................................26
protection circuits......................152
protection diode..........................77
prototype shields........................35
pull-down resistor......................119
pull-up resistor..........................121
pull-up resistors..........................81
PWM..123
PWM frequency...........................84
PWM pins.....................78, 82, 123
PWM signal..............................191

Q

quartz crystal..............................74

R

R3..46
reference voltage...................87, 89
References.................................56
relay..117
repair......................................182
reset button.................28, 74, 75
reset pin............................78, 138
RESET-EN................................167
resettable fuse.............69, 148, 152
resistor....................................104
resources............................20, 56
REV3...46
reverse connection protection...35, 207
reverse polarity protection..........152
revisions....................................46
RISC...63
RS-232.............................131, 133
RS-422....................................131

RS-485..131, 133
RTC..68
RX LED..29, 75
RX0..85

S

safety-critical applications........................39
SCK..128
SCL..125
SD card..129
SD card adapters......................................130
SD cards..66
SD library..130
SD mode...67
SDA..125
serial bus interfaces..................................33
serial data...194
Serial Monitor window..............................52
serial port..85, 131
Serial Port Demonstration........................52
series resistor....................................46, 104
shared pins...93
shield compatibility.................................210
shields.....................................33, 76, 206
short circuit protection...........................152
silkscreen..47
siren...116
sketches...20, 31
SMD..24
software serial library.............................135
solder pad jumpers..................................177
solder pads...142
SPI..68, 87
SPI bus pins..128
SPI library..130
SPI mode...67
SPI pins...98
SPI signals..198

SRAM...64
SS...128
stack...64
startup delay...49
static electricity..42
static sensitive..42
static shielding...42
stk500v2 bootloader................................163
strip-board..36, 208
supporting website.....................................20
switch...119

T

technical specifications..........................223
template file..208
thermal shutdown....................................152
through-hole...24
TQFP..62
trademark...40
trademarks...38
transistor..115, 149
TTL..131, 133
tutorials...57
TWI...68
TWI bus pins...125
TWI pins..86, 94, 98
TWI signals...196
TX LED..29, 75
TX0...85

U

UART...53, 85, 131, 194
UART test..194
UGND...148
unity gain op-amp......................................75
Uno...211
unused pin..77
USART..86, 131
USB..133

USB 2.0...69
USB bridge...29
USB bridge chip...................................85
USB connector....................................27
USB microcontroller circuit...............171
USB power..147
USB programming device.................156
USB to serial bridge..........................157
USB to serial bridge firmware..........159
USB to UART bridge...........................41

V

Veroboard....................................36, 208
Vin...71, 77
Vin pin..137, 148
virtual COM port..................................40

volatile memory..................................64
voltage..44
voltage measurements....................185

W

warranty...39
weak pull-up resistor.......................122
width..202
Wire library................................69, 127
Wiring..26, 58

Z

Zero..211

#

#define..79

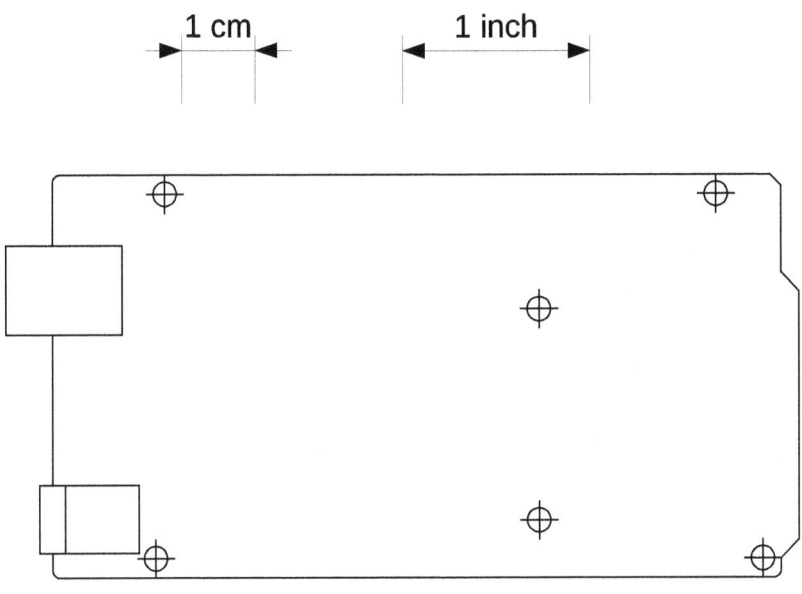
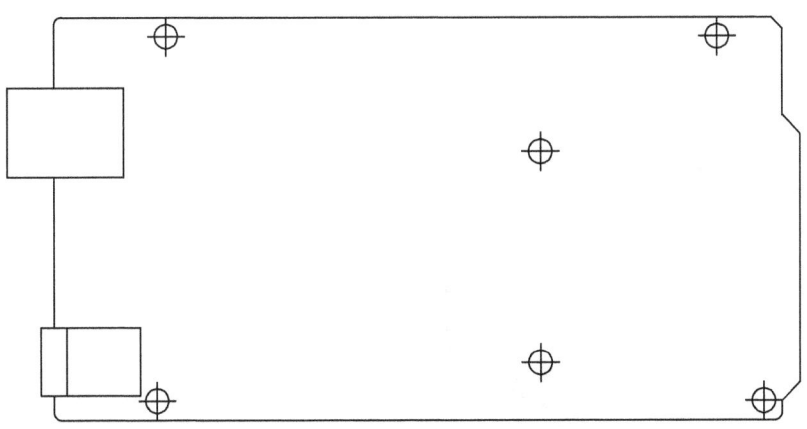

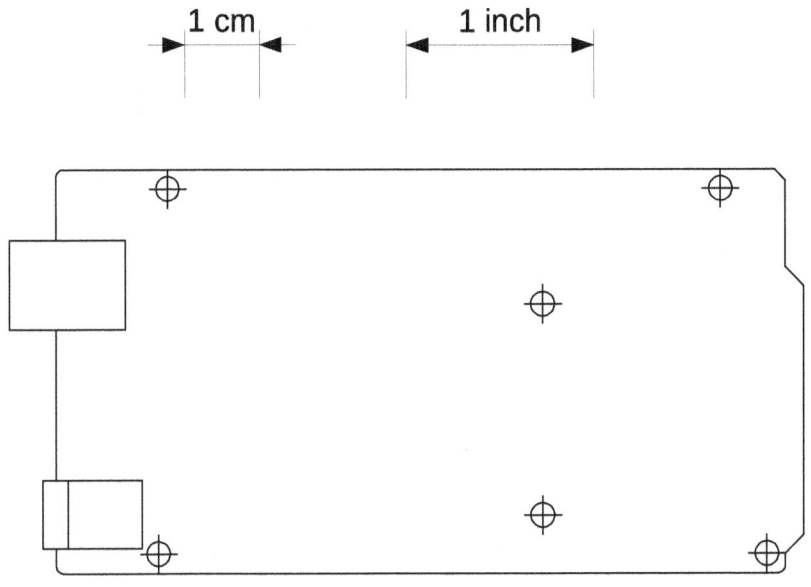

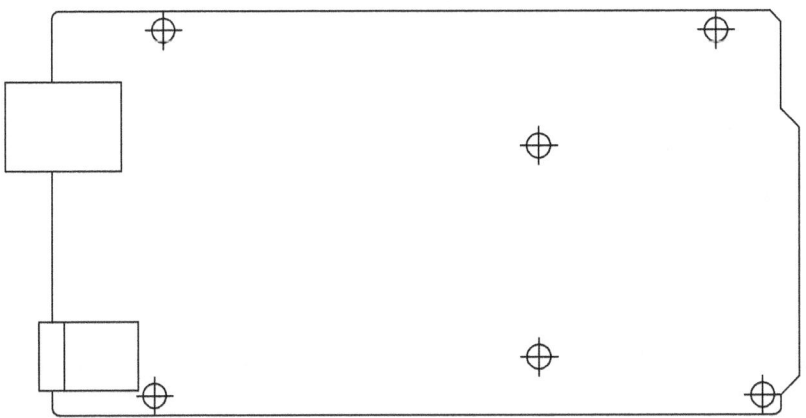